Remaking Chinese America

Remaking Chinese America

IMMIGRATION, FAMILY, AND COMMUNITY, 1940–1965

XIAOJIAN ZHAO

Rutgers University Press

New Brunswick, New Jersey, and London

Library of Congress Cataloging-in-Publication Data

Zhao, Xiaojian, 1953–
 Remaking Chinese America : immigration, family, and community, 1940–1965 /
Xiaojian Zhao
  p. cm.
 Includes bibliographical references and index.
 ISBN 0-8135-3010-5 (cloth : alk. paper)—ISBN 0-8135-3011-3 (pbk. : alk. paper)
 1. Chinese Americans—Social conditions—20th century. 2. Chinese American
families—History—20th century. 3. Chinese American women—History—20th
century. 4. Sex role—United States—History—20th century. 5. United States—
Emigration and immigration—History—20th century. 6. China—Emigration and
immigration—History—20th century. 7. World War, 1939–1945—Chinese
Americans. 8. World War, 1939–1945—Social aspects—United States. 9. Cold War—
Social aspects—United States. I. Title.

E184.C5 Z43 2002
305.895'1073'0904—dc21

                                                                    2001019844

British Cataloging-in-Publication information is available from the British Library.

Manufactured in the United States of America

To my mother
and the memory of my father,
and to Hai and Sue

CONTENTS

ILLUSTRATIONS

FIGURES AND TABLES

xi

ACKNOWLEDGMENTS

Many people provided indispensable assistance at various stages of this project, for which I am deeply grateful. I would like to thank all those who helped me with my research, especially the individuals who generously shared their time, records, and memories. Him Mark Lai has shared numerous sources, and his insightful knowledge of Chinese American history has saved me from many mistakes. The hospitality of Laura Lai made my trips to San Francisco both fruitful and enjoyable. Maggie Gee helped me to understand what it was like for a woman to work in the defense industry and in the military during World War II, and I still miss the wonderful Christmas dinners at her house. I first met Peter Lew in the summer of 1994, before moving from the San Francisco Bay Area to Santa Barbara. He took an immediate interest in my work, and in the course of his own research unearthed documents that proved to be of immense value. The late Joy Yee not only shared her own stories but also helped me make the acquaintance of many Chinese "Rosie the Riveters." Munson Kwok and Suellen Cheng generously shared their knowledge and archival materials, and they introduced me to members of the Chinese American Citizens Alliance. The stories of Maurice Chuck have been a constant inspiration, and his encouragement over the years pushed me to finish this book. Janice Chow persuaded her mother, Luella Louie, to accept my request for an interview, and arranged for her young daughter, Andrea L. Chow, to assist my work. Thanks are also due to Roger Hong, Elizabeth Lew Anderson, Betty Lew, Jade Snow Wang, Nancy Woo, and many members of Berkeley's Chinese Congregational Church, the Longgang Association, and the Chinese American Citizens Alliance.

A large part of the research was conducted in libraries and archives, and a number of librarians and archivists deserve special mention. Neil Thomsen, Claude Hopkins, Rose Mary Kennedy, Kathleen O'Connell, and other staff members at the National Archives' Pacific Sierra Branch in San Bruno, California, provided the most valuable assistance, and they warmly welcomed my then seven-year-old daughter during my visits to the repository. I would like to thank Michael McReynolds and Robert Ellis at the National Archives in Washington, D.C., and Marvin Russel and Fred Romanski at the National Archives II, College Park, Maryland, for locating and declassifying the Chinese Confession Program files with great efficiency. Advice from Mary Dudziak, Laura Kalman, and Peter Irons, who all have conducted research at the National Archives for documents of the Justice Department, proved to be most helpful. Special thanks also to Marian Smith, the historian of the Immigration and Naturalization Service in Washington, D.C., Wei Chi Poon of the Asian American Studies Library at the University of California, Berkeley, and staff members at the headquarters of the Longgang Association in San Francisco, the Bancroft Library at the University of California, Berkeley, the Hoover Institution on War, Revolution, and Peace at Stanford University, and the Archives of the University of Washington.

The librarians at the University of California, Santa Barbara, accepted my seemingly endless requests for interlibrary loan materials. The assistance I received from Lucia Snowhill, the legal reference librarian, was invaluable. I also benefited greatly from the assistance of Gerardo Colmenar, who never turned down any of my requests. Ma Xiaohe at the Harvard-Yenching Library responded to my last-minute inquiries with unusual care. He helped me locate the necessary sources that I could not find elsewhere, and he compiled circulation data for Chinese-language newspapers for me.

Bangwei Zhu deserves special thanks for relieving me of some of the work involved in hunting down sources from microfilmed issues of the *Chung Sai Yat Po*. I am also grateful to my student research assistants, especially Karen Fan, who assisted me during my visit to the National Archives at San Bruno and who shared with me the excitement of finding fascinating sources. Nancy Jeu helped with bibliographical research and carefully coded the war brides data. Several students provided assistance with oral history interviews, especially Kristen Martin, Jeff Wong, Denise Yee, and Briton Yee. Lainey Abe, Trang Huynh, Jennifer Lee, Mike Vu, and Wenjin Wan also helped with various research tasks.

The University of California, Santa Barbara, has been generous with research funds. Two career development grants and several grants from the Committee on Research and the Interdisciplinary Humanities Center provided money and leave that enabled me to travel and write.

I want to acknowledge that portions of chapter three are based on two previously published essays: "Chinese American Women Defense Workers in World War II," *California History*, 75:2 (Summer 1996), and "My Silver Wings," *Gender Camouflage: Women and the U.S. Military*, edited by Francine D'Amico and Laurie Weinstein (New York: New York University Press, 1999).

My deepest appreciation goes to Roger Daniels, who has provided several years of mentorship. The sources that he offered and helped me obtain are too numerous to be listed. At critical stages he read drafts of the entire manuscript, and his suggestions helped improve it significantly. His advice, his patience, and his constant support have been more important to my development as an Asian American historian than he can ever know.

Constructive and critical suggestions from friends and colleagues have also helped improve this book. Douglas Daniels, Paul Harvey, Gail Hershatter, Him Mark Lai, Peggy Pascoe, Paul Spikard, and Judy Yung each read the entire manuscript closely. Their detailed comments reshaped my thinking and enabled me to correct many errors. Advice from Douglas Daniels on language and style of argument has been especially beneficial. Bryna Goodman listened with patience and understanding to many of the stories that appear here. She read parts of the manuscript at different stages and repeatedly offered encouragement and helpful suggestions. I would also like to thank Sue Fawn Chung for her careful reading of the manuscript. Many of her critical suggestions were incorporated in subsequent revisions. The book also benefited from comments from Scott Wong and Zuoyuen Wang. Gail Tinsley and Zhiyun Guan both read the manuscript as well, and I am grateful for their editorial advice.

I am fortunate to have had the opportunity to discuss parts of the work with my colleagues at the interdisciplinary Asian American Studies Department at the University of California, Santa Barbara. Conversations with Susan Koshy helped me put individual stories in chapter six into a broader context. Sucheng Chan, who introduced me to the field of Asian American history, suggested that I take a closer look at postwar immigration files. Her keen interest and enthusiastic support in the early stages of this project are very much appreciated.

I want to thank Leslie Mitchner at the Rutgers University Press for expressing interest in my work several years ago and for her unusual efficiency in expediting the publishing process. Assistance from Theresa Liu and Marilyn Campbell at the press has also been invaluable. I am especially grateful to Elizabeth Gilbert for her meticulous copyediting. And I express my appreciation as well to Karen Hewitt and Jennifer Hammer for their support.

Although only a small portion of the materials used in this book came from my dissertation, I am deeply indebted to my graduate advisors at the University of California, Berkeley. My thesis director, Paula Fass, has been a constant source of inspiration for many years, and her unwavering support has played a critical role in the development of my career. No words can express my enormous debt to Leon Litwack. Through the years working as his graduate student, teaching assistant, and research assistant, I began to understand what it takes to become a historian. More than anything else, he showed me that a good scholar can also be a kind human being. His warmth and generosity, as well as that of Rhoda Litwack and the entire Litwack family, have provided more than can ever be thanked. Aihwa Ong was the first to encourage me to expand my research by utilizing Chinese-language sources.

Without the friendship of many individuals, my journey in pursuing a graduate degree in U.S. history and then a career in Asian American history after I left college in China would have been very lonely and far more difficult. I want to thank all of my friends who helped along the way, especially Ruth and Burt Dorman, Maggie Gee, Bryna Goodman, Sharman Haley, Paul Harvey, Gail Hershatter, Emily Honig, Kathy Nonoshita, Katherine Swatak, and Nancy Quam-Wickham. Several colleagues and individuals at the University of California, Santa Barbara, also assisted with the completion of this project in ways that they may not fully realize. I want to thank especially Christine Allen, Jacqueline Bobo, Elliot Brownlee, Patricia Cohen, Jon Cruz, Ellen Friedkin, Mark Elliott, Laura Kalman, Shirley Lim, Kathy Lowry, Claudine Michel, Patricia Miller, Cedric Robinson, and Denise Segura.

Members of my family have sustained me with their emotional support through all the years. My mother, who devoted her earlier years to a teaching career and had little time to care for her own children, provided three years of indispensable labor taking care of my daughter so that I could finish graduate school. Although geographical distance and busy schedules have prevented me from seeing my sister and brothers often, their support has always been evident in all my personal and career pursuits. My only sorrow is that my father, who was interested in writing, is no longer alive to see this book in print, for he would have been the first to read it. Hai and Sue, who have been there from the very beginning, have spent most of their vacations accompanying me on research trips. They have shared with me both the burdens and the joys of the process and have assisted with research and many other tasks. In the days of her early childhood, Sue learned to read her own books quietly in libraries and archives. And by age eleven, she began to proofread my numerous drafts and write her own stories. Without the unfailing love and support of Sue and her father, this book would not have been possible.

Note on Romanization and Pseudonyms

This book uses pinyin to romanize Chinese names and terms from Chinese-language sources. The Wade-Giles spellings of Peking and Toisan, for example, are rendered as Beijing and Taishan in pinyin. Exceptions to the pinyin system have been allowed for a few names such as Sun Yat-sen and Chiang Kai-shek. The other notable exception to the use of pinyin in this book is in the titles of Chinese-language community newspapers, books, authors' names, and names appearing in English-language archival records; they have been cited as presented. For example, *Zhongxi ribao* is rendered as *Chung Sai Yat Po*. An English, Chinese, and pinyin glossary appears at the end of the book.

A few people who were interviewed by the author requested pseudonyms. Each pseudonym is indicated with an asterisk in the Selected Bibliography.

Remaking Chinese America

Introduction

❧❦❧

*W*orld War II and the cold war profoundly altered the lives of Chinese Americans. Between 1940 and 1965, what had been a predominantly male Chinese immigrant community was transformed into a family-centered American ethnic community. This study traces the changing basis of that community, focusing on immigration, family, gender relations, and the development of ethnic identity. The book explores the forces that unified all Chinese living in the United States into one group, even though internal conflicts within the community never ceased.

One of the major changes in the Chinese American community in the 1940s was the growth and transformation of families. From the late nineteenth century, seeking to bring their families to the United States, Chinese Americans had repeatedly challenged the country's exclusion laws in the courts. Beginning in the 1920s, they also lobbied Congress to gain admission for their family members, but achieved only minimal success. Not until the exclusion acts were repealed in 1943 and alien Chinese became admissible did the struggle for family unification begin to gain significant momentum. The 1945 War Brides Act allowed the admission of alien dependents of World War II veterans without quota limits. A June 1946 act extended this privilege to fiancées and fiancés of war veterans. The Chinese Alien Wives of American Citizens Act, enacted in August 1946, granted admission outside the quota to Chinese wives of American citizens.[1] These legislative reforms opened the door to a broader echelon of Chinese immigrants. Women constituted the majority of the newcomers and significantly changed the sex ratio of the Chinese American population. In 1940 there were 2.9 Chinese men for every Chinese woman in the United States (57,389 men versus 20,115 women). By 1960 this ratio was reduced to 1.35 to 1 (135,430 men versus 100,654 women).[2]

During and after World War II, the Chinese American community was pressured to grant women more serious consideration. A significant improvement in gender equality took place during the war, as many Chinese women, most of them born and educated in the United States, entered nontraditional occupations outside the home. A subtler, perhaps more important change along the same lines occurred within the family. A woman's importance in the traditional Chinese family had been largely associated with her ability to reproduce. Because most Chinese women gained admission to the United States as dependents of their husbands, they had been expected to subordinate their individual interests to those of their family members, especially to those of their husbands. Such expectations, however, were challenged in the postwar years. After thousands of Chinese war brides reunited with their husbands, the community came under increasing pressure to help Chinese American couples negotiate domestic tensions and improve the status of women within the family.

The postwar years also witnessed the relocation and dispersion of the Chinese American population, which changed the physical boundaries of the community. Chinese Americans since the early twentieth century had been mostly an urban-centered ethnic group, and they experienced extreme residential segregation in Chinatowns throughout the United States.[3] By 1940 71 percent of Chinese Americans lived in cities with a population greater than 100,000, and most of them were in the segregated sections.[4] World War II and postwar development, however, enabled Chinese American men and women to purchase property outside Chinatowns. Residing in small towns or suburbs of large cities and working for non-Chinese-operated firms, they became less dependent on their traditional clans and district and benevolent associations.

At the same time the political situation in China became more complicated, creating a new challenge to the Chinese living in the United States. The Communist victory in the Chinese Civil War in 1949 significantly altered U.S.-China relations and intensified conflict among Chinese American political groups. When the Chinese People's Volunteer Army confronted American military troops under General Douglas MacArthur in Korea in 1950, China became an archenemy of the United States. Caught in the middle of a war between the country of their ancestors and the country of their residence, many Chinese Americans had conflicting emotions and lived in fear of political accusation and government investigation. Tension within the community intensified, mirroring that between the Nationalists on Taiwan and the Communists in mainland China. The Nationalist government was highly influential among Chinese American merchants, who largely controlled the community power structure. In a bid to exterminate their political opponents, right-wing community leaders collaborated with the FBI and the Immigration and Naturalization Service (INS) in the investigation of Chinese American leftists. This collaboration, however, ultimately facilitated the U.S. government's effort to break up the old community networks that for decades had helped circumvent exclusion laws.

As political conflict deepened in China, more members of the community realized the importance of shifting their energy from China politics to the struggles for racial equality in the United States. When the cold war made the entire Chinese community a target for the investigation of Communist subversion, it also forced Chinese Americans to form a united political front. In this complex political environment a sense of group identity began to develop among Chinese living in the United States.

Scholars have studied a number of Chinese settlements in the United States. In a study of Chinatown in San Francisco, Stanford Lyman examined the different forms of social, economic, and institutional control that dominated the lives of ordinary Chinese immigrants in the late nineteenth and early twentieth centuries.[5] In *Chinese Gold*, Sandy Lydon vividly illustrated the lives and struggles of the Chinese in the Monterey Bay region of California.[6] Studies by Clarence E. Glick, Paul Siu, Peter Kwong, Renqiu Yu, Judy Yung, Victor G. Nee and Brett de Bary Nee, Yong Chen, and others have recaptured the past of Chinese Americans in Hawaii, Chicago, New York, San Francisco, and elsewhere.[7] Works on contemporary urban Chinatowns have also contributed to our understanding of the importance of ethnic enclaves to the socioeconomic advancement of post-1965 Chinese immigrants and the complexity of race relations in America's multiethnic society.[8] These studies laid foundations for subsequent work in the field of Chinese American history.

Unlike previous studies, this book examines the Chinese American community beyond the confines of a particular Chinatown. It also focuses on a time period—from World War II through the cold war era—that has not yet been carefully studied. After the war, as the Chinese population spread out, the traditional community organizations such as *huiguan* (district associations) and family associations became less important in the day-to-day lives of Chinese Americans. The ties of Chinese America were now built upon a shared ethnic identity that was based on a common cultural sentiment and moral consensus, reinforced by pressures from the larger society.[9] Community newspapers thus became increasingly important. They were read by Chinese inside and outside Chinatowns and helped build a sense of community that transcended one locale. Chinese in the United States shared the experience of separation from family members and relatives in China, and as members of an ethnic minority group living in the United States, they faced the same difficulties. Individually and collectively Chinese Americans networked and struggled to gain the rights provided to all Americans in the language of the U.S. Constitution.[10]

Community newspapers, most in Chinese and some in English, and mostly published in the United States, were therefore major primary sources for this study. Other sources include INS immigration case files and investigation files at the National Archives, U.S. statutes and legal cases, congressional hearings, publications of community organizations, genealogical documents, and oral history interviews.

When data are available, statistical analysis is used to present a broader picture of the Chinese American experience, while personal documents and oral history interviews provide evidence of people's feelings, intentions, and reactions. A great effort has been made to include the average and sometimes less visible groups of Chinese Americans, even though source material for community leaders, politicians, scholars, and other notables is much more available. A primary aim is to provide the reader with some sense of what it was like to be a Chinese living in the United States during this particular period.

This book examines the years from 1940 to 1965. Although the first two chapters deal with issues of family and gender before World War II and much of the narratives in the later chapters are discussed in a historical context, the book does not attempt to cover the entire history of Chinese America since 1850. There is a relatively large body of literature on Chinese American history before World War II, which provided a solid basis for the historical analysis here. This study approaches the Chinese American experience topically, although an effort is made to organize the discussion chronologically. The book begins with a historical account of the efforts of male Chinese Americans to bring their wives to the United States. Within the past few years, our understanding of Chinese immigration during the period of exclusion has increased significantly. Several scholars have examined government restrictions on Chinese immigration, and George Anthony Peffer has demonstrated that as early as 1875, after the enactment of the Page Law, the U.S. government made it extremely difficult for Chinese women to join their husbands in America.[11] It is clear that harsh laws prevented many Chinese immigrants from family reunion, but little attempt has been made to explore the individual and collective actions taken by Chinese Americans to reverse the difficult situation. Taking a different approach from previous studies, chapter one draws upon federal legislation, legal cases, and records of congressional hearings to unveil the decades-long struggle of the Chinese to bring their wives to the United States, their hard-fought court battles and political campaigns that aimed to establish families.[12]

Drawing on genealogical documents that have been overlooked by most scholars as well as oral history interviews, chapter two examines the immigration strategy of Chinese immigrant families as it has been influenced by U.S. immigration laws. With the exception of the very early period, many (if not all) Chinese wanted to have their families with them. With a clear understanding of the exclusion laws, however, they also tried to find ways to maximize the number of new entries. As a result more male boys were brought to the United States than girls. Although the wives of immigrants were less visible in Chinatowns before World War II, they played some of the most important roles in the family emigration plans. They shaped the political life of the community and linked it closely to the immigrants' villages in China.

Chapter three focuses on the impact of World War II on the Chinese American community through the experience of women. Only in recent years have scholars begun to examine women's experiences in Chinese American history. *Unbound Feet* by Judy Yung, published in 1995, is the first in-depth historical study of Chinese American women. And Yung's recently published *Unbound Voices* documents these women's experiences in their own words. Yung's meticulously researched work covers the first half of the twentieth century and ends with World War II, convincingly describing the war as a turning point that offered Chinese American women great opportunities to expand their gender roles, helping them "unbind their feet" and their socially restrictive lives.[13] Picking up the story where Yung ends her book, this chapter examines World War II as the beginning of a new era; it places women at the center of community development in a critical period. Employment in the U.S. military and the defense industry enabled Chinese women to interact with women of other ethnic backgrounds, and they took on the responsibility of connecting the community with the larger society.

Chapter four examines the unique experience of the Chinese war brides—most of whom had been separated from their husbands during the exclusion—who came to the United States after World War II. The admission of thousands of Chinese women in the postwar years was indisputably crucial to the transformation of the Chinese American community. Although scholars have studied European, Japanese, and Korean war brides, little has been written about the Chinese.[14] This chapter analyzes 1,035 immigration cases, which consist of biographical sketches and the women's recorded testimonies at the ports of entry. The story is unromantic, but it shows the ability of these women to expand immigration networks by utilizing the new opportunities available to them in the post–World War II years.

Chapter five explores internal political struggles in the Chinese American community and argues that although the Nationalist government in China helped the Chinese Consolidated Benevolent Association (CCBA) secure its dominance in the 1930s and early 1940s, the reputation and influence of the CCBA declined in the postwar years largely because of its deep involvement on the losing side of China politics, which prevented the institution from providing leadership for the entire community. Independent community newspapers, in contrast, flourished during World War II and began to reach out to Chinese Americans residing in different parts of the United States. Recent studies of ethnic identity, influenced in particular by the theoretical work of Benedict Anderson, have emphasized the role and significance of the press in identity formation.[15] In the case of the Chinese American community during this period, it was the press that urged Chinese Americans to sever their ties with political parties in China and focus their energy on building their own community in the United States.

Chapter six treats the reunions of husbands and wives after exclusion. Once the long-separated wives and newlywed brides joined their husbands, domestic conflicts followed. To a large extent, these conflicts reflected a collision of two different cultures. When the confused and frustrated couples sought help from newspaper columnists, private problems of marriage, family, and gender relations became topics of public debate. The maneuvers of the newspapers to help the couples make compromises reflected the changing character of the Chinese American community.

Chapter seven explores the cold war era. During this period the government launched an all-out effort to break up Chinese immigration networks in the name of investigating Communist subversive activities. The purposes of this investigation are made clear in the recently declassified INS files on Chinese document fraud.[16] The investigation of Communist activities and illegal immigration deeply divided the Chinese American community; even family members were pressured to turn against one another.[17] These difficult circumstances, however, created urgent pressures for unity. Chinese Americans were compelled to remove themselves from China politics and devote their full energies to the construction and strengthening of a Chinese American community.

The stories told in this book offer only one perspective of the Chinese American experience. There is still much more to be written on issues such as class and generational conflicts, the differences between U.S.-born and China-born Chinese Americans, and the relationship of Chinese Americans to other American ethnic groups. There is also a rich mine of primary sources remaining to be explored. For a period of one hundred and fifty years, for example, Chinese in the United States and Canada have published more than two hundred newspapers, but only a fraction have been studied by the relatively few scholars in the field.

This book demonstrates the ways in which the Chinese American experience has been shaped by events and conditions in both the United States and China; it seeks to contribute to our understanding of how an individual Chinese becomes a Chinese American, how one Chinese living in the United States is identified with another, and how the Chinese American community was made and remade over time.

CHAPTER 1

The Struggle for
Family Unification
during the Exclusion

❧❦❧

On May 26, 1924, President Calvin
Coolidge signed a major piece of U.S. immigration legislation. It made no
direct mention of China or ethnic Chinese: by then Chinese exclusion acts
had barred Chinese immigration into the United States for forty-two years.
Nevertheless, the new law made persons ineligible for citizenship inadmissible, and thus raised legal questions about whether American citizens could
bring in their Chinese wives.[1]

When the law went into effect on July 1 of that year, a young Chinese
woman, Jee Shee, was en route to the United States with her new husband,
Paul Yee, an American citizen born in San Francisco. When the couple arrived in San Francisco on July 23, immigration authorities admitted Paul but
blocked Jee Shee's entry, invoking the new immigration law.[2]

Jee Shee was one of thirty-five Chinese women who had married U.S.
citizens but were denied entry in San Francisco and Seattle in July of 1924.
When she left China, she was unaware that a new law would prevent her from
joining her husband's family in America.[3]

Jee Shee did not return to China, however. She and the other thirty-
four wives petitioned the court and won temporary releases on bond, which
they were able to extend several times. On February 3, 1926, Jee Shee gave
birth to a son in Oakland, California.[4] Not until six years after their arrival,

when a new law was passed to admit Chinese wives of American citizens who had married prior to the approval of the 1924 Immigration Act, did Jee Shee and the other Chinese wives officially gain entry.[5]

The Chinese community in America was a predominantly male society before World War II. In 1860 there were more than eighteen Chinese men to every Chinese woman. By 1940 the male majority had dropped to 2.9 to 1. Scholars have sought to tie the extremely skewed sex ratio to Chinese family economy, kinship, and cultural values. Some have posited that there was a strong sojourner mentality among the Chinese immigrants and suggested that the father-son family structure provides evidence of a long-term strategy.[6] Others have seen less incentive for women to immigrate since California, known by the Chinese as the Gold Mountain, provided economic opportunities only for men, and remittances from the United States allowed immigrants' wives to live a comfortable life in China.[7] Gender roles in Chinese society have been viewed as yet another obstacle that prevented women from immigrating, for married women in a patriarchal, patrilineal, and patrilocal Chinese society were expected to bear children and serve their parents-in-law. Some scholars have argued that by leaving their wives behind in China, the men overseas assured their families of their familial loyalty.[8]

Others have challenged the assumption that cultural restraints were responsible for the skewed sex ratio of the Chinese immigration community. Both George Anthony Peffer and Sucheng Chan have examined the special situation in the United States, finding that harsh laws, strictly enforced and often supported by the courts, made it extremely difficult for Chinese women to gain entry.[9] The establishment of the so-called bachelor society, in their view, was not a choice made by the Chinese; it was the result of discriminatory legislation against the Chinese in the United States.

The reaction of the immigrants as a group to the pressure of anti-Chinese legislation, however, has not been carefully examined. The exclusion laws made the immigration of Chinese women difficult, but the Chinese were not passive victims of the discriminatory treatment. This chapter examines the legal and legislative struggles of Chinese Americans as a response to what Elaine Kim describes as "genocidal" American laws.[10] It demonstrates that family unification was one of the most important issues for the Chinese American community in the early twentieth century. Regardless of strong opposition from society at large, Chinese Americans were determined to build families in the United States. For several decades before World War II, simply trying to win admission for female spouses consumed much of the political energy of the community. It took six years of legal action and legislative struggle to win admission for Chinese wives of citizens such as Jee Shee, and this was only one episode in the larger battle for family unification.

Utilizing the Judiciary System: Moving from Laborers' Wives to Merchants' and Citizens' Wives

In the early decades of Chinese immigration beginning in 1850, for reasons that have been discussed elsewhere, many immigrants did not bring their wives and children to the United States. A large proportion of early Chinese female immigrants were poor girls who had been sold into prostitution. As early as the 1850s and 1860s, San Francisco's municipal officials made attempts to close down Chinese brothels, and in 1870 the California legislature passed a law to "prevent the kidnapping and importation of Mongolian, Chinese and Japanese females for criminal or demoralizing purposes." The state commissioner of immigration utilized the law to deny entry to all Chinese women, but the Chinese brought their cases to court. In 1874 this law was struck down by the California Supreme Court as a result of litigation filed by the Chinese on behalf of twenty-two women. In 1876, in *Chy Lung v. Freeman*, the U.S. Supreme Court also ruled that the law was unconstitutional because it interfered with the federal government's control over the regulation of foreign commerce.[11]

A year earlier, in 1875, the federal government had enacted the Page Law, which forbade the entry of Chinese, Japanese, and Mongolian contract laborers, prostitutes, and felons.[12] The effectiveness of this law has been documented in Peffer's studies and supported by Chan's research.[13] Although the Page Law stipulated an end to the importation of contract laborers and prostitutes, its strict implementation, with the collaboration of American consuls in Hong Kong, also made it extremely difficult for the wives of Chinese immigrants to come to the United States. Female applicants were charged fees for their applications and had to undergo examinations by the American consuls at the port of departure. Many women were turned away. The combination of the financial burden and the humiliation that they were subjected to in the process discouraged many Chinese women who had legitimate reasons for leaving from applying for entry.[14] Although the number of Chinese women immigrating fluctuated year by year, the overall rate declined significantly after 1875. From 1869 to 1874, for example, an average of 626 Chinese women were admitted annually to the United States. In contrast, only 265 were admitted between 1875 and 1881.[15] As Chan has pointed out, the law was so effectively enforced that the entry of Chinese women became a nonissue in the later campaigns to exclude the Chinese.[16]

The Chinese Exclusion Act of 1882 suspended the immigration of Chinese laborers for ten years, and it also officially prohibited state or federal courts from granting citizenship to any Chinese person. Those who were already residents in the country or might come within ninety days after the enactment of the law were allowed to stay and reenter after a temporary absence. New admissions were granted only to government officials and members of treaty-exempt classes—merchants, teachers, students, and tourists.[17] The 1882 act did not specifically prohibit women from entering the United States. Since women did not usually work for wages in China, they were not considered laborers. At that time, no restrictions were imposed on men who had already immigrated on bringing in their wives and establishing families.[18]

In 1884, however, an amendment was added to the act. It required each exempt Chinese applicant to present a Section 6 certificate issued by the government of which the Chinese person was a subject and endorsed by an American consul.[19] Because the new wives of the returning immigrant laborers—who had gone back to China to visit and to marry—lacked such documents, immigration authorities denied them entry.

The Chinese went to court immediately. The first petitioner, Ah Quan, came to the United States with her husband, a Chinese laborer who had resided in the United States before the Chinese Exclusion Act went into effect. The Federal Circuit Court for the District of California ruled that Ah Quan's husband would be admitted if he had a certificate issued by the collector of the port for reentry or if he could provide sufficient evidence of his residence in the United States between November 17, 1880, and June 6, 1882. Judge Lorenzo Sawyer, representing the court, however, argued that admitting a Chinese laborer did not mean providing unrestricted entry permits for his wife and children. Ah Quan would be admitted only if she possessed her own certificate or her name appeared on her husband's certificate. In other words, she had to prove that she herself had resided in the United States before June 6, 1882. Moreover, the justice argued that the wife and minor children, who had not adopted the occupation of laborer, "should be deemed to belong to the class to which the husband or father belongs."[20]

A month later the same court turned down the petition of Ah Moy, also the wife of a Chinese laborer. Ah Moy's husband, Too Cheong, had left the Unites States for China in late 1883. He married Ah Moy during the visit and brought her over when he returned. Too Cheong was admitted, for he had a certificate for reentry issued by the collector of the port, but Ah Moy did not gain entry. Delivering the opinion of the court, Justice Stephen J. Field backed the immigration authorities with the following statement:

> If such Chinese laborer has a right to bring into the country with him a wife who has never been here before, he must, upon similar grounds, be entitled to bring with him all his minor children; and under this right, the number of Chinese laborers who are entitled to come to the United States will be greatly extended beyond the number who can enter by virtue of their own individual rights. . . . The conclusion I reached, after considerable reflection, was that the husband is not entitled to bring his wife into the country, she being in fact a Chinese laborer, and never having been here before; and that, upon the marriage of the petitioner in this case with a Chinese laborer, she took upon herself the *status* of the husband as one of the *class* who are not now permitted to enter the United States, without reference to her former *status*.[21]

The court not only denied a laborer the right to bring in his Chinese wife and children, but also decided that a woman should be accorded laborer status upon her marriage to a laborer even if she had never worked outside the home. Once they were classified as laborers, these women became inadmissible based on the plain language of the 1882 act. Therefore Chinese Americans had to abandon references to laborers in their legal attempts to bring in their wives.[22]

The U.S. government, in the meantime, had further tightened Chinese immigration through a number of exclusion amendments.[23] The 1888 Scott Act canceled all outstanding certificates that allowed reentry of Chinese who had left the country to visit their families in China.[24] The 1892 Geary Act extended the exclusion for ten years and required every Chinese immigrant in the United States to register for and then carry a certificate of residence.[25] A 1902 amendment extended the exclusion for yet another ten years.[26] Finally, in 1904, the exclusion of Chinese immigrants became a permanent government policy.[27]

The exclusion laws would have compelled male Chinese immigrants to separate from their wives and children permanently unless they chose to give up their residence in the United States.[28] To Chinese immigrants, these laws were passed to separate families, reduce the Chinese population, and eventually rid the country of all Chinese.[29] Finding a way to bring in new entries and establish families therefore became requirements for the community's survival.

Although the wives of Chinese laborers were legally barred from entry, wives of Chinese treaty merchants domiciled in the United States could still enter with their husbands.[30] Immigration officials attempted to reject several merchants' wives' applications by raising questions about the legality of Chinese marriage customs and the age gap between Chinese spouses, but the court supported the Chinese in most of the cases.[31] In *United States v. Mrs. Gun Lim*, Justice Rufus W. Peckham held that wives and minor children of Chinese merchants domiciled in the United States might enter the country without the certificates required by the 1884 act.[32] Some Chinese therefore, to increase the number of new entries, pooled resources to start businesses and created partnerships with their friends and relatives. Establishing merchant status required more resources than the average laborer could acquire, however, even in combination with his fellows, and it was thus beyond the reach of the majority of Chinese immigrants.

These restrictive and discriminatory laws compelled Chinese Americans to fight back collectively. In the process, the Chinese Consolidated Benevolent Association in San Francisco, also known as the Chinese Six Companies, emerged as the voice of the community. One of the CCBA's most successful efforts to mobilize the community was a rigorous battle challenging the 1892 Geary Act, as Lucy E. Salyer has documented in *Laws Harsh as Tigers*. Immediately after the enactment of the Geary Act, which required all Chinese immigrants to register and carry their certificates or face the danger of being deported, the CCBA registered a strong protest with the collector of internal revenue, John Quinn, calling the new law "an unwarranted and unnecessary insult to the subjects of a friendly nation . . . an insult that has not been inflicted upon the subjects of any other nation." At the same time the CCBA posted circulars in Chinatowns throughout the United States, calling upon Chinese to stand together and not to register. The organization hired a team of eminent American attorneys to contest the law. Each Chinese American was asked to donate a dollar for the legal fees. According to Salyer, one month before the deadline for registration, only 439 of an estimated 26,000 applicable Chinese residing in San Francisco had applied for certificates following the requirement of the government. The majority of the Chinese immigrants were convinced that they could win the case.[33]

Although the CCBA was confident that the Geary Act was unjust, the Supreme Court, in a five-to-three decision, upheld the constitutionality of the act in 1893. Writing for the majority, Justice Horace Gray ruled in *Fong Yue Ting v. United States* that there is a distinction between the rights of aliens and those of citizens, and that Congress could devise any procedures it saw fit to register and deport the resident Chinese aliens. The defeat of the CCBA caused the prestige of the organization to suffer, and for some years thereafter the CCBA involved itself in a power struggle with the secret societies, the tongs.[34]

The struggle for family reunions, however, never stopped. In 1902 Chinese Americans successfully established a case in the Circuit Court of Appeals for the Ninth Circuit in which an alien Chinese wife of an American citizen gained the right to reside with her husband according to existing laws for married women. The appellant, Tsoi Sim, had come to the United States at age three with her father, a laborer, before the 1882 exclusion act went into effect. She attended both public and private schools in California, and she never left the country. She was nonetheless arrested for deportation in 1902 on the grounds that she did not have the certificate of residence required by the Geary Act. However, Tsoi Sim was married to Yee Yuk Lum, a Chinese born in the United States, a citizen. Delivering the opinion of the court, district judge Thomas Porter Hawley concluded that a citizen of the United States should be entitled to greater rights and privileges than an alien merchant. Upon marriage, Tsoi Sim's husband's domicile became hers, and therefore she was entitled to live with her husband and remain in the country. "If the appellant were to be deported," the judge reasoned, "she would have the unquestioned right to immediately return, and would be entitled to land, and remain in this country, upon the sole ground that she is the lawful wife of an American citizen."[35]

The principle established in *Tsoi Sim v. the United States* was extremely important to the Chinese. As the argument shifted from the rights of an immigration applicant (an alien excludable) to the rights of her sponsor (an American citizen), a small door for the wives of Chinese Americans opened. The ruling implied that any male American citizen of Chinese ancestry could go back to China, get married, and then bring his alien Chinese wife back to America, even if he was a laborer. After the 1906 earthquake and fire in San Francisco destroyed many of the city's civil documents, some Chinese immigrants falsely claimed U.S. citizenship by birth. They then used this claimed status to bring in their wives. Only 44 Chinese women were admitted to the United States in 1902; in 1924, 938 were admitted (table 1.1).[36] This group of women was crucial to the early development of family life in the Chinese American community.

Tsoi Sim v. United States stood for about two decades, until the Immigration Act of 1924 added new criteria that further excluded Asians. The new legislation was a triumph for the forces of American nativism. By introduc-

TABLE 1.1   *Chinese Women Admitted to the United States, 1900–1930*

Year	Total	Wives of U.S. citizens
1900	9	n.a.
1901	39	n.a.
1902	44	n.a.
1903	40	n.a.
1904	118	n.a.
1905	88	n.a.
1906	88	7
1907	64	23
1908	86	37
1909	135	98
1910	172	110
1911	183	80
1912	241	88
1913	330	126
1914	302	122
1915	287	106
1916	277	108
1917	280	110
1918	300	132
1919	272	91
1920	429	141
1921	713	290
1922	843	396
1923	835	387
1924	938	396
1925	195	0
1926	193	0
1927	221	0
1928	263	0
1929	271	0
1930	249	0
Total	8,505	2,848

SOURCES: *Annual Report of the Commissioner General of Immigration to the Secretary of Labor*; U.S. House of Representatives, *Hearing before the Committee on Immigration and Naturalization on H.R. 2404, H.R. 5654, H.R. 10524,* 71st Congress, 2nd sess.
NOTE: Besides wives of U.S. citizens, other groups of women admitted included children of citizens, wives and children of merchants, and students. Data for these subcategories are not available in the annual reports.

ing a national quota system, it effectively limited the number of immigrants from the less desired eastern and southern European countries. The new legislation also had a grave impact on immigration from Asia. Section 13(c) of the act, using the same language in California's alien land laws and the 1922 Cable Act (see chapter two), stipulated that "no alien ineligible to citizenship shall be admitted to the United States."[37] This provision was added to satisfy the anti-Japanese forces in western states. As a result, Japanese immigration was virtually cut off, even though Japanese were not named in the act.[38] Chinese were not named in the act either, since they had been officially excluded after 1882. Because the 1882 exclusion act also barred Chinese immigrants from naturalization, Section 13(c) provided legal grounds for immigration authorities to turn down any immigrant applicants from China. Shortly after the law went into effect, some thirty Chinese wives of merchants and citizens arrived at the port of San Francisco aboard the ship *President Lincoln.* Immigration authorities refused to admit the women, and the district court in California backed the charges brought by the Department of Labor against them.[39]

The Chinese American community burst into an uproar upon learning the ramifications of the 1924 Immigration Act. The CCBA chapters in New York, Boston, and Seattle sent telegrams to the CCBA in San Francisco, urging the organization headquarters to take the lead in protesting the new law. This time the CCBA decided not to act alone. Instead it tried to form a united force with other community organizations throughout the United States, especially affiliates of the Chinese American Citizens Alliance (CACA) and the Chinese Chamber of Commerce. On October 30, 1924, a fourteen-member Boli ju (Committee to Challenge the 1924 Immigration Act) was formed to lead the struggle. Its top priority was to raise money to hire lawyers and secure admission for the wives of citizens and merchants.[40] The Boli ju took immediate action. Between December 1, 1924, and February 18, 1925, it raised $7,000 and hired three prominent attorneys to appeal to the higher court.[41]

The appeal for the merchants' wives was successful. In *Cheung Sum Shee et al. v. Nagle* in 1925, Justice James Clark McReynolds, sitting on the United States Circuit Court of Appeals for the Ninth Circuit, argued that an alien who came to the United States "solely to carry on trade" under an existing treaty should not be considered an immigrant and therefore should not be excluded under the 1924 act. Although wives of resident Chinese merchants did not come to carry on trade, by "necessary implication" they would be admitted with their husbands under the treaty and the door remained open for them.[42]

The same court, however, turned down appeals by citizens' wives. In *Chang Chan et al. v. John Nagle*, Justice McReynolds denied the petitioners the spousal privilege that was granted to the merchants. Although the petitioners were all citizens of the United States, the justice argued that their wives "did not become citizens and remained incapable of naturalization," and according to the Immigration Act of 1924, "no alien ineligible to citizenship shall be admitted to the United States."[43] The ruling reaffirmed the principle established in the Cable Act two years before, in which female U.S. citizens would not only not have the right to bring in their husbands, but would be deprived of their citizenship upon their marriage to aliens ineligible for citizenship.

The new law and the court interpretation of it closed one of the only two avenues for the wives of Chinese Americans. In 1924, 938 Chinese women had been admitted to the United States; a year later, the number declined to 195. During a nineteen-year period from 1906 to 1924, 2,848 Chinese women entered as wives of citizens; between 1925 and 1930, not a single one in the same category was allowed in (table 1.1). Of the total number of 24,782 married Chinese men in the United States in 1920, 21,736 of them (about 88 percent) had wives abroad.[44] Under the new law, even American-born Chinese would face great difficulties in marrying and starting families because of the skewed sex ratio of the Chinese population in the United States. There were 18,532 Chinese American citizens in 1920, but only 5,214 of the total were female. Among the 30,868 citizens in 1930, only 10,175 were female. Interracial marriage was not an option either; it was illegal in many states.

Lobbying the Congress: Securing Admission for Citizens' Wives

Scholars have noted that most lawsuits filed by the Chinese against the exclusion laws involved the immigration of men rather than of women.[45] This does not, however, suggest that Chinese Americans were not interested in bringing in women and establishing families, for litigation is by no means the only way to challenge laws or administrative policies. After the U.S. Supreme Court handed down its 1925 decision in *Chang Chan et al. v. John Nagle*, it became useless for Chinese Americans to address their grievances to the court. Community members thus took another tack and shifted their energy to political lobbying. To focus on the argument of citizens' rights, it was decided that the Chinese American Citizens Alliance, an organization of American-born Chinese who had the right to vote, should take the public spotlight in the legislative struggle, while the CCBA and other community organizations would offer their support behind the scenes. At its 1925 national convention, the CACA appointed twenty-six-year-old Y. C. Hong, a San Francisco–born Chinese, as its campaign spokesperson. Hong, who had worked for the INS since 1918, received his law degree from the University of Southern California.[46] In "A Second Plea for Relief," a pamphlet drafted by Hong and issued in 1926, the CACA declared:

> There is no other remedy for the hardship under which the American citizen of the Chinese race suffers in his separation from his wife but relief from Congress. He went to the courts believing that the courts would hold that an American citizen had an inherent, natural, and constitutional right to have his wife with him in the country of his citizenship, that his domicile was her domicile, and that his home was her home. But the United States Supreme Court in the test case of *Chang Chan et al. v. John D. Nagle* decided otherwise, and his only hope of relief is in following the intimation contained in the decision of the court to the effect that Congress alone can remove the hardship from which he suffers.[47]

Indeed, in *Chang Chan et al. v. John Nagle*, Justice McReynolds cited an earlier decision, one from *Chung Fook v. White*, that "the words of the statute being clear, if it unjustly discriminates against the native-born citizen, or is cruel and inhuman in its results, as forcefully contended, the remedy lies with Congress and not with the courts."[48]

A lobbying campaign was quickly mounted to repeal the law that barred the entry of Chinese wives of citizens. The CACA wrote to prominent American citizens and organizations for support and circulated its pamphlet to members of Congress. In 1926, the Sixty-ninth Congress received a Senate bill (S. 2358) through Democratic senator William H. King of Utah and a House bill (H.R. 6544) through Republican representative Leonidas C. Dyer of Missouri to amend the 1924 Immigration Act. By the time Congress formed the Committee on Immigration and Naturalization, the Chinese had obtained written support from more than forty prominent American citizens, including Ray Lyman Wilbur, president of Stanford University; Nicholas Murray Butler, president of Columbia University; Walter D. Scott, president of Northwestern University; and spokespersons for a number of church groups and missionary associations.[49]

Appearing before the Committee on Immigration and Naturalization of the House of Representatives were active members of the CACA, including George Fong, Peter Soo Hoo, and Wu Lai Sun. Some of them were veterans of World War I. Trying to reestablish the principles of *Tsoi Sim v. United States*, they repeatedly argued that an American citizen should have the right

1. Y. C. Hong, lawyer for the Chinese American Citizens Alliance and spokesperson during the lobbying effort to win admission for Chinese wives of American citizens. *Courtesy of Roger S. Hong, trustee, Youchung Hong and Mabel Chin Hong Archives.*

to his wife's companionship, that his domicile should be hers, and that Chinese American citizens should be entitled to no less protection than alien Chinese merchants. If Chinese merchants could bring their wives to live with them in America under the treaty between China and the United States, the same should be allowed to American citizens of Chinese ancestry.[50]

As a political strategy, Chinese Americans tried to convince the House committee that their request would not lead to an influx of Chinese immigrants, since the number of American-born Chinese was very small, and that Chinese women would not compete with American workers for jobs. They also argued that letting Chinese American citizens have their families would discourage interracial marriage and ensure that these men's income would be spent in the United States.[51] Wu Lai Sun of CACA's Portland Lodge made the following argument: "So far as the laborers are concerned, I will admit that their presence here in large numbers is not good for the country, but we are not asking for the importation of Chinese laborers that come to compete with the labor in this country. These wives of Chinese-American citizens are not brought in here to work as laborers. . . . It is a question of breaking up the family and the possibility of the Chinese intermarrying here or remaining in a condition of celibacy the rest of their lives."[52]

Members of the House committee did not pay much attention to what the Chinese said, however; they were apparently more concerned with the issues raised in a 1925 report from the immigration commissioner. The report stated that the 1924 Immigration Act had been effective in curbing Chinese immigration; the only problem was that the court ruled in favor of Chinese merchants. The commissioner suspected that a greater number of Chinese women might take advantage of the court ruling and try to gain entry as merchants' wives.[53] The congressional members were more interested in keeping out an undesirable race than in supporting the rights of a certain ethnic group of American citizens. Few committee members bothered to rebut the points made by supporters of the bills; they simply ignored their requests.

The Chinese Americans would not give up. They strongly believed that their efforts would not be "in vain."[54] In 1928 they introduced similar bills to the Seventieth Congress through Senator King and Congressman Dyer (S. 2271, H.R. 6974), and they repeated their arguments at the hearing of a Senate subcommittee. Once again Congress refused to act.[55]

After two failed attempts to amend the 1924 legislation, the CACA made a third effort. In early 1929 the CCBA and some fifteen community organizations teamed up to aid the campaign. A new thirty-member Boli ju was formed to raise money and look into new venues for litigation.[56] To exercise its political power more effectively, the community urged American-born Chinese to participate in local and state elections and to endorse candidates who appeared sympathetic to Chinese immigration issues.[57] San Francisco's Republican congresswoman Florence P. Kahn, a supporter of the Chinese and a majority member of the Committee on Immigration and Naturalization for the Seventy-first Congress, acknowledged that a large number of Chinese American citizens had participated in elections in her district.[58]

Waiting for the Seventy-first Congress in 1929 was another Senate bill (S. 2826, Bingham, Connecticut) and two House bills (H.R. 5654, Houston, Hawaii; H.R. 12379, Dyer, Missouri) requesting yet again that American citizens of Chinese ancestry be accorded the same rights as alien merchants regarding the entry of their wives. Eager to achieve at least some positive results, representatives of the Chinese community worked with legislators to modify their demands. Recognizing that the overriding concerns of Congress were the possible influx of Chinese women and the probability that Japanese Americans would take advantage of the proposed amendment, both the Senate bill and the House bill introduced by Houston asked only for the admission of Chinese wives of citizens (instead of all alien wives of citizens) who had married before 1924. The Senate bill was finally passed by both the Senate and the House, and it was signed into law by President Herbert Hoover.[59]

The act of June 13, 1930, amended section 13(c) of the 1924 Immigration Act by granting entry to alien Chinese wives of U.S. citizens who had married prior to May 26, 1924. Because of this new law, Jee Shee and the other Chinese wives of American citizens who had been released on bond since 1924 finally gained entry, but those citizens who married after 1924 were still separated from their alien Chinese wives.[60] Between 1931 and 1941 an annual average of only 60 Chinese women entered as citizens' wives.[61] This was, however, the best deal that Chinese Americans could negotiate in 1930. Of a total of 210 Chinese admitted from July 1932 to June 1937, only 9 were men. The majority, 201 of them, were women.[62]

The story behind the passage of the 1930 act reveals the difficulties and complexities of the legislative struggle. It also shows the strength of the Chinese American community and the power it could exercise. Throughout the 1930s and early 1940s, Congress busied itself with restricting further immigration. As the worldwide depression continued and unemployment among American citizens rose, demands for the liberalization of immigration policies were often ignored. In 1935 the congressional delegate Samuel W. King of Hawaii introduced a bill to the Seventy-fourth Congress asking that the privilege of citizens to bring in their wives be extended to all races ineligible for citizenship. The bill passed in the House but failed in the Senate,[63] as was the case in the next Congress.[64] For many years after 1930, Chinese wives of citizens who married before 1924 could enter the United States, but Japanese, Korean, and Asian Indian wives of American citizens could not.

After 1930, the CACA continued to raise funds in hopes of further amending the 1924 act.[65] Waiting for the Seventy-eighth Congress in 1943 were two new bills authorizing the admission of alien Chinese wives of American citizens regardless of the date of marriage (S. 691, Downey, California; H.R. 1607, Lesinski, Michigan).[66] By then, the United States had entered World War II and Congress was under pressure to end Chinese exclusion as a goodwill gesture to its war ally China. In order to win the repeal, which would change the political status of all Chinese in America, the CACA let the two bills be pushed aside.

The lobbying campaign to abrogate the exclusion acts was led by the Citizens' Committee to Repeal Chinese Exclusion (CCRCE), organized by a group of "friends of China," instead of the Chinese American community.[67] Some Chinese American organizations, including CACA, CCBA, the Chinese Hand Laundry Alliance in New York, and the Chinese Women's Association in New York, had expressed a desire to pressure Congress and had written to members of Congress, but other than that the community, following the advice of the CCRCE, kept a low profile during the congressional debate. The CCRCE had in fact limited membership on the committee to non-Asian citizens to convince Congress that it was the white Americans rather than the Chinese who demanded an end to the exclusion. Only two Chinese Americans testified before the House committee: Dr. Li Min Hin from Hawaii and Paul Yee, an electronics engineer working for the War Department. They both emphasized the significant contributions the Chinese had made and the assimilability of the Chinese into the American way of life. Several Chinese Americans who spoke at public meetings focused on various aspects of racial equality but were careful not to make their views sound as if they were advocating an open door immigration policy.[68]

The repeal campaign was also helped by Japanese propaganda that sought to weaken the Sino-American alliance. Radio Tokyo broadcast documented evidence of U.S. policies against the Chinese in an effort to discredit America's influence in Asia.[69] For instance, Chinese children who listened to a "children's hour" program broadcast from Tokyo on March 17, 1943, were told in Chinese that "while white people are free to live in China, the Chinese cannot enter the United States."[70] The Nationalist government was reminded by their Japanese enemies that in the United States the few Chinese exempt from the exclusion laws were "forced to undergo the most humiliating and discourteous treatment and detention at the various immigration stations," that Chinese immigrants had to live in segregated Chinatowns located in the most disreputable districts, and that the Chinese were rigidly excluded from attaining American citizenship by naturalization, a right that was accorded the lowliest immigrant from Europe.[71] This fact-based propaganda greatly embarrassed the United States: its treatment of racial minorities did not square with its condemnation of Hitler's racist theories. The suggestion that discriminatory policies might cause the Chinese and other Asians to join Japan in its "Asia for Asiatics" campaign alarmed American lawmakers.

To some Americans, the repeal was a military necessity. Speaking at the House hearings for the repeal, Admiral H. E. Yarnell, commander of the Pacific Fleet from 1936 to 1939, warned of the grave possibility that the Chinese Nationalist government might collapse and urged Congress to act: "The most effective method is to consider, by act as well as by word, China as an equal in every respect with the other three Allied Nations, in the conduct of the war and in the postwar settlement. A step in this direction has been made in the announced intention of annulling the treaties regarding extra-territoriality and the special privileges. A greater step will be the repeal of the Chinese exclusion laws."[72]

Still, the repeal bills faced strong opposition. During the debate, several congressmen spoke against making any changes in immigration policy during the war; they argued that such changes would give the Chinese no material assistance. Opposition also came from the American Federation of Labor, the American Legion, and the Veterans of Foreign Wars: their concerns had largely to do with labor standards and postwar unemployment. At the end of the first session of the Seventy-eighth Congress the House committee voted nine to eight against repeal, and the matter was tabled.[73]

When Congress reconvened in September, three new repeal bills had been introduced. Sitting on the sidelines, Chinese Americans had watched Congress take every possible measure to ensure that the repeal would not make it any easier for Chinese to immigrate. The *Chinese Times*, the official newspaper of the CACA, expressed dismay at the difficulties encountered by a bill granting Chinese immigration to a token 105 newcomers per year.[74] Eager to win support for his bill (H.R. 3070), Democratic congressman Warren G. Magnuson from Washington sent a telegram to William Green, the president of the American Federation of Labor, stating that "the quota system amply puts brakes and complete control over any migrant labor," and that the "purpose of the bill is not in any sense to allow migrant labor, merely to put Chinese, our allies, on equal basis with other countries."[75] On October 11, 1943, President Franklin D. Roosevelt urged Congress to take action, noting that by repealing the Chinese exclusion laws, the United States could "correct a historical mistake and silence the distorted Japanese propaganda." In answer to those who feared an influx of Chinese immigrants after the war, the president pointed out that the Chinese quota would be only about one hundred immigrants per year, and he emphasized that "there can be no reasonable apprehension that any such number of immigrants will cause unemployment or provide competition in the search of jobs."[76] On October 21 the House passed the Magnuson bill. A month later the Senate gave its approval. Sixty-one years of Chinese exclusion finally ended when the president signed the repeal bill into law on December 17. Having been involved in the legislative struggle for decades, Chinese Americans well knew that the repeal was only a wartime strategy of the government. They nevertheless thanked Congress for taking the action. According to the historian Him Mark Lai, who lived in San Francisco's Chinatown at the time, there was no public celebration in the Chinese American community.[77]

The repeal act made the Chinese eligible for naturalization and opened the door to Chinese immigration. At the same time, however, the act imposed additional racial restrictions to ensure that the quota of Chinese immigrants from all parts of the world would be limited to 105 annually. The new law stipulated that all people of Chinese origin, regardless of their place of birth, were subject to the quota allocation, even though the 1924 Immigration Act had classified immigrants for quota purposes by place of birth rather than by citizenship or nationality except for "aliens ineligible to citizenship." A Chinese quota would be deducted for a Chinese born in Hong Kong who came with a British passport, and no Chinese who was a native of a Western Hemisphere country could enter as a free immigrant.[78]

Most ominously, the repeal act cast a new shadow on the immigration of Chinese women and children. Existing laws had allowed Chinese children of American citizens to enter outside the quota limit, and the 1930 legislation granted the same privilege to Chinese wives of American citizens married before 1924, but the new law required every Chinese person entering the United States (with the exception of merchants, teachers, students, tourists, and government officials) to come in under the quota. In contrast, no such limits were imposed on European families.[79] Although the repeal made the Chinese "admissible," under the quota system the actual number of new entries might be reduced. Fred W. Riggs, who researched the congressional debate on the repeal, argued that the failure to include Chinese wives in the repeal was because of "a technicality of drafting" rather than a racist intent to keep the limit low.[80] Given that the issue had been presented to Congress so many times without results, however, Chinese Americans had to be skeptical about the government's intentions. Writing shortly after the repeal bill passed both Houses, Gilbert Woo, then an editor of the *Chinese Times*, told his readers that it was pure luck that the exclusion acts were rescinded. He doubted that the repeal would have been possible if its opponents had been able to delay the matter for a few more months until the victory of the Allies was at hand.[81]

The significance of the repeal act, nevertheless, should not be overlooked. The new law changed the status of Chinese from inadmissible to admissible and thus entitled them to equal treatment under general immigration laws. The repeal also made Chinese immigrants eligible for citizenship. Between 1937 and 1942, an annual average of fewer than 38 Chinese aliens became naturalized citizens; they were children born in China of parents who were already American citizens. Between 1943 and 1949, the numbers ranged from 497 to 927 per year.[82] Now both Republican and Democratic candidates began placing campaign ads in local Chinese newspapers. Aware of the Chinese voters' growing strength in their state, California representatives introduced seven bills requesting more relaxed policies on Chinese immigration to the Seventy-ninth Congress in 1946. Six of these bills urged unlimited admission of alien Chinese wives of American citizens, and the last one concerned the reentry of Chinese laborers and their wives and children.[83]

General postwar immigration legislation also helped ease the immigration of Chinese women. The War Brides Act of 1945 granted admission to alien spouses of World War II veterans on a nonquota basis.[84] Because the Chinese had become admissible after 1943, they were one of the first qualified Asian groups to bring in their spouses.[85] After the passage of Fiancées and Fiancés of the War Veterans Act of 1946, Chinese women who intended to marry war veterans could also gain temporary admission.[86] Because the War Brides Act was applicable to all foreign spouses of war veterans regardless of when the marriage took place, between 1945 and 1948 several thousand Chinese women were reunited with their families. The picture of Chinese immigration thus began to change. In late 1946 Congress finally acted on the bill reintroduced by Democratic congressman George P. Miller of California, and the act of August 9, 1946, granted all Chinese American citizens the right to bring their wives as nonquota immigrants.[87] This act brought to an end the twenty-year battle to win admission for citizens' wives. It was the combined effort of litigation and legislative struggle that enabled a small number of Chinese women to enter the United States under extremely difficult circumstances.

Mobilizing the Community: Protecting the Rights
of Citizens to Bring in Wives

The struggle to win women's admission brought a sense of unity to a community that was often not harmonious; it also drew many Chinese Americans' attention to congressional activities and the legislative process in Washington. In early 1949, the House considered a bill introduced by Walter Judd, a Republican congressman from Minnesota, that would "make immigration quotas available to Asian and Pacific peoples in accordance with the national origins provisions of the 1924 Immigration Act." When the Chinese learned that this bill would negatively affect the immigration of Chinese women, the entire community organized to block it.[88]

Congressman Judd was no stranger to Chinese Americans. Born in Rising City, Nebraska, he had lived and worked in different parts of China as a medical missionary for ten years, and he had lectured throughout the United States on American foreign policy and interests in the Pacific before being elected to the Congress in 1942. Judd had been sympathetic to the causes of Asian Americans. In early 1943 he had worked with the INS on a comprehensive bill that would make members of all races eligible for citizenship and apply the quota system to all Asians. When it became clear that his bill would not pass at the time, Judd joined other members of Congress to repeal the Chinese exclusion acts. He was one of the key witnesses who testified for the repeal before the House committee, and his eloquent testimony filled twenty-five pages of the *Congressional Record*.[89] In 1948, after Chinese exclusion ended, Judd worked on a new bill that aimed to end Japanese and Korean exclusion (H.R. 5004). Chinese Americans supported his efforts wholeheartedly, although no action was taken by Congress at the time.[90]

When Judd reintroduced his bill in 1949 (H.R. 65), representatives of the Chinese American community were in Washington working on a new piece of legislation that would give permanent resident status to wives of merchants. They were shocked to learn, after the bill passed the House in early February, that Judd had added a new section limiting nonquota alien spouses and unmarried children of citizens only to nations with more than a 200–person quota.[91] Apparently the representative from Minnesota had revised the bill to increase its acceptability in Congress. If the bill were to become law, Chinese Americans would be pushed back to where they had been in 1943. The 1946 victory would be wiped out, and Chinese wives of American citizens would again be placed under the 105–person quota limit.[92] At the time, about twenty thousand wives and children of ethnic Chinese who were citizens of the United States were still in China, and taking away their nonquota privileges would make reunion extremely difficult for these families.[93]

On March 4, 1949, representatives of the CACA, the CCBA, the Chinese Chamber of Commerce, and the Chinese War Veterans Association convened an emergency meeting at the CCBA headquarters in San Francisco. The meeting called for immediate action to defeat the Judd bill by utilizing all possible human and financial resources.[94] In the next few weeks, the entire community was mobilized.[95] Telegrams were sent to several senators in hopes of convincing them to delay the Senate debate, and a long letter was sent to President Harry S Truman and Attorney General Tom Clark, demanding equal treatment for the Chinese under general immigration laws. Legal teams working on Chinese immigration cases in Washington protested to the Justice Department and other government agencies. [96] Special fund-raising drives were launched, and individual community members reached deep into their pockets.[97] Organized by the Zhonghua zhong xuexiao (Chinese Central High School) in San Francisco, Chinese students mounted a "ten thousand signatures" campaign and approached both Chinese and non-Chinese educators, students, and residents. Meanwhile, a sixteen-member delegation representing Chinese Americans from different parts of the country went to Washington to work with members of Congress, and their progress was reported in community newspapers.[98]

These all-out efforts were enormously effective. Several members of Congress offered their support to Chinese Americans almost immediately. In a letter to San Francisco's CCBA, Democratic senator Sheridan Downey of California promised that he would do everything possible to block the bill.[99] Meeting with members of the Chinese delegation, Walter Judd admitted that he made a mistake. After several Chinese Americans, including Henry Lem, Albert Chow, William Jack Chow, and Y. C. Hong, testified before the Senate hearings of the Eighty-first Congress, Judd requested that his own bill be amended, calling Section 3 "unfair" and "discriminatory" to countries with low quota allocations. As advocates became opponents, the bill died in the Senate in July.[100]

*I*t is plausible to argue that many early Chinese immigrants never intended to make the United States their permanent home: examples are not difficult to find, especially during the late nineteenth century. The exclusionists hoped that by separating Chinese men from their wives, those who had already resided in the United States would either return to China or eventually die off. The legal and legislative struggles that were carried out by the Chinese American community, however, illuminated the determination of Chinese Americans to settle in the United States and to accept the challenges that the democratic system posed. The victories that they won were limited at times, but hardly any opportunity was missed. The community's ability to utilize limited resources and to negotiate with law-enforcement officials and legislators under difficult circumstances played an important part in Chinese American history, one that should not be ignored.

One may still argue that a sojourner mentality dominated the Chinese immigrant community before World War II, because Chinese brought significantly more male children than female children to the United States throughout the exclusion period. The following chapter will examine the relationship between the gendered immigration pattern and Chinese immigrants' desire to establish families.

CHAPTER 2

Gender and Immigration

During the first half of the twentieth century the Chinese brought a significantly larger number of male children than female children to the United States. During the second quarter of 1925, for example, all but 3 of the 256 Chinese men with American citizenship returning through San Francisco had wives in China, and at the port of entry these men claimed to have a total number of 719 children—670 boys and 49 girls, a ratio of 13.7 to 1.[1] My own study of Chinese immigration files between 1945 and 1952 shows a similar trend. Of the 1,004 married women entering, 877 claimed 1,788 children—1,483 boys and 301 girls, a ratio of 4.9 to 1. Such discrepancies cannot be interpreted as statistical aberrations.[2] Apparently some Chinese immigrants did not claim their daughters as dependents, and a large number of others claimed biologically unrelated boys as dependents.

As chapter one documented, the Chinese American community had fought vigorously to gain admission for married women for decades. As far as children were concerned, however, they preferred bringing boys to girls. Scholars have given various explanations for this gendered immigration pattern. They argue that patriarchal cultural values, a sojourning mentality in the early period, and better opportunities for boys than for girls in the United States are important factors that contributed to the immigration patterns of the Chinese.[3] This chapter examines the gendered immigration pattern as influenced by the immigration laws. Combining genealogical documents with immigration files, it argues that the Chinese brought more boys than girls to the United States as a means of maximizing the number of new entries to the country. Although this practice separated family members from time to time, in the long run it enabled more families to emigrate to the United States.

Boys and Girls: Patterns of Chinese Immigration

In 1997 Peter Lew, a retired Chinese American machinist who had been born and raised in Oakland, compiled a family genealogy and immigration history dating back to his grandfather, Lew Chuck Suey, who immigrated to the United States in 1877.[4] The result of Lew's two years of painstaking research is more than seven hundred pages of documents containing the immigration papers of three generations of his family, as well as correspondence, photographs, and family trees. In tracing the immigration history of the Lew family, the collection details the sponsoring role of each family member and relative. The story of the Lew family encapsulates one hundred years of the experience of a Chinese American family, and it provides insight into the struggles of Chinese Americans to establish families and communities in the United States.

The Lew family's immigration history began when seventeen-year-old Lew Chuck Suey set sail for America in 1877 from Guangzhou (Canton), China. He came as a laborer but later achieved merchant status. Between 1891 and 1903 Lew visited China three times. During these visits he got married and fathered one daughter, Lew Gay Heung, and two sons, Lew Wah Chew and Lew Wah Chuck, who remained in China with their mother. Lew Chuck Suey returned to China again in 1907, after the death of his first wife, and married a second time. When he came back to the United States in 1908, he claimed that he had a $1,900 share of the Pacific Coast Canning Company and was a partner in Oakland's Hop Wah Lung & Co. As a merchant, he was now entitled to bring in his family.[5]

There were problems, however. When Lew Chuck Suey returned to the United States in 1892, he reported that his first wife had given him a son, Wah Doon, even though the child had not yet been delivered and would in fact be the girl who was named Gay Heung. When the second child, a son, Wah Chew, was born, Lew claimed him upon his return to the United States. Coming back from China in 1903 on the third trip, he was unaware that his wife had become pregnant with his third child, Wah Chuck, and did not claim any new offspring at the port of entry. His own immigration records, therefore, allowed him to sponsor only two male children. Since his daughter and his younger son were eleven years apart, Gay Heung's slot could not be used for Wah Chuck, so along with his older son Wah Chew, Lew brought in his nephew under the name of Wah Doon.[6] After he and his second wife settled down in Oakland, Lew Chuck Suey fathered eight children. Later on, he was

2. Lew Chuck Suey's U.S. family in 1914. From the left are his sons Wah Chuck and
William, his wife, Kong Shee, his daughter Annie, Chuck Suey, his daughter Jennie,
and his son George. *Courtesy of Peter Lew.*

able to bring in his younger son by his first wife, Wah Chuck, as the paper
son of another Chinese.[7]

Gay Heung, Lew's oldest daughter, never joined the family in the United
States. One might argue that this was because girls were not considered important in traditional Chinese society, for only male offspring could carry on

the family name. Lew's sons and nephew were the ones who would continue the family lineage, so he had to bring them to America. His daughter, on the other hand, would hypothetically marry and bear children for a different family, so it would be pointless for the father to make the effort to bring her over. It is true that Chinese families traditionally valued boys over girls: in some cases, extremely poor Chinese families even sold their daughters. The Lew family, however, was well off, and it is very unlikely that someone like Chuck Suey would abandon his first child simply because she was female.

A careful reading of Lew's genealogy reveals information that adds detail to the picture of the family's immigration history. Over several decades Chuck Suey and his family did whatever they could to bring members of the clan to America. Seventy-four people were able to come after Chuck Suey, including twenty-seven of Chuck Suey's own family members and their descendents, thirty-three members of his siblings' families, six members of his cousins' families, and eight other fellow villagers. Many of them used fictive ties or fraudulent kinship. Most of these latecomers were Lews, but there were also Wongs, Toys, Chois, Lees, and others. Those who arrived before 1930 were mostly young men, but they all later brought in their wives. The family also sponsored Chuck Suey's baby sister, Po Chu, who had married a Wong.[8]

There were special circumstances surrounding Gay Heung's failure to join the family in the United States. For Gay Heung to come after Lew Chuck Suey had failed to claim her as his offspring, arrangements would have to have been made for her to take another person's slot. Sending for a "paper" child using false papers, however, was a difficult, expensive, and risky endeavor. After he and his family settled down in the United States, it had taken Chuck Suey five years to save enough money to bring over his son Wah Chuck, who arrived in 1913. By then, Gay Heung would have been twenty and almost certainly married.[9] Had her father been able to purchase a slot for her, Gay Heung would have had to assume an identity that was not her own and conceal both her age and her marital status, which would be extremely difficult for an adult married woman. Negotiations with her husband and parents-in-law could further complicate the matter. In any case it is not known whether Gay Heung would have wanted to be separated from her husband and children to go live with her father and brothers. The family did eventually sponsor Gay Heung's only surviving child, a son, to come to the United States in 1947.[10]

Then why did Lew Chuck Suey claim that he had a son before Gay Heung was even born? The fact that the Chinese claimed so many more boys than girls suggests that what Chuck Suey did was more than an innocent mistake. As far as minors were concerned, the Chinese did seem to prefer boys to girls.

The practice of sending more boys was an important tactic used by the Chinese to expand their community in the United States during the exclusion. Most of the early immigrants were male, since there was a better chance for a man to succeed. It took time for a man to find work and save money before he could send for his wife and children. As Peffer has argued, however, this situation would not have lasted for long if the government had not interfered.[11] Yet if the statutory exclusion had indeed blocked all new Chinese entries except for members of the exempt classes, most of the earlier immigrants probably would have returned to China. But the exclusion was hardly a complete success; the Chinese found ways to circumvent the discriminatory laws, which gave them the hope of eventually establishing families in the United States.

Chinese immigration was a network-driven process operated by clan or kin and friendship ties.[12] In rural areas of China, assisting individual migrants was traditionally viewed as an economic investment for the clans as well as for the families concerned.[13] It was a group rather than an individual decision, as Haiming Liu argues.[14] Lew Chuck Suey was the oldest son of a family of eight children (five sons and three daughters).[15] He was sent by his family to the United States as a teenager, probably with the help of his relatives in planning and financing. Both his parents and his clan expected a return on their investment.

When Chuck Suey first came to the United States, he needed to earn money; his family was probably in debt after paying for his voyage. As the representative who had started the family's journey to Gold Mountain, he probably also wanted to make sure that he would be followed. He would not have wanted to retire until these two goals had been achieved.

These factors explain why when Chuck Suey returned from a brief 1891 visit to China (he had most likely been called back by his kin to get married), he claimed that his unborn child was a male. If the child indeed turned out to be a son, he would follow in his father's footsteps. There was no point in claiming a spot for a girl. If the child were a female, she would stay in the village with the family, since there was little chance for a girl to make it on her own in a foreign land. It was important for Chuck Suey to secure a future immigration slot: whether it was for his own son or another male relative made little difference.

When Chuck Suey went to China to marry his second wife in 1907,

3. Lew Chuck Suey's children and their families in the United States in 1950. *Courtesy of Peter Lew.*

he was not yet ready to retire. He had just obtained merchant status and was on his way to making more money. He also now had the privilege of bringing his family back with him. His immigration records could not be revised, however, and he had to leave two of his children behind. But he made a major contribution to his clan: because his daughter could not enter as a boy, Chuck Suey was able to bring his nephew with him, thus planting roots in the United States for a member of his brother's family.

In the decades that followed, Lew Chuck Suey and other members of his family helped many members of his clan settle in the United States. He tried to help his siblings' families first. He brought in a nephew and two of his brothers, and his brothers helped his youngest sister come. Except for two of his older sisters who had married before he left for the United States and a brother who never fathered a child, Chuck Suey's siblings all had their own family members in the United States by 1940. Chuck Suey also helped several of his cousins come to the United States. His children did the same. One of Chuck Suey's American-born sons, Wah Sing, got married in China and later brought two clan members back as his sons. Wah Sing's younger brother Wah Git brought in three paper sons. The immigrating clan members were mostly young men. They had come to the United States and then looked for opportunities for members of their own families and kin.[16]

At the same time, Chuck Suey and his children struggled for their own family reunions. The immediate family members they sent for included wives and both male and female children. The Lew family proper never left another female child in China.[17]

A similar strategy may be seen in Lisa See's study on the Fong/See family. The patriarch of this family, Fong See, came to California in 1871. Unlike his father, a sojourner who later returned to his village in China, Fong See married a white woman (even though he had a wife in China) and fathered five children in the United States. During one of his visits to China, Fong See married again and formed yet another family. After he divorced his second wife, he brought all members of his newer family, his wife, sons, and daughters, to the United States. As a well-to-do merchant, he also helped a number of his relatives to immigrate, and most of these entries were male.[18]

The story of Hwong Jack Hong, a cook in San Francisco who came to the United States in 1921, was similar to that of Lew Chuck Suey. During his home visit, Hwong Jack Hong got married and fathered two children. His younger child, a girl, was born after he returned to the United States and was recorded in his immigration papers as a son. In 1947, when Hwong Jack Hong went to China to retrieve his children after the death of his wife, his immigration papers allowed him to bring only his son, Maurice. In Maurice's autobiographical novel *Benliu*, the author describes the heartbreaking moment when he and his father had to leave his sister behind in China.[19]

The immigration history of the Lew family may be seen as a struggle to establish both family and clan networks. The unbalanced sex ratio resulted from the many slots that Chuck Suey and his children had created to help other families emigrate. No evidence suggests that any female children of these families were abandoned, even though under special circumstances they sometimes had to make significant sacrifices.

Men and Women, Sponsors and Dependents

Lew Chuck Suey, like many other Chinese immigrants, selected boys over girls when he had the opportunity to sponsor someone outside his immediate family in part because it was relatively easier for boys to find employment in the United States and make money, as a number of scholars have documented. In addition to the economic concerns, this gendered immigration practice also indicates that the Chinese had a clear understanding that the American laws and immigration system were biased against women in the immigration process. Chuck Suey, his sons, and his other male relatives each brought a number of new entries to the United States in the early decades of the twentieth century; several of them also brought in their wives. But not until 1947, after gender-biased legal provisions were removed from the statutes, did Chuck Suey's U.S.-born daughter Jennie become the first woman in the family to sponsor her own dependents.

American legislation historically had classified women as dependents of their husbands, as it did with minors. A brief analysis of these laws will illustrate how legal restrictions had long crippled the eligibility of American women to sponsor their alien spouses and children in entering the United States.

The first law regarding women's status was the Married Women Law of 1855. It granted an alien woman American citizenship upon her marriage to an American citizen. Nothing was said about the status of female citizens who married alien husbands.[20] The 1907 Expatriation Act stipulated that "any American woman who marries a foreigner shall take the nationality of her husband." The woman, as the law provided, "may resume her American citizenship" only upon "the termination of the marital relationship."[21] Interpreting the law eight years later, the Supreme Court ruled that a female citizen became an alien upon marriage to an alien even if the wedding took place in the United States and the couple decided to reside there.[22] Thus a woman's citizenship and nationality were determined by those of her husband.

The Expatriation Act and the decisions of the court were criticized in the early decades of the twentieth century as part of the political debate surrounding the suffrage movement. The issue of independent citizenship for married women could no longer be ignored after American women won the right to vote in 1920, after the ratification of the Nineteenth Amendment. How could the government disfranchise native-born women because their husbands were aliens, while foreign-born women could vote if their husbands were American citizens?[23] Few white reformers related the issue of independent citizenship to that of immigration at the time, since few restrictions were imposed on Europeans, but gendered nationality rights had deprived American-born Chinese women in transnational marriages the right of sponsorship.

Once American women citizens gained the right to vote, they pressed Congress to amend the 1907 Expatriation Act. The commitment of the reformers to the principles they had set forth in debates over government policies, was, however, rather weak. The goal of maintaining their own nationality concerned white women more directly, and the issue of justice for women of all racial backgrounds was pushed aside.[24] The result, the Cable Act of 1922, seemed to honor the principle of gender equality by making a woman's citizenship independent of that of her husband. This significant reform measure was nonetheless racially discriminatory, for the new law made a woman's nationality and citizenship contingent upon her husband's eligibility for naturalization, and a woman who married a person "ineligible for citizenship" would still have to forfeit her American citizenship.[25]

Legal prejudices against both women and ethnic Chinese worked together to deprive female members of Chinese American families of their basic rights. This was apparent in the case of a woman named Fung Sing. Born in Port Ludlow, Washington, in 1898, Fung Sing went to China with her parents and siblings in 1903. While in China she married a Chinese man. Fung Sing came back to the United States in 1925, after the death of her husband, but immigration officials in Seattle denied her entry. Only then was Fung Sing informed that she had lost her citizenship upon marriage and was ineligible for repatriation. She immediately sought release under a writ of habeas corpus.[26]

Interpreting the 1907 Expatriation Act, the 1922 Cable Act, and the 1924 Immigration Act, District Judge Jeremiah Neterer argued that "citizenship is a political status" that "may be defined and the privilege limited by Congress." He noted that according to the 1907 act, "any American woman who marries a foreigner shall take the nationality of her husband" and reiterated that the Cable Act stated that a woman who has lost her citizenship by reason of her marriage before 1922 might be naturalized only if the alien husband were eligible for citizenship. Further, he argued that the 1924 Immigration Act stipulated that "an immigrant born in the United States who has lost his United States citizenship shall be considered as having been born in the country of which he is a citizen or subject." The judge therefore ruled that although Fung Sing had been born in the United States, by marrying a citizen of China, she also became a citizen of China. She could not regain her American citizenship since her husband was an alien ineligible for citizenship, and once she became an alien ineligible for citizenship herself, Fung Sing should be barred from entering the United States.[27]

Another woman, Huang Cuilian, was born in San Francisco. She went to China with her mother in 1913 and married Ma Bingchang in Hong Kong in 1917. After giving birth to five children, Huang was abandoned by Ma, and she returned to her family in the United States in early 1930. Immigration authorities denied her entry, arguing that the Cable Act had stripped Huang of her citizenship upon her marriage to a Chinese alien, and denied her the right to regain her citizenship. Therefore she was barred from the country of her birth, but she had no home to return to in China. Her hard lot gained her great sympathy in the community, and the immigration lawyer Y. C. Hong offered his services free of charge. In court Hong argued that although Huang lived with Ma and had five children, she had never been legally married. The only legitimate marriage for Huang, a Christian, would be one that was registered and licensed according to Western customs: this was also required by the marriage laws of Hong Kong. A traditional Chinese wedding ceremony, while sufficient proof of marriage for any ordinary Chinese, would not be valid for a Christian, and therefore there was no legal ground for taking away Huang's U.S. citizenship in the first place. Hong also called a number of witnesses, including several white women who were members of the local Presbyterian church that both Huang and her mother attended, to testify that she was indeed a Christian. Only then did the court reverse its earlier decision and order the INS to admit Huang.[28]

Nationality laws of the United States had also prevented children from deriving their citizenship from their American-born mothers. The principle for derivative citizenship first became law in 1802 and was later strengthened in 1855 and 1878. The revised statute of 1878 provides that "all children heretofore born or hereafter born out of the limits and jurisdiction of the United States, whose fathers were or may be at the time of their birth citizens thereof are declared to be citizens of the United States."[29] Accordingly, a child born in China of an American father could gain both admission to and citizenship of the United States, but a child of an American-born mother was not entitled to such privileges.

The combination of these racially discriminatory and gendered immigration laws severely handicapped Chinese women in transnational marriages. Two of Lew Chuck Suey's U.S.-born children, daughter Jennie and son Wah Git, married alien Chinese while attending school in China. Such a marriage did not prevent Wah Git from coming back to the United States, and he later brought his wife in as a war bride. The convoluted legal restrictions against Chinese women in transnational marriages, however, compelled Jennie to give up her residence in the United States for many years.[30]

The legalized prejudice dogging Chinese women in transnational marriages had a great psychological impact on Chinese immigrants. Lew Chuck Suey's two older sons from his first marriage both married alien Chinese. Wah Chew later became a merchant, which allowed him to bring in his young wife and establish a family in the United States. Wah Chuck, who came later as a paper son, was less fortunate. Because he entered as a minor and did not report that he was married, he could not claim his son as his dependent. He then bought a paper slot, but got caught. Because of that, he was unable to unite his family until the early 1970s, many years after his wife had passed away. Wah Chuck did go back to visit his son, however.[31] Had Lew Chuck Suey's daughter, Gay Heung, managed to come to the United States as a paper daughter, as Wah Chuck did, after she was married, she would not have been able to reenter if she visited China, and she would have had no chance to bring in her husband and children. In addition, it would have been extremely difficult for a Chinese woman to live alone in the United States, work to support herself, and save money to send to her husband and children in China. After he failed to claim her as a dependent, Chuck Suey might have hoped Gay Heung could marry someone in the United States and come as a dependent, but it would have been nearly impossible for any of his male children to gain entry through marriage.

Not until the Cable Act was rescinded in 1930 did U.S.-born Asian women win the right to independent nationality.[32] After that, American feminists made amending derivative citizenship laws a focus of their legislative reform. This time, however, immigration emerged as a main issue of concern. Reform opponents were especially worried about the possibility that Asian women might use the opportunity to bring in foreign-born children of alien fathers.[33] Not until May 1934, when President Roosevelt signed an equalization bill into law, could a foreign-born child of an American mother also claim American citizenship if he or she entered the United States before the age of eighteen.[34]

Some new laws enacted in the 1940s used gender-neutral language. The War Brides Act, for example, uses the word "spouse,"[35] making the few Chinese women who served in the armed forces during the war eligible to send for their family members. In the three years that the War Brides Act was in effect, a total of 5,726 Chinese spouses and dependents of war veterans were admitted to the United States as permanent residents, but only 5 were male spouses (see table 2.1). The Chinese Alien Wives of American Citizens Act of August 1946 allowed the entry for citizens' wives outside the quota; it made no mention of Chinese husbands of American citizens, however. In other words, although postwar legislation facilitated the immigration of Chinese women, it continued to restrict Chinese women's ability to sponsor their family members.

The gender-selective strategy, to a large extent, was used by the Chinese

TABLE 2.1. *Chinese Spouses of War Veterans Admitted under the War Brides Act, 1945–1950*

Date admitted	Total	Husbands	Wives	Children
Dec 28,1945–June, 1946	155	1	150	4
July 1, 1946–June 30,1947	1,098	1	966	131
July 1, 1947–June 30, 1948	2,873	2	2,643	228
July 1, 1948–June 30, 1949	1,561	1	1,340	220
1950	39	0	33	6
Total	5,726	5	5,132	589

SOURCES: *Annual Report of the Immigration and Naturalization Service,* 1946, 1947, 1948, 1949, and 1950.
NOTE: The War Brides Act expired on December 28, 1948. Those added thereafter were fiancées or fiancés who adjusted their visa status. Of the 119,693 alien spouses from all countries admitted under the act, 333 were men, in contrast to 114,691 women and 4,669 children.

to maximize the number of new entries. The price they had paid to establish their community in the United States was high. Behind the successful example of Lew Chuck Suey were many Chinese immigrants who never had the resources to unite their families. Even within the Lew family, several members were separated from their spouses and children for decades. This not only affected the structure of the Chinese communities in the United States, but also had a lasting impact on the demographic components of the immigrants' villages in China. A 1989 study by Fang Di shows that some female members of overseas Chinese families never had the chance to come to the United States. The county censuses of Guangdong Province in 1964 indicate a significantly higher female-to-male ratio in the thirty-five-year-old age group in the three main home counties of Chinese Americans (Taishan, Xinhui, Kaiping) than in neighboring counties, and the discrepancy was even more prominent for older age groups.[36] The gender-selective immigration strategy, nonetheless, seemed to be crucial to the development of the Chinese American ethnic community during the exclusion.

Men and Women in the Transnational Families

The difficulties Chinese women faced in coming to the United States and the gender-selective immigration process for Chinese children created a large number of what scholars describe as split households in the Chinese American community before World War II.[37] Adam McKeown sees transnational families as creations of the Chinese migration network to ensure quick and predictable returns on their investments.[38] Madeline Yuan-yin Hsu, who also applied the concept of transnationalism in her study of Taishan County in Guangdong, found that a class of well-to-do Chinese families lived on money sent from family members abroad. Because of the favorable exchange rate for U.S. dollars, the average income of the Gold Mountain families was double or triple those who had no overseas connections.[39]

While marrying a Gold Mountain emigrant seemed economically desirable for village women, the wives in these marriages often had to shoulder many more responsibilities than others. Mary Yee, who came from a village where many men had gone overseas, remembered that the wives usually had to manage all the daily activities in the family, even though most of them received financial support from their husbands. During the ten years that her husband was in the United States, she had to till the rice field—a job traditionally done by men.[40]

Not all immigrant families received regular remittances from their overseas members. Wives who received no money from their husbands were compelled to become the breadwinners for their families. As Lisa See recorded in *On Gold Mountain*, Shue-ying Fong, her great-great-grandmother, received neither letters nor funds from her husband in the United States for over a decade. She had to carry people on her back from village to village to make a living for herself and her son.[41]

In rural China, where law enforcement was almost nonexistent, young wives who lived by themselves were often targets for rape or seduction.[42] Their families were also vulnerable to robbery and kidnapping. Mary Yee, whose father immigrated to Chicago when she was young, recalled that her mother would tie her and her siblings to the bed at night because so many children of Gold Mountain families were kidnapped.[43] In 1923 bandits attacked a school in Shui Bo village in Taishan County and kidnapped forty-three children of overseas immigrants. Among them was Lew Chuck Suey's American-born son Wah Git. The children were held for ten months, and released only after a large ransom was paid.[44] In the late 1930s when Japanese troops raided the villages in Guangdong, residents were forced to abandon their homes and go into hiding. Reunification in the United States then became an even more pressing concern for members of transnational families.

In the absence of their husbands, Chinese women became the heads of their households. They made the decisions, assumed responsibility for their aged in-laws, and controlled the family income. Tewdy Yee, who married a Gold Mountain immigrant at age fifteen, had to flee with her parents-in-law

4. Tewdy Yee and her son, Danny Gin. During World War II Tewdy lost touch with her husband, a cook in Santa Barbara, California. To support her family, she smuggled goods between Hong Kong and Japanese-occupied Taishan before coming to the United States in 1947. *Courtesy of Danny Gin.*

and her son when Japanese soldiers attacked her village in 1937. The Japanese invasion had broken off communications between her and her husband, a cook in Santa Barbara, California, and cut off her source of income. To feed the family, Tewdy smuggled goods between Hong Kong and Japanese-occupied Taishan. It was very dangerous for a young woman to engage in such an enterprise, but this experience turned a well-to-do housewife into an independent entrepreneur who later ran her own business in the United States.[45]

Sandra Wong, who conducted field research in San Francisco's Chinatown in 1987, found from oral history interviews that the concept of *jia* (family) changed in the process of immigration, for immigrant Chinese women often included their own parents and siblings, in addition to members of their husbands' families, as their family members.[46] The traditional patrilocal structure of the Chinese family often broke down when married couples lived separate lives. When Tewdy Yee smuggled goods between Hong Kong and Taishan, she was unable to live with her in-laws in the village. Thus instead of living with his paternal grandparents, Tewdy's son spent most of his childhood in Hong Kong, under the care of his maternal grandmother and uncle, while his mother worked outside the home.[47]

Gay Heung, Lew Chuck Suey's oldest daughter, had maintained close ties to her own family in the United States even though she had married a Toy. As Chuck Suey's only offspring in the village, she became the most important figure in the Lew family's Chinese center. After her sister-in-law passed away and her brother, Wah Chuck, failed to bring his son to America, Gay Heung took care of her nephew for many years. She also provided motherly care to her American-born half brothers and sisters while they attended school in China.[48]

Most male immigrants maintained close contact with their families in China. Quilted coats, soft cotton-bottomed shoes, and comforters hand-stitched by their wives in China kept the men warm in the United States. Letters from home often lifted their spirits. It was their families in China that gave their hard labor in their new home a sense of purpose. They looked forward to each home visit, to fathering more children, and to future family reunions. A sense of dependence on their wives also developed, since the women were the ones left behind to take care of their families in China. Even though some men married again in the United States, they were still bound to life in the villages in China, where their parents and relatives lived.

Marriages and families across the Pacific Ocean made the Chinese American community a transnational entity. Events in China were of critical concern to the men living abroad. In addition to providing national news coverage of both the United States and China, Chinese community newspapers usually had sections covering Chinese American settlements throughout the United States (Benfu xinwen) and the home villages (Jiaxiang xinwen).[49] This transnational connection played an important role in shaping community politics

5. A 1937 studio photograph of some of Lew Chuck Suey's children and grandchildren. In the center is Gay Heung, Chuck Suey's oldest daughter, who was never able to come to the United States. After Chuck Suey and his second wife died, Gay Heung cared for her American-born half brothers and sisters while they were studying in China, and this picture was taken just before some of them returned to America. *Back row:* Alice, Annie, Mae, Nancy; *front row:* Diane Louie Lew (wife of William), William, Toy Bay Oak (Gay Heung's son), Gay Heung, Toy Thuin Ock (Gay Heung's son, who later came to the United States as Jennie's son), Jennie, and Sik Tong (Wah Chuck's son who failed to come as a paper son). *Courtesy of Jennie Lew Quan.*

and social activities. In the 1930s and early 1940s, the community mobilized to support China's war against Japanese military aggression even though there was disagreement regarding which political forces should receive support.[50] As reports of natural disasters, war atrocities, political turmoil, and human suffering became more common, the Chinese in the United States sped up the immigration process for their family members by circumventing and challenging discriminatory immigration laws. The overarching struggle against the discriminatory immigration policies and practices of the United States, especially the struggle for family unification, brought all community groups together.

A well-knit immigration network was also established on both sides of the Pacific Ocean. Between 1881 and 1940, when the exclusion laws were in effect, an average of 2,553 Chinese entered the United States each year.[51] The fact that the Chinese had continued to come despite extremely harsh immigration laws puzzled Congress.[52] Because most Chinese immigrants were subject to interrogation and investigation by immigration authorities, the success of each entry depended largely upon the collective effort of family members, friends, and relatives in preparing immigration papers and providing supporting evidence and testimony.[53] Like Lew Chuck Suey, many early immigrants sponsored not only their own family members but also their fellow villagers.[54] They tried whatever they could to create new entry slots, while family members back in the villages did their part by selecting or preparing the right persons to fill the slots.

Chiu Chun (Ma) Wong, whose grandfather, father, and uncle went to Canada, recollected that after her mother died, the villagers whom she addressed as aunties were her guardians in every stage of her life: "Whatever the aunties said, went." The aunties had been looking for a man from the United States for Chiu Chun because she was a member of a Gold Mountain family. In early 1947, they learned that Tommy Wong, an American war veteran from a nearby village, was looking for an eligible young lady to take to the United States as his bride. After these women checked out Tommy's background, they took Chiu Chun shopping at a local store to be seen by Tommy and his relatives. To assure them that the potential bride was not mute, the aunties asked her to purchase a spool of thread. Everything went smoothly thereafter, and Chiu Chun came to the United States after her wedding later that year.[55]

Although women were not usually selected as the first ones in the family to emigrate, as siblings, wives, and mothers of the immigrants, their roles in making male family members' emigration possible should not be overlooked. Before Cai Fujiu (Henry Tsoi) made his journey to the United States impersonating the son of his cousin, his wife Qiu Guanyin helped him memorize facts about his new identity and family ties. She and other friends pretended to be immigration inspectors and made up questions so that Cai could prepare for his interrogation at the port of entry.[56] Although Qiu knew that she and her daughter would endure much hardship after her husband left, she supported his decision to emigrate, for it was an opportunity for the family.[57]

Immigration files show that a large number of Chinese women who arrived in the United States after World War II also claimed dependents other than their own children.[58] These women must have known the risks involved, but their loyalty to their family and kin left them little choice. They understood that it was the network's support that had enabled their men to go abroad in the first place. It was therefore their duty to help other clan members when their turn came.

Jennie, Lew Chuck Suey's U.S.-born daughter who had married in China, sailed back to the United States in 1947, after the death of her husband. In addition to her own daughter, she brought Toy Thuin Ock as her son Quan Wing, who had died in infancy. This required tremendous courage and careful preparation because Thuin Ock, who was born in 1930, had to declare his birth as 1934. It was difficult for a seventeen-year-old to impersonate a thirteen-year-old, but Jennie was determined to take the risk for her family: Thuin Ock was the only surviving child of Gay Heung, Jennie's half-sister, whose slot had been lost forty years earlier. Immigration records indicate that both Quan Wing (Toy Thuin Ock) and Jennie's daughter were admitted under the Nationality Act of 1934, which granted derivative citizenship to children born abroad to one citizen parent.[59]

In 1948, a woman who was entering as a war bride arrived at San Francisco claiming eighteen-year-old Liang Wangxin as her son. She was caught by the immigration authorities since she and her thirty-year-old husband Liang Yongyuan were too young to be the young man's parents. Further investigation by the INS revealed that Liang Yongyuan had originally entered the United States in 1930 using the identity of the son of a San Francisco merchant. He was convicted of a felony and sentenced to five years' parole plus a $500 fine. If Liang Yongyuan's wife had not claimed this young man as the couple's son, the INS would probably never have found out about his earlier fraud. His wife, however, was obligated to assist Liang Wangxin, for the latter's grandfather was the merchant who had sponsored Liang Yongyuan in 1930.[60]

The family has been the basic social unit in Chinese society for thousands of years. It was not, however, the dominant feature of Chinese American society until after World War II. Immigration changed family structures and gender roles, allowing Chinese immigrants' wives in China to gain the independence and power that had traditionally been reserved for men. These women lived an ocean apart from their husbands for many decades, but they worked with their men to achieve the same goal. In this sense they had been an integral part of the Chinese American community, serving as the links between the Chinese American community and immigrants' home villages in China. World War II and postwar developments would profoundly change Chinese Americans' family lives. But before we examine such changes, the next chapter will take a close look at the impact of the war on Chinese American women who were born or educated in the United States.

CHAPTER 3

Women and World War II

THE MAKING OF A NEW GENERATION

⚜

*I*n early 1943 the *San Francisco Chronicle* and several defense industries in the San Francisco Bay Area sponsored an essay contest on the topic of wartime production. The winner was a twenty-two-year-old Chinese American college graduate named Jade Snow Wong. An employee of Marinship, Jade Snow received a fifty-dollar war bond and the privilege of christening a Liberty Ship. Her essay, concerning the problem of absenteeism, was also used in a congressional report to the president of the United States. The success of a Chinese person in the American world generated much excitement in San Francisco's Chinatown, where Jade Snow had grown up. As her picture and stories about her appeared in mainstream newspapers and her voice was heard on the radio, Jade Snow became a community celebrity. Even her parents, who believed that the main duty of a Chinese woman was to get married and have children, began to view their daughter in a different light. They were pleased that she had glorified the Wong family name. April 16, 1943, was a day of festivity in Henry Kaiser's Richmond shipyards and in San Francisco's Chinatown. As Jade Snow smashed a bottle of champagne to launch the SS *William A. Jones*, she showed the audience and her community that a Chinese woman could be as capable as any man.[1]

The ship-launching ceremony, which made the news in the *Chronicle*, however, was at first not mentioned in the *Chinese Times*, now a major Chinese American community newspaper in San Francisco. Not until three days later, after friends and relatives of the Wong family protested, did the newspaper print Wong's story and offer a public apology. During the war, only the *Chinese Press*, an English-language community newspaper run by American-born Chinese Americans, regularly covered Chinese American women defense workers. Major Chinese-language papers paid more attention to women's roles in fund-raising and Red Cross work than their work in shipyards and the military.[2]

Scholars have long recognized the importance of World War II in the lives of women in the United States. Since the release of the documentary film *The Life and Times of Rosie the Riveter* in the late 1970s, popular interest in the topic has been increasing as well. Most observers, however, have overlooked the impact of the war on Chinese American women. In part because of the scarcity of English-language sources, some have assumed that Chinese American women did not share the experiences of Rosie the Riveter.[3] Not until recent years have scholars begun to examine these women's participation in World War II. In her 1995 book on Chinese American women in San Francisco, Judy Yung convincingly argued that it was the combined war effort of China and the United States that enabled Chinese American women to fall in step with their men and society at large.[4]

World War II profoundly changed the lives of Chinese American women. For the first time, the larger American society welcomed the contributions of most ethnic and gender minorities. Chinese American women entered the armed forces and were hired by industries previously dominated by white males; they worked side by side with men and women of different ethnic backgrounds. The war altered American attitudes toward Chinese in the United States as well as the Chinese community's attitudes toward women. The Chinese American women who participated in the war effort found themselves even more changed. The story of their involvement in the war is not just the story of how much they contributed to the war effort. It is also the story of the creation of a new generation of Chinese American women.

Possibilities and Limitations: The Prewar Experience

There were more male Chinese than female Chinese in the United States before World War II: 285 males for every 100 females in 1940. Because laborers' wives were barred during the Chinese exclusion, a fairly large number of female Chinese immigrants were wives of men who had merchant status. Few of these women's families were affluent, however. Many merchants' wives started to work immediately after they arrived, and most Chinese business owners would not have been able to make ends meet without the free labor provided by their spouses.[5]

While wives of Chinese merchants labored alongside their husbands in family-operated businesses whenever they were not occupied with household duties, most wives of Chinese laborers found work sewing, canning fruit, or shelling shrimp. The flexible working arrangements of Chinese-operated businesses made it possible for women to combine wage earning with family obligations. In Chinatown garment shops, babies slept in little cribs next to their mothers' sewing machines, and toddlers crawled around on the floor.[6] Many women also did piecework at home. These arrangements were important in maintaining the traditional order of the family and community. Women were paid lower hourly wages than men, and they had to shoulder many household responsibilities. Not until the early 1940s did nursery schools begin to appear in San Francisco's Chinatown. Few Chinese American families, however, were accustomed to the idea of leaving their children at childcare facilities. Nor did most Chinese women in the United States have their parents nearby to help out with childcare, which left them as their children's primary caretaker.[7] While Chinese men were free to play a large role in the community, the double burden of wage earning and household responsibility kept women occupied.

The isolation of the Chinese community also limited Chinese women's dealings with the outside world. In the late 1930s, only 4 percent of the Chinese families in San Francisco had cars, and few women knew how to drive. Most immigrant women living in Chinatowns in large cities were familiar only with the areas within walking distance of their homes. Some never ventured outside their communities without their husbands.[8]

The 1900 U.S. Census recorded 2,353 Chinese females living in the country who either were born in the United States or had gained derivative citizenship from their fathers, but these women, too, found their lives isolated.[9] Ah Yoke Gee's father, Jung San Choy, was a pioneering fisherman in the Monterey Bay area.[10] Ah Yoke grew up in the small Chinese fishing community there, lived in San Francisco's Chinatown after she got married, and later settled down in a racially mixed neighborhood in Berkeley with her family. Even though she could read and drive, Ah Yoke found her life was confined within the Chinese American community. She was a member of Berkeley's Chinese Presbyterian Church and a frequenter of San Francisco's Chinatown. In 1930, after her husband died, Ah Yoke became the breadwinner for a family of six children. She took in sewing through a Chinese subcontractor in Oakland and worked at home while taking care of her offspring.[11]

Most American-born Chinese women of Ah Yoke's age had little education, and many of them did not receive any public schooling whatsoever because they were systematically rejected by the public school system. Some went to segregated schools, the first of which was established in 1859 in San Francisco. After the facility was closed down by the school board in 1871, however, the city's Chinese children were excluded from public education for fourteen years. In 1885 the California Supreme Court ruled in *Tape v. Hurley* that Chinese children were entitled to public education, but the San Francisco Board of Education successfully campaigned to pass a state law imposing separate education on these students. The segregation of black children, in contrast, had ended ten years earlier. Following San Francisco's example, several other districts in the Bay Area also established segregated schools for Chinese pupils.[12]

By the 1920s, however, school segregation policies were breaking down and younger Chinese American children were gaining access to public education. Most Chinese American women who came of age on the eve of World War II had gone to high school, and some had attended college. As Ah Yoke Gee's daughter, Maggie Gee, recalled, going to college seemed to be a way of life for youngsters in Berkeley, where the central campus of the University of California was located. Her family was by no means affluent, but to save money Maggie lived at home while enrolled in the university, and she paid the twenty-eight-dollar quarterly fees and bought school supplies out of her own earnings from odd jobs. Ah Yoke never dreamed of higher education for herself, but sending Maggie to college was simply a matter of "setting her daughter's bowl of rice on the table" a few years longer, and she could not say no.[13] Jade Snow Wong, who received no financial assistance from her parents, went through college on a scholarship and the wages from a part-time job. Aimei Chen, the daughter of a Chinese restaurant waiter, enrolled in a community college in Stockton, California. She did not know what she would do with a college degree, but since she did not have a full-time job, she decided to take advantage of the opportunity.[14]

The educational opportunities available at the time differentiated this generation of Chinese American women from their mothers. The racially diverse educational institutions provided them not only with academic knowledge but also with experiences that encouraged their desire for more equitable race and gender relations. In the classroom, Chinese women competed with their non-Chinese peers, and some excelled academically. They learned that they had rights as individuals and deserved respect from others.

The liberal academic world was stimulating. At Mills College, a school for women in Oakland, Jade Snow Wong developed friendly relationships with the students, professors, and administrators through small classes, social activities, and her live-in work arrangement in a dean's home. She enjoyed participating in a world in which she was well liked and her intelligence was recognized. She was glad to have found a place where she fitted well as an individual, and she felt at ease outside the strict bounds of Chinese American society.

The rewards of education helped Chinese women realize and value their own strength. They learned much about what they could do in an environment that recognized individual talent and academic achievement. Before she attended Mills, Jade Snow Wong was honored as the most outstanding female student of California's junior college system, and she was selected as class salutatorian. In her address she told the audience that "college has developed our initiative, fair play, and self-expression, and has given us tools for thinking and analyzing."[15] But where would this lead?

Many young Chinese American women faced difficulties assessing their future after graduation. They did not accept the idea that race or gender, rather than individual quality, made them different in the eyes of others. Yet they had seen for themselves that racial discrimination prevented Chinese Americans from participating in many areas of American society. Chinese students were excluded from most of the extracurricular activities in high schools. They could not dance with white children, and only a few of them had been invited to parties organized by non-Chinese people. Luella (Chinn) Louie, who graduated from Oakland Technical High School in the late 1930s, recalled that all of her extracurricular time was spent at Wah Ku, a club for Chinese girls. The Wah Ku girls played basketball and volleyball against Chinese or Japanese girls' teams in Oakland and San Francisco, but they never competed with non-Asian groups.[16]

Racial discrimination in the job market compelled young, qualified Chinese Americans, frequently rejected by American firms, to turn to their ethnic community.[17] In New York City in 1938, Louise Chin and Helen Wong headed a Chinese Youth Council. In addition to social gatherings and war relief activities, the council held seminars to discuss employment issues facing ethnic minorities. Realizing that opportunities in the larger business world were few, the council encouraged young Chinese Americans to help the community create new jobs.[18]

By 1940 the number of American-born Chinese women was almost triple that of their parents' generation.[19] Within the community, however, they could find employment only in places such as garment shops, laundries, canneries, and restaurants, the same businesses where their mothers had worked.

Many Chinese children grew up working alongside their mothers. Jade Snow Wong began working in her family's garment shop when she was ten, helping load clothes on pick-up days. By age eleven, she had a sewing machine next to her mother's.[20] Elizabeth Lew, Lew Chuck Suey's granddaughter, remembered her mother's job as a routine activity in which all family members except for her father participated. Her mother usually sewed dresses while the children worked on jeans. Those who were not tall enough to operate the sewing machine helped snip the threads. Elizabeth learned to sew at almost the same time she learned to read, and it was not long before she was hired in a garment shop in Oakland's Chinatown:

> When I was ten years old, my sister Pearl and I, when we got out from school, would go straight to the factory. The windows were all painted white, but they had a little hole-scratch for the door, and they could see who was there when we rang the door bell, so others won't go in. We went in after school. Some women who worked there during the daytime had gone home because their kids had got home from school. We came from school to take over their machines. We worked until ten o'clock every night. We worked there during school vacations as well. Between the two of us we made twenty-one dollars per month. We sewed our fingers with the sewing machines, would think nothing of it, pull the broken needles up, and continue to sew. The boss's sons had to work too. They ran button-hole machines. Everyone worked. We ran machines, they [the boss's sons] had to fold everything.[21]

Aimei Chen, who had come to the United States in her infancy as a paper daughter, grew up in the small Chinese community in Stockton. She worked as a waitress in a Chinese café while attending junior college. Other girls her age were hired by local dime-stores, ice-cream parlors, and department stores, but none of these jobs were available to a Chinese girl. Taking business classes in college, she did not think much of her future. It was unlikely that she would find a job outside her community, and Stockton's Chinatown was too small to provide full-time employment for Chinese women.[22]

Yulan Liu, who was born in Oakland, was a grocery clerk's daughter. She began working in a laundry when she was twelve, following in her mother's footsteps. She never had time to play with other children, and she did not recall ever having been invited to a house outside the Chinese community.[23]

The educated young Chinese women had higher expectations than their mothers, however. They would not be satisfied by working at the same jobs as their mothers, marrying young, and having numerous children. Some girls planned to go to China for their future careers; others hoped that one day the world outside academic institutions would also recognize and reward individual merit.

World War II: The Turning Point

Ironically it was the attack on Pearl Harbor, one of the most tragic events in the history of the United States, that allowed Chinese Americans to take part in the larger society. On December 7, 1941, Maggie Gee went to study in the campus library. As she entered the usually quiet reading room, she was surprised to see that no one was reading. People were talking loudly and emotionally. Maggie sensed that something important had happened, and she soon learned of the Japanese bombing of Pearl Harbor in Hawaii.

For Chinese Americans, World War II had begun when the Japanese invaded Manchuria, in northeastern China, on September 18, 1931. Maggie was a fourth grader at the time. She and her sister had planned a trip to China with their uncle, but the trip was canceled after the Japanese invasion. When the Japanese attacked Chinese troops at Lugou qiao (Marco Polo Bridge) near Beijing on July 7, 1937, the war against Japan was joined by overseas Chinese in most parts of the world. Maggie and her siblings accompanied their mother to many rallies and fund-raising drives in San Francisco's Chinatown. She was extremely upset by the atrocities that took place during the 1937 Nanjing Massacre. She was surprised and disturbed that her classmates knew little about what was going on in China and also by their lack of interest in what had happened. Pearl Harbor, however, brought China and the United States together against a common enemy. Suddenly everyone was talking about the war. Maggie's support of the war effort in China became an indication of her loyalty to the United States.[24]

Many Chinese Americans have mixed feelings about World War II. Without the bombing of Pearl Harbor, the isolation of the Chinese American community would have lasted much longer. During the war Japanese Americans were seen as enemy aliens and were sent to internment camps. Because resistance against the Japanese was crucial to the Allied victory, the Chinese people were portrayed positively by the American media. On December 22,

1941, a short article was published in *Time* magazine to help Americans differentiate their Chinese "friends" from the Japanese. According to the magazine, the facial expressions of the Chinese were more "placid, kindly, open"; those of the Japanese were more "positive, dogmatic, arrogant."[25] World War II, considered by the American public to be a "good war" against fascists who had launched a racist war, put pressure on the government to improve its domestic race relations. Discriminatory legislation against the Chinese in the United States, as noted in chapter one, was an embarrassment to the United States during its wartime alliance with China. Chinese Americans, too, recognized the racial dimension of this war. "It is fortunate," said an editorial in the *Chinese Times*, "that this war has the white race and the yellow race on both sides and therefore will not turn into a war between the two."[26]

The wartime shortage of workers helped lower racial barriers in the military service and in the defense industry. In May 1942, defense establishments in the San Francisco Bay Area began advertising jobs in local Chinese newspapers. The Kaiser shipyards in Richmond announced that they would hire Chinese regardless of their citizenship status or English skills. In a recruiting speech, corporation president Henry J. Kaiser urged Chinese to work in his shipyards to support the war effort. The Moore Dry Dock Company in Oakland hired Chinese-speaking instructors in its welding school and provided a shuttle bus service between the shipyard and Oakland's Chinatown for Chinese trainees.[27]

After decades of isolation imposed by anti-Chinese legislation and sentiment, the Chinese American community lost no time in seizing these opportunities. Participation in the war effort could build up the nation's defense and help defeat the enemies of both China and the United States. Military service would qualify Chinese immigrants for U.S. citizenship, breaking through the restrictions of the exclusion acts. Employment in defense industries, suggested the *Chinese Times,* also paid well and could be used for draft deferment. Moreover, defense employees could apply for government-subsidized housing, which would afford Chinese Americans the rare opportunity to move out of Chinatowns.[28] Thousands of Chinese American men and women answered the government's call. Their wartime employment would forever change their own lives as well as the development of the community.

Chinese Rosie the Riveter

News reports and oral history interviews suggest that by 1943, about five thousand Chinese Americans were at work in defense jobs in the San

Francisco Bay Area, and between five and six hundred of them were women. Chinese American women in other parts of California and around the nation also joined in defense work, especially in Los Angeles, Portland, Seattle, Chicago, New York, and Boston.[29]

Chinese American women were a familiar sight at most defense plants in the Bay Area. As early as May 1942, the *Chinese Press* reported that eighteen-year-old Ruth Law was the youngest office staff member at Engineer Supply Depot, Pier 90, and her co-worker Anita Lee was an assistant to the company's chief clerk. Fannie Yee, a high school senior, won the top secretary award at the Bethlehem Steel Corporation's local headquarters in San Francisco. In Oakland, Stella Quan was recognized by Army Supply. Both Jenny Sui of San Francisco and Betty Choy of Vallejo started as messenger girls in the Mare Island shipyard, but they were quickly promoted to clerk-typists. Before Kaiser's shipyards in Richmond and Bechtel's Marinship in Sausalito began production work, the Moore Dry Dock Company in Oakland, the Naval Air Base in Alameda, the Mare Island Navy Shipyard, and the Army Department at Fort Mason in San Francisco were the primary defense employers for Chinese women.[30]

The majority of the Chinese American women who joined in defense work had grown up in the United States. Of the seventy-six named in published sources and the twenty-four interviewed, only four were over the age of forty at the time of the war and very few were married.[31] With relatively few household responsibilities, these women had the freedom and independence to work outside the home.

It was the combination of economic opportunity and patriotism that led Chinese women to work in defense jobs. When Ah Yoke Gee was forty-six, employment outside the Chinese American community became possible for the first time, and she jumped at the chance to serve the country of her birth.[32] Elizabeth Lew was hired at the Naval Air Base in Alameda, making twenty-five dollars a week, four times more than she had made in the sewing factory.[33] Defense employment was an undreamed-of opportunity for Aimei Chen. With her college education, she landed a secretarial job at the Stockton Army Depot.[34] Yulan Liu had just graduated from high school in the summer of 1942 when her brother got a job at Moore Dry Dock Company and encouraged her to try as well. Yulan went to the yard the next day and became a welder.[35]

Married women had to find ways to combine work and household responsibilities. Because her youngest child was already in high school, Ah Yoke Gee's household chores were manageable. Working the swing shift in the shipyard, she cooked the whole day's food in the morning, and shopped and did the laundry on Sundays.[36] Jane Jeong, married for only four months, took a job at Richmond Shipyard Number Two. Her husband was a merchant seaman, so Jane was free to work outside the home.[37]

Some married women worked with their husbands and families. Mannie Lee worked with her two daughters and a daughter-in-law in the electric shop at a Richmond shipyard. Her husband was a graveyard shift welder there and her two sons and a son-in-law were in the military. Mannie had worked with members of her family on a vegetable farm in Fresno, California. The difference now was that everyone worked fewer hours and earned more money. Moreover, the family members enjoyed the publicity the company gave them because of their singular example.[38] Mrs. Yam joined the Mare Island Navy Shipyard with her husband in June 1942, shortly after her graduation from San Jose High. She became an electrician's helper in Shop 51 and her husband became a pipefitter. The young couple commuted by bus to Vallejo from San Francisco's Chinatown every day. On December 18, 1942, Mrs. Yam was selected by the company to christen a Liberty Ship. Accompanied by six young Chinese American girls, she smashed a bottle of champagne to launch HMS *Foley* (built for the British navy) before thousands of her colleagues. She felt that she was "the proudest and happiest girl in the world."[39]

Fore 'n' Aft, the weekly magazine of the Kaiser Richmond shipyards, wrote about Lena Chiang, a female employee who came from China during the war. A shipfitter at Richmond Shipyard Number Three, Lena claimed to be a second cousin of Chiang Kai-shek, the leader of Nationalist China. A Chinese university graduate, Lena had accompanied her husband, Major Pei Lun Chiang, to the United States in 1941 for medical treatment. When her husband entered a military academy, Lena worked in the shipyard.[40] Although some Chinese immigrant women found jobs in defense plants, most, because of the language barrier, were hired as laborers.[41]

Some young Chinese women entered defense work before they finished college. Miaolan Ye, an Oakland resident, was an agriculture major. She took time off from school during the war to work as an inspector in a defense plant in San Leandro, California.[42] Maggie Gee started a graveyard shift job, welding at Richmond Shipyard Number Two, while still in college.[43]

Honolulu-born Betty Lum had been a nurse before the war, but she thought that "shipbuilding is the present must industry of America" and left her nursing job to learn acetylene welding at a Richmond shipyard. According to *Fore 'n' Aft,* three factors pushed Betty to support the war effort: she was an American citizen, she was Chinese, and she had a nephew who was

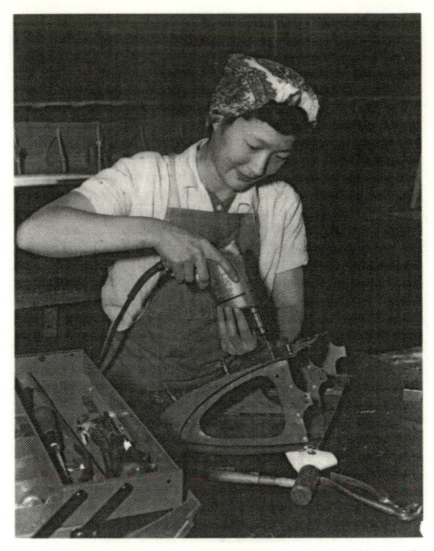

6. As a riveter, Luella Louie also drilled, welded, and operated machinery at the Alameda Naval Air Base during World War II. *Courtesy of Luella Louie.*

killed during the attack on Pearl Harbor. Betty's two sisters also went into defense work while her brother, a dentist, prepared to join the U.S. Army.[44]

Although Jade Snow Wong began to realize her hopes in college, when she stopped at the college placement office in 1942 seeking career advice after graduation, she was told not to expect any opportunities in "American business houses" and to look only for places within her ethnic community. Stunned, Jade Snow felt "as if she had been struck on both cheeks." She was determined to get a job outside Chinatown, and Marinship offered her the opportunity. Twenty-four hours after she submitted an application, she was hired.[45]

Wartime employment brought tangible benefits to many Chinese Americans. Although Chinese American women had labored hard at home and outside the home before the war, their productivity was neither recognized nor rewarded. Many girls had no say in discussions about spending the money they gave to their families. Elizabeth Lew had worked with her sister in a garment factory since she was ten to supplement her family income. "Payday Pearl and I would go to the Safeway store on the way home," she recalled. "Payday we would spend three cents each" for a push-up popsicle. During the war several of Elizabeth's sisters and brothers were employed by defense plants, which helped pull their family out of poverty. Elizabeth finally had a little money to call her own. She spent many Sundays in movie theaters and at an ice rink.[46] "For people who used to have very little money," said Aimei Chen, "the war was a time of great economic opportunity." She brought home kitchenware and other household items, things that were considered luxuries in the past, and she was free to purchase clothing she liked.[47]

Compared with their jobs before the war, most Chinese women found the so-called men's jobs easy. Joy Yee, a San Francisco–born high school graduate, was the second daughter of an Oakland garment shop owner. She and her sisters had sewed in the shop, but her mother told Joy that she was no good at sewing and that she would never succeed as a seamstress. At Alameda Naval Air Base, Joy became a metalsmith. She learned to use different tools and operate machinery, and she was excited about having a job that she was good at.[48] Before the war, Yulan Liu had worked ten hours a day, seven days a week, in a laundry. "There was nothing heavier than the iron," she said, "Sometimes my arm was so sore at night that I could not hold my chopsticks." "The welding torch," as she remembered, "was lighter," especially since she did not have to hold it for as many hours. She was able to work in different areas on the ships, and she often chatted with people between assignments.[49] Luella Louie, hired as a riveter, also drilled, welded, and operated machinery at the Alameda Naval Air Base after two weeks of training.[50] Ah Yoke Gee no longer sewed late at night. She worked eight hours a day, six days a week, and took Sundays off.[51]

Going to college during the day and working in the shipyard at night was not easy for Maggie Gee. It was difficult to stay awake, and there were few people to talk to. The work went slowly at night and she sometimes fell asleep, but it was so cold in the yard that she never slept well. Dissatisfied with her welding job, she got a day job at the Mare Island Navy Shipyard as a draftswoman after she graduated in 1942. At age twenty, Maggie wanted to experience as much as she could and find her own potential. During the war, there seemed to be many opportunities and possibilities.

With Silver Wings

The Chinese American community's efforts toward building military power for China in the early decades of the twentieth century had prepared some men and women for military service in World War II. According to Him Mark Lai, aviation clubs first appeared in the community in the 1910s, inspired by the idea of "National Salvation through Aviation" advocated by the Chinese government. After Japanese military forces occupied Manchuria, training pilots for the Chinese Air Force became one of the major concerns of the Chinese in America. Several Chinese American aviation schools and clubs were established with money solicited from community members, and some accepted female trainees. Chinese communities in San Francisco, New York, Portland, Los Angeles, Chicago, Pittsburgh, Boston, Tucson, Phoenix, and Honolulu all sponsored flying instruction programs, and some even bought training planes. Young Chinese American volunteers studied at these community-sponsored facilities, and about two hundred pilots who had no chance to apply their skills in the United States before World War II went to China for aviation careers.[52]

In March 1932 Katherine Sui Fun Cheung, who took flying lessons with the Chinese Aeronautical Association in Los Angeles, became the first Chinese American woman to receive a commercial flying license in the United States.[53] A year later, she joined Amelia Earhart's Ninety-Nines Club for women pilots and began entering air races. Katherine also spoke publicly about Chinese women's flying: "I don't see any reason why a Chinese woman can't be as good as a pilot as anyone else. We drive automobiles—why not fly planes?" In July 1937 the Chinese American community raised seven thousand dollars to buy a Ryan ST-A plane for Katherine to fly to China to teach Chinese volunteers. But before Katherine was scheduled to take off, her cousin, who had been her first aviation teacher, took a test flight and was killed when the airplane crashed. As a result Katherine's father, on his deathbed, made her promise that she would never fly again.[54]

With the financial backing of the community, Ah Ying (Hazel) Lee, the daughter of a Chinese immigrant, and Huang Guiyan (Virginia Wong) began training in Portland. They were among the first thirty-two graduates of Portland's Chinese Aeronautical School in 1932. In 1933 Ah Ying and Guiyan sailed to China to serve in the Chinese Air Force. Most of their male classmates were accepted into the Chinese military, but Ah Ying and Guiyan were turned down. Despite the high demand for trained pilots, the Chinese military was not ready to accept women aviators. Disappointed, Guiyan found a job as a typist and Ah Ying went to teach in the village where her father was born. Life in rural China with her father's clan was not easy, and the rigid social structure made Ah Ying realize that she was an American. She soon returned to the United States and went to work in New York City.[55]

In the summer of 1942, Ah Ying learned that Jacqueline Cochran's Women's Flying Training Detachment (WFTD) was being set up in Houston to train pilots for the Air Transport Command. She immediately applied. Serving her own country, she thought she might also ferry some aircraft that would fly in combat against the Japanese in China.

In August 1943 the Women's Auxiliary Ferrying Squadron and the WFTD were officially merged as the Women Airforce Service Pilots (WASP), and Ah Ying entered the first class. Most of her fellow students came from wealthy American families who could afford the luxury of private aviation lessons for their daughters or wives, and many of these women had attended distinguished colleges. Marianne Verges, who has researched the life and times of the WASP, gives Ah Ying a special introduction in *On Silver Wings*:

> When the trainees from 43–W-4, which had been in Houston, flew their PT-19s cross-country to join their classmates at Avenger, one member of the combined class stood out from the rest: Hazel Ah Ying Lee, a scrawny, boisterous, brown-skinned Chinese girl from Portland, Oregon. Her classmates agreed that Ah Ying was homely. She had buck teeth, flat features, and an even flatter chest. She wore her pitch-black hair yanked back or poked up under her cap, and from a distance it was hard to tell if Ah Ying was a man or a woman. But her handy, hearty laugh made her the favorite of everyone on the base. She also had an off-kilter brand of luck that could draw mishaps like a lightning rod.[56]

Training at Avenger Field in Sweetwater, a small town in west Texas surrounded by ranches, cotton fields, and a few oil wells, Ah Ying had a hard time picking out landmarks. She got lost several times. Once she landed in a field that was too small to allow her to take off again, and the plane had to

7. Hazel Ah Ying Lee and her classmates in the Women Airforce Service Pilots. *Courtesy of Woman's Collection, Texas Woman's University Library, Denton.*

be taken apart and shipped back to Avenger. When she landed in a cotton patch, a frightened farmer approached her, brandishing a hoe. Ah Ying had to convince him that she was not a Japanese spy, but a Chinese American flier for the U.S. military. Despite her slow start, Ah Ying caught up with the rest of the class, graduated, and went on active duty.[57]

Working as a draftswoman at the Mare Island Navy Shipyard, Maggie Gee became close friends with two of her co-workers: Jean, a white girl, and Mary, a Filipina. Every day at lunch, the trio met in the sitting area adjoining the lady's room. They had all been to college, and they thought that they could do more than just drafting. Mary, who had taken a few flying lessons, suggested that they become pilots. Maggie, who had gone with her father to the Oakland Airport to watch airplanes take off and land, had read about women who flew, but the possibility that she could be one of them did not seem real. Now she learned that all she needed was eight hundred dollars to enroll in an aviation school in Nevada. That was a lot more than she had paid to get a college degree, but the job at the navy shipyard paid her over a hundred dollars a month, and she began to save every penny she could to learn to fly.

In late 1943 Maggie and her friends took a temporary leave from their jobs and boarded a bus to Nevada, where they got their first exposure to the glamour and excitement of flying. Two months later, they completed the training program and were interviewed by the WASP. While their files were under review, they went back to their jobs at Mare Island. The girls were now the center of attention. People asked many questions about flying, often with a touch of envy, because Maggie and her friends were doing something that most people only dreamed about. The calls from the army arrived shortly after. Mary was not accepted because she was nearsighted, but Jean and Maggie were recruited. Everyone in Maggie's family was proud of her. Although concerned about Maggie's safety, Ah Yoke Gee told her daughter that if she were twenty years younger, she would have wanted to fly too.

Maggie arrived at Avenger Field in February 1944 and became the second Chinese American woman, after Ah Ying Lee, to join the WASP. She was the only Chinese in a class of 107 young women, but that did not make any difference. In her Santiago blue uniform, she was one of them. Very few non-white women were able to join the WASP. The eight black women applicants had all been turned down because it was felt that integrating blacks into the unit would trigger more controversy at a time when even the establishment of the WASP was generating resentment. Moreover, the South was still segregated, and the WASP training field was in Texas. The war allowed

8. Maggie Gee, wearing her WASP silver wings and Santiago blue uniform. *Courtesy of Maggie Gee.*

Maggie, a Chinese American girl, to become a member of this elite group of American women pilots. It took her a while to believe that it was true.

Life in the WASP was memorable. As Maggie recounted, "We marched to the mess hall, we marched to the gym, we marched to classes. You had to line up and march to everywhere you went. We used to sing when we marched, just like in the movies." The training program was intensive, and there were many tests. One day Maggie flew back to the base a little behind schedule. As many of her classmates looked on, she thought she would show off. She managed a nice landing, but due to her lack of concentration, the airplane ground looped in a circle. Maggie was almost washed out because of the incident. The WASP had accepted about 2,000 women, of whom only 1,074 graduated. Maggie's friend Jean was among those who did not make it. Maggie completed the program and was awarded her silver wings. At the WASP squadron at the Las Vegas Army Air Force Base, she gave flying lessons to male pilots and ferried military aircraft.[58]

As the war neared its end and the Allied victory became apparent, women were no longer needed in the military. In October 1944, the WASP was ordered to disband. All the WASPs were disappointed by the army's decision and confused about their future. Once again, Ah Ying Lee thought about flying for China. She may have felt that the Chinese Air Force would take her more seriously because she had served in the U.S. military. She probably learned that the Chinese military had also changed as the war progressed and that some Chinese women had been accepted since she had been turned down in 1932.

Ah Ying never flew for China. During the final weeks of the WASP program, she took every opportunity she could to ferry military aircraft. One morning in late November 1944, Ah Ying was flying a Kingcobra and got caught by a storm in Bismarck, North Dakota. Unable to land, as all the airports in North Dakota, Minnesota, and Wisconsin were closed down, she headed north toward the Rocky Mountains. She reached East Base in Great Falls, Montana, along with a dozen airplanes at about two o'clock in the afternoon. She had no idea that there was another Kingcobra slightly above her when she approached the ground. When Ah Ying was told by the ground controller to distance herself from the other aircraft, she responded by pulling up. The other pilot, however, had apparently not heard the instruction. His Kingcobra straddled Ah Ying's, and both exploded. Ah Ying's plane was engulfed by flames as it skidded down the runway.

The doctors at the base hospital tried to save Ah Ying's life while the army attempted to reach her family. Her husband, Yin Cheung Louie, was with the Nationalist Air Force in Chengdu, China. As the WASP was about to disband, no one thought to contact her classmates, who knew she had family in Portland's Chinatown. Ah Ying died quietly but alone in the base hospital, and her body remained unclaimed at the military morgue in Great Falls for almost a year.[59]

In addition to military aviation, a small number of Chinese American women also served in the Army Nurse Corps, the Women's Army Corps (WAC), and the WAVES (Women Accepted for Volunteer Emergency Service). Altogether 15,998 Chinese Americans served in the military between 1940 and 1946, and among them 1,621 served in the navy. Over the course of the war 214 Chinese American military personnel gave their lives for their country.[60]

Forging Interracial Links

The Chinese in America had become more urban centered after the 1880s, when mob attacks and anti-Chinese agitation made it difficult for them to survive outside urban ghettos. By 1940, 71 percent of Chinese Americans lived in large cities, and 38.1 percent of the 55,030 large-city Chinese lived in San Francisco and Oakland.[61]

Behind the invisible walls of the Chinatowns, the Chinese had little contact with citizens of other racial backgrounds. Most of the non-Chinese city population of San Francisco, for example, had never met a Chinese socially before the war. A contemporary observer found San Francisco's Chinatown a counterpart to black ghettos such as New York's Harlem, Chicago's South Side, and Detroit's Paradise Valley.[62] Within the confines of the Chinatowns, the Chinese lived among people who shared the same dreams and hardships. They relied on one another for comfort and companionship, shopped in their own stores, worshiped in their own temples and churches, and celebrated traditional as well as Western holidays among themselves. Chinese community organizations, which provided mutual aid and protection, controlled the day-to-day lives of the community members.

In addition to being victims of residential segregation, Chinese Americans were excluded from the American industrial labor force between 1880 and 1940. Chinese labor had been the basis of light industry in western cities in the 1860s. In areas where there were few women, cheap Chinese labor enabled the shoe, cigar, and garment industries to compete with eastern manufacturers. In the heat of the labor agitation of the late 1870s and early 1880s, however, the jobs held by the Chinese were gradually taken away by white workers.[63] As David R. Roedinger points out, "The labor and anti-Chinese movements overlapped so thoroughly as to be scarcely distinguishable in California."[64] Except for menial labor and domestic work, the larger American economy offered no employment opportunities for Chinese Americans.

With few employment opportunities in industry and limited networks for further geographical movement, the Chinese had to make the best of an onerous situation. They pooled their money through rotating credit associations for entrepreneurship, and most Chinese entrepreneurs selected businesses that required little capital investment and provided services or products with the least profit margin because they were not allowed to compete with white businessmen. In addition to developing laundry and restaurant enterprises, some Chinese contracted with wholesalers for small-scale manufacturing and provided employment for members of their own community.[65]

It was through domestic service rather than governmental or industrial employment that Chinese American women found the opportunity to interact with members of other races. In the late nineteenth century, some Euro-Americans hired male Chinese cooks or house servants. In the early decades of the twentieth century, many Chinese American girls took part-time jobs as housemaids. They became acquainted with their employers and used their connections to find better jobs or educational opportunities.[66] At Mills College, as we have seen, Jade Snow Wong lived and worked in the dean's house. It was an advantage to work with the dean because she was generous, well connected, and knowledgeable, but Jade Snow noticed that when she and the dean talked, the latter's words were usually "a command, not a suggestion."[67] Although this type of relationship sometimes appeared to be friendly or intimate, it was based on the personal subordination of the maid to the mistress and lacked the basic foundations for mutual understanding.

Employment opportunities during World War II, in contrast, provided Chinese American women with the chance to interact with people of different racial backgrounds. There were no masters or servants, only colleagues and co-workers, and everyone worked for the military or companies under government contract. In shipyards, the workers addressed one another by their first names regardless of rank or ethnicity.

Wartime media coverage that dealt with events in China or Chinese people also helped promote public acceptance of Chinese, and defense companies especially acknowledged Chinese workers' contributions. In early 1943 the Marinship in Sausalito launched a Liberty Ship named *Sun Yat-Sen,* after the first president of the Chinese Republic. The Marinship's in-house magazine, *Marin-er,* published a special issue entitled "The New China" to commemorate the event. The issue profiled more than two dozen Chinese workers, all of them "normal humans" who were "well-behaved, law-abiding, intelligent, economical, and industrious." The shipyard workers were also told that Chinese food was "healthful & delicious," and that they should learn from "Chinese culture and philosophy."[68]

The fact that most Chinese Americans were West Coast urbanites also differentiated them from the migrant workers of the rural South and Midwest. Katherine Archibald, a sociologist who worked in the Moore Shipyard in Oakland during the war, noticed many incidents of prejudice against blacks and Okies, but according to her observations, the Chinese were well tolerated.[69]

Chinese women were more readily accepted in defense companies than their men. The women had been hired to solve the manpower shortage and to meet the demands of defense production during the war. As thousands of Rosies worked at men's jobs, the news media opened a public debate on gender differences, women's morale, and social order that effectively set female workers apart from their male counterparts. It was understood that black, white, or Chinese women were employed not to replace men but to release them for the cause of Democracy, and would not threaten skilled labor once the war was over.

Competition between women and men in the defense industry was made almost impossible by the wartime training programs. Women were taught to do mass production work, and few were offered the chance to obtain sufficient skills for long-term employment. Seen as temporary help, they did not create potential problems for either their employers or their unions.

In contrast, companies did find themselves pressured to change racially discriminatory policies in hiring, training, and promoting male minority workers.[70] Male Chinese were often resented by white workers because of their apparent ability to compete. These workers too received very little job training. Many of them, however, were well educated, and some had college engineering backgrounds.[71] These men had a broad knowledge of industrial production and mastered their jobs quickly, but they often found that promotions went to less-qualified white workers. They were told that they could not be moved up because no one would want to work under a Chinese. One male Chinese American at a Richmond shipyard had years of work experience with an excellent performance record. But he saw several less-qualified white workers promoted to foreman positions ahead of him, and no one listened to his complaints. He finally quit the job.[72]

Many shipyard workers had never interacted with an Asian woman before, and found the Chinese women in the wartime workplace of special interest. Leong Bo San, a middle-aged Chinese American woman from San Francisco, was described in *Fore 'n' Aft* as a "tiny, doll-like figure" who "walks with the dainty, mincing gait of the upper class Chinese lady whose feet once were bound" in her "flat rubber-soled shoes of the shipyard." She attracted much attention on the graveyard ferry trip from San Francisco to the East

Bay. On her assembly line, Leong Bo San worked with "an energy that amazes people twice her size." Her boss, James G. Zeck, reportedly said that he wished he "had a whole crew of people like her."[73]

In February 1945, when the story of the Richmond shipyards appeared in *Fortune* magazine, Ah Yoke Gee was one of the eight featured employees. The caption under her photo read: "Chinese woman: she hasn't missed a day's work in two years."[74] When Ah Yoke posed for the shipyards' weekly magazine, however, she was designated simply as one of the "oldest crew members of the yard." [75] The fact that she was a Chinese and a woman did not seem to matter too much to those who worked with her. As one of the first production workers hired by the yard, she introduced many of her colleagues to their jobs, and they viewed her as one of them.

Most Chinese women adapted well to their wartime employment. The shipyard was very different from college, but Jade Snow Wong entered the new work environment with ease. Her boss, a white man, not only had a good sense of humor but could also "match in wit the 'smart' suggestions." Later she had the opportunity to research the working conditions of defense plant employees and embraced it enthusiastically. She developed confidence in her own capabilities and in dealing with the people with whom she worked.[76]

Recognition from the larger world helped improve Chinese women's status in their families and community. When Jade Snow Wong questioned her parents' authority by invoking Western ideas of individualism that she had learned from her professors, she angered her parents. The elder Wongs warned their daughter that she would learn her lesson the hard way, through the realities of the racially discriminatory American society.[77] Her parents were pleased with her performance in college, but most Chinese parents expected their children to be successful in school. What Jade Snow did in Marinship, in contrast, opened her parents' eyes and helped them realize that their old ways of thinking about women were wrong.[78] Chinese women's access to jobs in the white world legitimized them in public roles, and their accomplishments brought honor to the community.

Because racial stereotypes were still a major obstacle to the integration of the Chinese into U.S. society, Chinese American women realized that their performance at work would have a direct impact on the status of all Chinese Americans. The images of Chinese immigrants presented by the media had played an important role in shaping public sentiment against the Chinese in the late nineteenth and early twentieth centuries. Many Chinese American women who engaged in defense work and military service believed that they had the responsibility to educate the general public, and they used their workplace—their access to the larger world—to showcase the strengths of Chinese tradition and culture and prove the intelligence and industriousness of Chinese people.

At work, Yulan Liu considered herself a representative of her community. She was well liked by her teammates. A small figure weighing only eighty pounds, she not only worked hard but was also the only member of the crew who could weld in the narrowest areas of the ships. She and her stories about the world she came from generated a keen interest in Chinese people and Chinese culture among her colleagues. At their request, she led her co-workers on a tour of San Francisco's Chinatown.[79]

Beginning in her college years, Jade Snow Wong had treated every social occasion as an opportunity to introduce Chinese culture and tradition to her friends. She and her family prepared carefully for occasions such as a sociology class field trip to their garment shop or a party for her college friends at which she served finely prepared Chinese foods, for she believed that in a small way she was helping others to understand her people. She also wrote about China and the Chinese people: in a special issue of the *Mariner* devoted to praise of Marinship's Chinese employees, she pointed out that Chinese immigrants, the workers that the shipyard seemed to value so much, were still barred from becoming American citizens.[80]

When Elizabeth Lew met a young merchant mariner, Wallace Anderson, at an ice rink, it was love at first sight. Elizabeth knew that her family would not approve of her marrying a white man, so she ran away. Her parents announced that they had disowned her. After she got married, she moved to Ironwood, Michigan, with her husband and lived with her Finnish parents-in-law. She even learned to speak Finnish. Not until her father fell ill five years later was Elizabeth permitted to come home to visit, and she eventually moved her family back to the Bay Area.[81]

A Growing Gender Consciousness

The daughters of Chinese American immigrants were quite aware that they were less privileged than their brothers. Many Chinese immigrants expected to live with their sons and grandchildren in the future, so they were more willing to give financial support to their male than to their female offspring. All the children in Elizabeth Lew's family worked when they were young. The girls sewed, and the boys shined shoes and delivered lottery tickets. While Elizabeth and her sisters had to give their parents all the money they made to cover household expenses, the brothers kept their money so that they could afford wives in the future.[82] Similarly, Ah Yoke Gee was an open-minded woman, but when money became tight, Maggie Gee and her sisters knew that only their brothers would be given family money for college.[83]

Jade Snow Wong bitterly resented the unequal treatment. In her autobiography, she wrote: "How can Daddy know what an American advanced education can mean to me? Why should Older Brother be alone in enjoying the major benefits of Daddy's toil? There are no ancestral pilgrimages to be made in the United States! I can't help being a girl. Perhaps, even being a girl, I don't want to marry, *just* to raise sons! Perhaps I have a right to want more than sons! I am a person, besides being a female! Don't the Chinese admit that women also have feelings and minds?"[84]

Chinese women's roles in the community were also limited compared with those of men. Women's hourly wages were usually lower than men's, so they often worked longer hours. Gender lines could also be found in community organizations and activities. Women had no voting rights in the Chinese Consolidated Benevolent Associations, district associations, or family associations. Men made the major decisions, while women were mostly involved in social gatherings, fund-raising, and Red Cross work.[85]

The Chinese community press was cautious in dealing with the issue of women's wartime employment. Chinese American men were more likely to be encouraged to join the army or do defense work; Chinese women's primary roles were still defined by the press as those of wives and mothers. Not one article or editorial in Chinese newspapers specifically called on Chinese women to enter the defense industry. Women's organizations and social clubs were active in roles more readily recognized and praised by the community. "It is the servicemen who will do the fighting for us," C. T. Feng, chairman of the American Women's Voluntary Service, told Chinese American women. "We must show our fighting men that we are absolutely behind them."[86] As part of its war effort, the Chinatown branch of the YWCA in San Francisco started a weekly class to teach women time-saving ways of preparing food. At a YWCA open house meeting, the Y's administrator, Mrs. Jane Kwong Lee, called upon Chinese American women to support the country by giving their families the "right nutritional food."[87]

Chinese American women did not need the approval of the community to respond to the nation's call for defense work and military service, however. They wanted to serve their country, and they wanted to demonstrate that they could do more than get married, have children, and work at women's jobs. They thought it was time for people to view women in a different light. Because Yulan Liu was so small, her work uniform looked awkward on her, but it was her favorite outfit. "I just wanted everyone to know that I worked in the shipyard," she explained.[88]

The women's horizons expanded. Ah Yoke Gee finally learned that she had other skills, and she never went back to sewing.[89] Neither did Joy Yee, who found sewing clothing difficult but metalsmithing manageable and fun.[90] After the war, Luella Louie preferred to take more traditional women's jobs, working as a restaurant hostess or a secretary so that she could combine work with household responsibilities, but she proudly exhibited photos taken at the Naval Air Base, which recalled some of the most precious moments in her life. She wanted her children and grandchildren to know that in addition to being an excellent cook and craftsperson, their caring, soft-spoken mother and grandmother was once a Rosie the Riveter.[91]

Chinese American women's wartime employment allowed them to mingle with other women, and some established long-term friendships with their colleagues. Maggie Gee considered Mary and Jean, whom she had met at the Mare Island Naval Shipyard, two of her best friends. The three of them stayed in touch for decades even though they moved to different places and led different lives after the war. As a member of the small, closely knit WASP group, Maggie lived, trained, and worked together with her classmates. It did not matter that many of the WASPs came from well-to-do families and that Maggie was one of the very few who had had to earn money to learn how to fly. The war and their common interests brought these women together, and they shared the most exciting experiences of their lives. Maggie stayed in touch with many of her WASP friends after the war and attended many group reunions. She kept a WASP address book and visited many of her colleagues throughout the United States, even some she had not previously met. "After all, I am one of them," she said.[92]

Ironically, it was through their wartime experience that Chinese women learned that gender inequality was more than a Chinese tradition. In the defense industries women worked as welders, burners, riveters, and machinists, but as the historian Mary Ryan points out, "rather than a genuine alteration in the rules of gender, the admission of women to the male job sector was regarded as an emergency measure, permissible 'for the duration only.'"[93] Women were recruited to provide temporary help in a place where they did not belong.

Women who were hired during the war were set apart from traditionally trained skilled workers through highly publicized wartime training programs. The demand for military equipment and supplies required the application of mass production methods and thus led to changes in the production process. A conventional shipyard, for example, was designed for one-of-a-kind production. During the war, however, it contracted with the government to build a large number of identical ships within a short period of time. To beat the deadline, the yard would break jobs down into small sequences and train its temporary employees to perform simple assembly-line tasks. The training the women received did not enable them to meet the standards set by companies for peacetime production.[94]

Despite tight schedules and the necessity for mass production during the war, the Maritime Commission and the Federal Committee on Apprenticeship urged companies to make "every reasonable effort" to continue the training of skilled workers.[95] The apprentice training programs expanded from the 760 men registered before the war to 5,818 in 1945. With the cooperation of over 34,000 companies, twenty-six states established official apprentice programs and developed training regulations.[96] Unlike the short-term programs, which taught only the basic skills needed for mass production, these apprentice programs trained workers for long-term industrial employment.[97] But women had no access to the programs. They acquired few skills aside from those needed to perform a specific task and received no general training, so they had little chance for promotion and postwar industrial employment.[98]

Maggie Gee did not consider herself a skilled worker. She found welding unchallenging, and she thought that her work at the Richmond shipyard was not much different from her mother's sewing. She felt it was easy, and that "everyone could do it."[99]

The WASP experience was different, however. Maggie and her classmates went through the same training program as the men, and she later gave flying lessons to male pilots. Most of the time she and the other women flew single-engine airplanes, which were more dangerous than the larger ones.[100]

Although all the women pilots were well trained and the WASP was under the jurisdiction of the army, whether women pilots should be given military status was a heated debate for several years. Maggie tried not to be bothered by it, but on October 3, 1944, she received a letter from General Hap Arnold notifying her of the Army's decision to disband the WASP. The general made the point that keeping women pilots in service would mean replacing young men, and he said, "I know the WASP wouldn't want that."[101] Maggie felt terrible: the military did not want the WASP simply because it was an all-female group. The WASP squadron in Las Vegas was shut down at the end of 1944, before the war ended. Although she had flown military airplanes and followed the rules of the army, Maggie went home without veteran status and could not enjoy any of the benefits specified by the G.I. Bill.[102]

It took Jade Snow Wong quite a while to see the gendered structure of defense industries. At first she thought she had learned to work the system and was achieving positive results. Often the only woman in a room full of men, she believed she was moving toward gender equality. Not until her boss was assigned to the main administrative office did Jade Snow, after being transferred from one menial office job to another, finally realize that she was trapped in a dismal situation.[103] Asked whether she would like to stay at Marinship after the war if she had the chance, she answered "no" without hesitation. "I decided to leave before they started to lay people off," she said. "There was no future for me, no future for women in the shipyard." At Mills College, Jade Snow had found a few female role models: her professors, the dean for whom she had worked, and the college president. She wanted to be a professional woman like them. But in the shipyard, she said, "a woman could only be someone's secretary. The bosses were all men." She wanted to have a career in which the fact that she was Chinese and a woman would be irrelevant.[104]

Toward the end of the war, the defense industry gradually reduced the volume of production, and the employees were free to leave their jobs. Jade Snow Wong was among those Chinese women who left right away, while Ah Yoke Gee and others stayed on. By the end of 1945, however, most of the nation's defense plants had either converted to conventional production or shut down. Thousands of workers were laid off. With no support from society and limited skills, few American women were able to compete with male workers for industrial jobs. In the San Francisco Bay Area, only the Alameda Naval Air Base let a few women keep their jobs. Marinship, all four Kaiser Richmond shipyards, and most of the other defense companies eventually disappeared.

The war, however, had changed the lives of many Chinese American men and women. Although the majority of white middle-class American women returned to domesticity, most Chinese American women continued to work, but they no longer relied on employment within their own communities. Lanfang Wong, a metalsmith during the war, landed a new job at an insurance company in San Francisco. She later married a war veteran and moved to Napa Valley to work on a farm.[105] After her yard was shut down, Ah Yoke Gee found a job at a post office in Berkeley.[106] Because the Alameda Naval Air Base continued to manufacture defense products in the postwar years, Joy Yee was able to keep her job until 1955, when she gave birth to her first child. She went back to work at the base in 1968 and remained for another seventeen years. To celebrate the fiftieth anniversary of the war, she

9. Elizabeth Lew Anderson, who was employed at the Naval Air Base in Alameda, California, during World War II, took another job there later when a position became available. This 1983 photograph captures her at work. *Courtesy of Elizabeth Lew Anderson.*

helped organize a reunion of all the base's Chinese Rosies.[107] Although Elizabeth Lew Anderson had spent years in different parts of the country and overseas because of her husband's job, she was able to go back to her job at the base during the Korean War and the Vietnam War while she was living in the Bay Area.[108] Yuk Wah Fu, also a base employee, kept her job until 1947, when she married. She later worked for the Pacific Bell Company.[109] Aimei Chen left Stockton's Chinatown and settled down in Berkeley. While her husband studied engineering at the University of California under the G.I. Bill, she worked as an office clerk.[110] Yulan Liu left Oakland's Chinatown and became a nursing aide in Vallejo after her husband found work at the Mare Island Naval Shipyard. Lili Wang, who had worked in a Richmond shipyard during the war, began medical school in 1946 and eventually practiced as a physician in Washington, D.C. [111]

*A*s many Chinese American women realized, what had taken place during the war was only the first step toward racial and gender equality. When Maggie Gee and her sister looked for an apartment in Berkeley in the early 1950s, a landlady refused to show them her unit when she saw that they were Chinese.[112] Jade Snow Wong, the girl who used to believe that only in the Western world could she enjoy a life as an individual, rediscovered her community while working in the shipyard. After the war she went back to San Francisco's Chinatown and opened a business so that she could make a living in a way she could "call her soul her own." She decided to write about Chinese Americans because she wanted the American public to develop a better understanding of the Chinese people. She also gave up her English name, Constance, the name that she had gone by in school and at Marinship. The girl in her autobiographical first book was called Jade Snow, a translation of her Chinese name.[113]

After she returned from the WASP, Maggie Gee wanted everyone to know that there wasn't anything in the world men could do that women could not. When she decided to go to graduate school to study physics, people told her that physics was a man's field, but she went ahead anyway. Many young Chinese Americans studied at the Berkeley campus of the University of California after the war, and a number of them had been in the army. They organized the Chinese Students Association, and Maggie served as its president for two years. In the late 1950s and most of the 1960s, she was the only female physicist in her group at the Lawrence Livermore National Laboratory.[114]

In 1972, the former members of the WASP held a thirtieth-anniversary reunion at Avenger Field in Texas. The reunion sparked five years of political lobbying for recognition of the WASP. On Thanksgiving Day in 1977, President Jimmy Carter finally signed the WASP amendment into law. Then on May 21, 1979, thirty-four years after the end of the war, the United States Air Force officially recognized the status of World War II women pilots and issued honorable discharges to WASP members.[115] By then, the educational benefits for World War II veterans provided by the G.I. Bill had long since expired. The WASP members, however, gained access to veteran hospitals and military cemeteries, and they now qualified for home loans from the government. Several hundred WASP gathered at Avenger Field to celebrate the victory. Maggie Gee, then fifty-four years old, marched to town with her fellow pilots in her Santiago blue uniform and silver wings. The group sang as they marched, just as they had almost forty years earlier. Although Ah Ying Lee was not able to experience the day, she had served in the U.S. military through the last moments of her life.

CHAPTER 4

The Family Reunited

THE COMING OF THE WAR BRIDES

*T*he resounding victory over fascism and the repeal of the Chinese exclusion acts signified the beginning of a new era, making the postwar years appear especially promising. Chinese Americans had made great sacrifices to make their country safe for democracy, and they expected significant improvement in the quality of their lives.

As Chinese American soldiers sailed slowly home, they were especially excited about the new prospects for their future: postwar immigration legislation favored family unification for World War II veterans. Because the 1943 repeal act made alien Chinese admissible, Chinese war veterans became the first qualified Asian group to send for their families. In a five-year period between 1945 and 1950, thousands of Chinese women immigrated to the United States, leading to a profound change in the Chinese American community. Having started its life in the United States as a bachelor society, the Chinese American community began to change into a family society.

Both the War Brides Act and the Alien Fiancées and Fiancés Act were gender neutral, granting men and women veterans the same privilege to sponsor their family members.[1] Fewer American women gained war veteran status, however. Under the War Brides Act admissions there were 114,691 female versus 333 male spouses (see table 4.1). The number of male adults who gained entry under these two pieces of legislation was so insignificant that both the INS and popular parlance categorized all of the war spouses as "war brides." The public's perception of the war spouses was vividly illustrated in a 1949 Hollywood comedy, *I Was a Male War Bride,* which is based on a

TABLE 4.1. *Alien Spouses and Alien Minor Children Admitted or*
Status Adjusted under the War Brides Act, 1945–1950

Origins	Number admitted	Husbands	Wives	Children
Europe	87,624	234	84,517	2,873
Asia	7,717	16	7,049	652
All other regions	24,352	83	23,125	1,144
Total	119,693	333	114,691	4,669
European countries				
Austria	2,302	8	2,180	114
Belgium	2,721	1	2,687	33
Czechoslovakia	1,348	11	1,236	101
Denmark	231	4	225	2
Estonia	219	2	214	3
Finland	112	0	102	10
France	8,744	23	8,581	140
Germany	14,931	6	14,175	750
Great Britain	35,469	53	34,944	472
Greece	1,469	15	1,301	153
Hungary	567	7	544	16
Ireland	1,245	3	1,224	18
Italy	9,728	21	9,046	661
Latvia	294	1	279	14
Lithuania	185	0	179	6
Netherlands	702	30	655	17
Northern Ireland	1,469	3	1,446	20
Norway	285	3	246	36
Poland	2,674	23	2,514	137
Portugal	237	1	211	25
Rumania	312	4	303	5
U.S.S.R.	808	3	795	10
Yugoslavia	500	3	395	102
Other Europe	1,072	9	1,035	28
Asian countries				
China	5,726	5	5,132	589
India	467	4	458	5
Japan	763	0	758	5
Other Asia	761	7	701	53
All other regions and countries				
Canada	7,541	44	7,254	243
Mexico	2,300	6	2,080	214
West Indies	1,327	7	1,230	90
Central America	518	1	464	53
South America	492	2	471	19
Africa	931	6	907	18
Australia	6,853	7	6,671	175
New Zealand	1,038	2	1,007	29
Philippines	2,485	1	2,215	269
Other countries	867	7	826	34

SOURCE: *Annual Report of Immigration and Naturalization Service, 1950.*

true story. After encountering many difficulties explaining his status as the married spouse of a member of the American military, the ex–French Army officer played by Cary Grant finally disguised himself as a woman in order to accompany his American bride (Ann Sheridan), an officer of the Women's Army Corps, to the United States.[2]

Together with the Chinese Alien Wives of American Citizens Act, the War Brides Act and the Alien Fiancées and Fiancés Act helped push the unbalanced sex ratio of the Chinese American community toward normalcy. The nonquota aspect of these laws was most significant for Chinese Americans. During the war 12,041 Chinese Americans had been drafted, and every one of them was eligible to bring in an alien spouse and children.[3] The War Brides Act alone enabled 5,132 adult Chinese women to enter within three years.[4] The Chinese Alien Wives of American Citizens Act admitted an additional 2,317 adult women between July 1947 and June 1950.[5] With thousands of families settling down in the United States, the chapter in the history of the Chinese American community as a predominantly male society came to a close.

The Chinese "War Brides"

Although few would dispute the importance of these new immigrant women to the transformation of the Chinese American community, the subject has received little scholarly attention.[6] The Chinese women who came in the late 1940s were generally referred to as "war brides" because most of them entered under the War Brides Act. Except for Rose Hum Lee's study on postwar Chinese families in the San Francisco–Oakland area, Arthur Dong's documentary film *Sewing Woman*, and a brief discussion in Judy Yung's *Chinese Women of America*, little has been said about the Chinese war brides and their position in the Chinese American community.[7]

In her study published in 1956, Lee found that the majority of the Chinese war brides did not wed Chinese American servicemen until the war was over: in her view, only after the War Brides Act went into effect did the approximately 6,000 Chinese American war veterans rush to China, get married, and bring their wives home.[8] For decades, the image of young brides who gained residential status in the United States by marrying Chinese American servicemen after the war has exemplified the Chinese women who came after the war, like Mei Oi, a fictional character in Louis H. Chu's popular novel *Eat a Bowl of Tea*.[9] But who were these women and how did they become involved with the Chinese American war veterans?

Immigration files, with their biographical information for each new entry, make it possible to examine the origins of Chinese immigrant women. The stories that these women told the immigration authorities are rich and detailed. They reveal not only who these women were and where they came from, but also how they became involved with their men and the Chinese immigration network. Because both academic and popular discourse have treated most postwar female immigrants as war brides, this study will not be limited to entries under the War Brides Act; women who applied for admission under the Alien Fiancées and Fiancés Act and the Chinese Alien Wives of American Citizens Act of 1946 are also included.[10] The 1,035 randomly selected files examined were created by the INS district offices in San Francisco and Honolulu between 1945 and 1950.[11]

The majority of America's postwar Chinese immigrant women were admitted under the War Brides Act, which is also reflected in the cases for this study. Seventy-three percent of the cases studied were spouses of war veterans, 2 percent were fiancées of war veterans, and 25 percent were wives of American citizens. The majority of these women's husbands had served in the U.S. military during World War II. In principle the war veterans could also have sent for their wives under the Chinese Alien Wives of American Citizens Act, since military service qualified Chinese Americans for U.S. citizenship. Most war veterans, however, used the War Brides Act to send for their wives, because once proof of the husband's service or his honorable discharge was in hand, no visa was required for the wife. Sponsors for applicants under the Chinese Alien Wives of American Citizens Act would include men who were too old or too young to be drafted; they gained their citizenship either through birth or through naturalization after 1943. Some of these citizens used the new law to reunite with wives they had married during the exclusion; others went to China to marry after the war was over.

Entry status, however, does not tell us much about the women themselves. The War Brides Act recognizes all marriages to World War II veterans, regardless of when the marriage took place. In other words, both the War Brides Act and the Chinese Alien Wives of American Citizens Act could be used by Chinese Americans to reunite with their wives and children who had been excluded before the war.

A more detailed picture emerges after the length of time these women had been married is examined.[12] Among the 1,035 cases, 798 applicants provided complete marriage information. As figure 4.1 shows, only 10 percent of the women had been married for a year or less by the time they arrived in the United States. Despite what Lee argued, this suggests that only a small

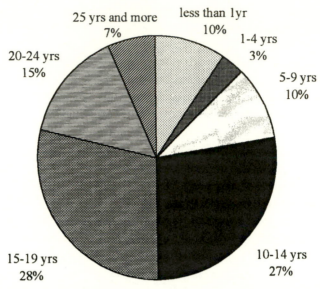

FIGURE 4.1. War bride marriage duration. Sample size: 798. (Records of the Immigration and Naturalization Service, Chinese Immigration Files, 1945–1952, RG85, National Archives, San Bruno, California.)

percentage of Chinese American war veterans went to China to find wives after the war. The number of Chinese Americans who courted and married during the war was even smaller, for only 3 percent of the women had been married between one and four years. Eighty-seven percent of the women, however, had been married for five years or longer, and 77 percent had been married for over ten years. In other words, the vast majority of these so-called war brides were not new brides but longtime wives of Chinese Americans in transnational families.

Chinese war brides were considerably older than those from other parts of the world. Jenel Virden, who studied the British war brides, estimated that the average age of British war brides was sixteen in 1939. These women would have been between twenty-three and twenty-five when they applied for entry under the War Brides Act.[13] Figure 4.2 indicates that, of the 991 women among the 1,035 Chinese applicants who provided age information, only 15 percent were twenty-five or under, the age group of the majority of war brides from Great Britain. A significantly larger number of Chinese war brides, 85 percent, were twenty-six or older. The average age of the postwar Chinese immigrant women, shown in figure 4.3, was 32.8, and most of them were between thirty and forty.

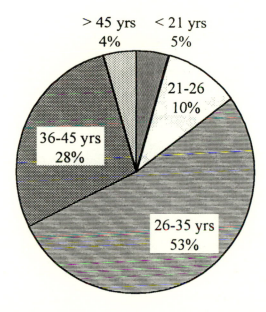

FIGURE 4.2. War bride age groups. Sample size: 991. (Records of the Immigration and Naturalization Service, Chinese Immigration Files, 1945–1952, RG85, National Archives, San Bruno, California.)

The length of their marriage and their age help explain the unique situation of the Chinese war brides. Their association with the United States had begun long before the war, and their marriages had little to do with the war. Without the war, however, these women would not have had the chance to be reunited with their husbands for many more years. Aimed at facilitating the immigration of European women who had married American G.I.'s, the War Brides Act incidentally opened the door for already married Chinese women.[14] At the end of the war, thousands of Chinese women who had lost touch with their husbands for years suddenly learned that they could join them in the United States as brides.

Entering the "Golden Gate"

Except for the attack on Pearl Harbor, the United States experienced World War II at a great geographical distance. Several million U.S. military personnel were engaged in combat around the globe for nearly four years. While 322,000 of them lost their lives, the war also facilitated romantic relationships between American soldiers and citizens of foreign countries. The

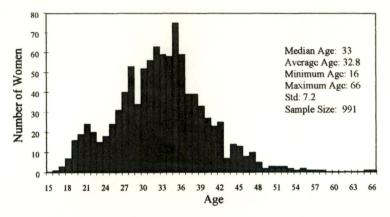

FIGURE 4.3. War bride age distribution. Sample size: 991. (Records of the Immigration and Naturalization Service, Chinese Immigration Files, 1945–1952, RG85, National Archives, San Bruno, California.)

INS estimated in 1945 that between 75,000 and 100,000 American soldiers married abroad, and the majority of these marriages took place in Europe. Great Britain alone was thought to have produced 40,000 to 55,000 American war brides. Pressure from the INS, the European governments, and the American soldiers to facilitate these women's entry into the United States generated some of the least restrictive immigration legislation in recent U.S. history.[15]

In addition to passing laws to make the immigration process less complicated, a group of INS officials was sent to England and France to expedite the admission process.[16] The U.S. government also provided transportation for war brides. As thousands of war brides and their babies arrived in the United States from Europe, Australia, or other parts of the world on "bride ships," they were embraced by their husbands, parents-in-laws, news reporters, and photographers. The publicity surrounding them was usually positive, and relatively few European brides encountered problems at their ports of entry.[17]

The possibility of an influx of Asian women under the War Brides Act did not seem to be an issue at first. American naval forces fought many battles in Asia, mainly on islands of the Pacific. A few thousand American soldiers were sent to the East Asian mainland, but most of them did not stay there for more than a year. Wartime marriages between American military personnel and Asians were fewer compared with those between Americans and Europeans, and Asian brides, except for the Chinese and Filipinos, were still inadmissible in 1945.[18] The War Brides Bill (H.R. 4857) passed both houses of Congress without a struggle, partly because no one anticipated that this new piece of legislation would be used by Chinese to reunite their families. The INS had supported the passage of the bill in order to simplify the immigration process for European brides and to reduce its own workload. Not until a few months after the new law went into effect did the INS regional inspectors find themselves confronted by hundreds of middle-aged Chinese women who possessed the required documents to enter the United States as war brides.

Checking the identity of each Chinese immigrant applicant at the ports of entry was routine for the INS. Because marriage certificates and birth certificates were not issued in rural China, the INS had established a system of investigation and interrogation to determine applicants' qualifications. INS inspectors were quite familiar with the tactics used by the Chinese, and they had developed certain strategies against document fraud. It was made the responsibility of each war bride to convince the inspector in charge that her case was genuine. Should any suspicion arise, the applicant would be detained.

Qiu Guanying would have had a hard time proving that she and her husband had married in 1937, because her husband, Cai Fujiu, had come to the United States in 1940 as his cousin's minor son and so did not report his marriage to the INS. When her husband and his fellow servicemen were called back to the United States from China in September 1946, Qiu and her daughter were able to return with them on a U.S. military vessel. The group was welcomed to Seattle, and her husband, who was still in uniform, handled all the questions from the immigration authorities. The following is recorded in Cai Fujiu's biography:

> Cai Nüliang resembled her father very closely. As soon as the officer saw her, he smiled and said, "Okay." But he had questions about Qiu Guanying's identity.
>
> The officer asked: "Mr. Cai, your daughter was born in 1937. Why did you declare yourself unmarried when you entered the U.S. in 1940?"
>
> Prepared for this question, Cai Fujiu answered calmly: "When I fell in love in China, my parents in America opposed it strongly. I married without getting their consent, and I had this daughter. I did not want to upset my parents, and therefore declared myself unmarried when I came. It was that simple."
>
> The officer laughed, "I see, very interesting." He then signed the entry permits.[19]

Tenley Chin married David Chin in February 1947 at her village in Taishan, Guangdong. Born in Barnstable, Massachusetts, David had been brought to China at age three. He was detained for a month when he returned to the United States six years later. He did not want his wife to go through the same ordeal, so the couple wed a second time, after David turned twenty-one, at the American consulate in China. Arriving in San Francisco with her newborn daughter on Christmas Eve of 1948, four days before the War Brides Act expired, Tenley carried all the documents required: an official marriage certificate issued by the American consulate in China, wedding photos, and David's military service record. Not many questions were asked, and she was granted immediate entry.[20]

The legacy of the exclusion era, however, had made it difficult for some Chinese women to face interrogation. The women knew they had every right to enter the United States, but their husbands might have used fictive ties when they first came over or have given false testimony to help other fellow villagers. To protect the immigration networks, these war brides had to involve themselves in their husbands' schemes. They had to furnish immigration authorities with the exact information that was already in their husbands' files. Failure to adhere to the recorded details would not only jeopardize a woman's own case, but also cause trouble for the many others who had helped her husband in the past. Whether a woman could gain entry in such cases would depend on how well she could conceal part of her own past.

Dong Zem Ping, documented in her son Arthur Dong's film *Sewing Woman*, married at age thirteen. When her husband came to America, most likely as a paper son, he did not report that he had a wife, much less that she was pregnant. Although his wartime military service qualified him to bring in his family members, his previous sworn testimony, as well as the testimonies of his sponsor and friends, prevented him from reclaiming his real identity. Dong therefore had to marry her husband a second time to apply for entry as a war bride. She had to pretend that she was a new bride when she came to the United States, and she could not reveal that she was the mother of an eight-year-old boy. Dong was admitted, but she had to leave her son behind in the village.[21]

Many Chinese women were detained at immigration stations before their husbands had a chance to greet them. The women were under pressure to perform well, for they were fully aware of the consequences if they were caught lying. Their feelings of helplessness and the uncertainty concerning their future created much frustration. The detained women were not allowed to see anyone from the outside, and not knowing what they were going to be questioned on or what their husbands might have said made life at the detention center most difficult.

Huang Lai, a forty-one-year-old woman who applied for entry as the wife of a citizen, arrived in San Francisco in January 1948. Because her story did not match that of her husband, Zheng Hele, in detail, the immigration inspectors suspected that they were not a married couple and decided to deport her. Waiting for the results of her appeal, Huang became desperate. On June 2, after being kept at the immigration station for almost six months, Huang climbed out of her cell window in an apparent suicide attempt. The scene of a woman about to jump from the fourteenth floor of the building housing the INS office attracted thousands of onlookers. It took the police three hours to rescue Huang. Only then was she able to reunite with her husband.[22]

A week later, on June 10, Liang Bixia, a thirty-two-year-old war bride, was detained. Liang did not do well in the cross-examination, and she was told that she would be deported. On September 20, Liang's husband, Wu Boxiang, flew to San Francisco from New York to meet her, but immigration authorities would not let them see each other. Frustrated and humiliated, Liang hanged herself at the immigration station the next morning.[23]

The immigration authorities' suspicions that many Chinese newcomers were involved in document fraud were not all groundless. Many war brides had been victims of the Chinese exclusion. Now that family reunification had finally became a reality for them, they considered it their responsibility to pave the way for other community members. Claiming additional dependents was a common strategy. The INS recorded that only 589 Chinese children were admitted under the War Brides Act, but the actual number of dependents claimed by Chinese war brides was much larger.[24] These women did not have to bring all the claimed children with them when they came: a minor's slot, once established in the parents' records, could be used at any time before the person was twenty-one. It was very likely that some women brought fewer children than they claimed to make their own entry less complicated. If a war bride's husband had entered the country illegally and the INS had no entry records, the couple would claim as many children as they thought they could get away with.

As table 4.2 indicates, there is a highly skewed sex ratio among the children claimed by Chinese war brides according to immigration records. Of the 1,784 children claimed by 877 women, 1,483 were boys and 301 were girls.

Previous involvement with immigration networks provided some war

TABLE. 4.2. *Dependents of Postwar Female Chinese Immigrants*

Number of women who claimed children	877
Total number of children claimed	1,788*
Number of boys claimed	1,483
Number of girls claimed	301
Boys to girls ratio	4.93

SOURCE: Records of the Immigration and Naturalization Service, Chinese Immigration Files, 1945–1952, RG85, National Archives, San Bruno, California.
NOTE: Sample size: 1,035.
*Four children's genders were not recorded.

brides with considerable knowledge in dealing with the U.S. immigration officials. Mary Yee, who married in 1934, came to the United States to join her husband, a paper son, in 1948. In addition to her own daughter, she claimed two sons. One of the boys was her nephew, and the other was the son of her husband's godfather. During her two weeks' ordeal at the immigration station in San Francisco, Mary was interrogated repeatedly, but she remained calm. She and her husband had carefully prepared for the interrogation, and they had ready answers for questions regarding the boys.[25]

In September 1948, a twenty-nine-year-old Chinese woman who had been married for eleven years was admitted as a citizen's wife. Admitted with her were one boy and two girls, including an adopted infant girl. In addition to these children, the woman claimed that she had left six of her sons in China. It is unclear how many of her claimed sons later came to the United States, but very likely most, if not all, did. Attached to her file is a confession by one of her alleged sons, who came in 1950. The young man admitted that the woman was not his biological mother and that his own family members were still in China.[26] It should be noted that this confession was made in 1969, three years after the termination of the Chinese Confession Program (see chapter seven) and a year after the 1965 Immigration Act went into effect.[27] At a time when McCarthyism was subject to criticism in U.S. political discourse, there was much less danger in Chinese immigrants' admitting their previous fraud. A voluntary confession would enable the young man to reclaim his true identity and kinship. He could then sponsor members of his family to the United States under the family unification principle of the 1965 Immigration Act.

Immigration officials were determined to deny entry to all whom they suspected of document fraud. They found, however, that the Chinese war brides were more difficult to deal with than they had expected. On the one hand, these women seemed to understand that their right to enter was guaranteed by law, since their husbands had indeed served in the military during the war. The INS, on the other hand, was no longer free to detain and deport Chinese applicants as it had done during the exclusion, because Chinese American war veterans had now gained public support.[28]

The difficulties the INS faced in dealing with the war brides are readily apparent from two failed deportation proceedings. The INS's most effective weapon was interrogation, and the inspectors could try to intimidate Chinese applicants by pressing them to admit to fraudulent schemes. In November 1947, a twenty-six-year-old war bride with a young boy was detained. Intimidated by the inspector in charge during the initial interrogation, she could not describe her own wedding. She also admitted, under pressure, that she was assuming the identity of her alleged husband's deceased wife. The next day, however, the woman regained her composure. She denied what she had said earlier and calmly described her wedding. Only then was she informed that her alleged husband had told the investigators that the two were not a couple. He confessed that he had been promised $1,000 for bringing in the boy, and he said that the woman's father, a laundryman in New York, had planned the whole affair.[29]

This would seem to be a clear-cut case for deportation, especially because the woman's alleged husband, the sponsor, turned against her, and her own earlier testimony in fact matched the man's confession. Obviously the woman failed to prove that her claim was genuine, which should have been sufficient for the INS to deny her entry. The increasing political strength of the Chinese American community in the postwar years, however, forced the INS to prove her guilt incontrovertibly, which was extremely difficult because the agency did not have the capacity to conduct investigations in China. Cooperation of the applicants was therefore crucial for successful deportation proceedings. Even though it was almost impossible for the woman to prove herself innocent, she insisted that she was the wife of her sponsor. Her alleged husband, she argued, was mentally ill. The case dragged on for fourteen months, but the INS could not prove the woman guilty beyond reasonable doubt. She and her alleged son were both admitted in January 1949.[30]

A second case involves a thirty-four-year-old war bride who came in June 1947. The woman said that she had been married for fifteen years, and she had a fourteen-year-old son who was now attending school in China.

Immigration records indicate that her alleged husband had originally entered the United States in 1926 as a minor son of a citizen. The young man visited China in 1930, returned a year later, and reported that he had married a woman whose name was the same as the one given by the applicant. It seemed a simple case. However, when the husband returned from the 1930 trip, he came with his father and a young woman the father claimed as his daughter. That woman was later deported, leaving a red flag in the young man's file. Immigration officials now detained his alleged wife and pulled the file of the deported sister. There they found two black-and-white photos of the woman, whom the investigators identified as the current applicant even though the picture had been taken some fifteen years earlier.[31]

Deportation proceedings were filed against the woman. Her alleged husband had been involved in a document fraud and was an untrustworthy sponsor. If the woman was indeed a party to the fraud, she had committed a felony and therefore was not admissible. The woman, however, would not give in. While her alleged husband argued that she was not related to the person who had attempted to enter as his sister, she insisted that the photo on file was not hers, that this was her first trip to the United States, and that she had no knowledge whatsoever about her husband's earlier fraud.[32] Two medical experts who examined photos of the war bride and the old photos on file confirmed that the two applicants were most likely one person, but they also pointed out that photos alone were not sufficient proof of a person's identity.[33]

As discussed in chapter one, laws during the exclusion did not permit Chinese women who married American citizens after 1924 to enter the United States. That this woman might have been desperate enough to try to enter fraudulently was understandable, especially because some Chinese had successfully come in as dependents of citizens.[34] The failed attempt, however, had not only led to her deportation but also destroyed the credibility of the ones involved. Her husband did not visit her once in the following fifteen years—probably because he knew it would be unwise: should suspicion arise when he applied for reentry, his derivative citizenship might be revoked.

The husband's military service record during the war, however, provided the couple with the chance to be reunited. His residence in the United States was now secure. Even if immigration authorities bothered to question his derivative citizenship, he was entitled to be naturalized anyway. The woman was apparently quite prepared for an extended interrogation, possibly because she had already experienced one. She made the same statements every time she was questioned, and she appeared completely ignorant about the deportation case of her husband's alleged sister. After a year-long investigation, the INS finally relented and admitted the woman.

Between September 14, 1946, and April 15, 1948, the INS detained 3,838 Chinese immigrant applicants, most of them women. The government believed that at least 75 of the detainees were involved in fraud, but proof of fraud was no longer sufficient for the INS to deport an applicant.[35] One thirty-six-year-old war bride was detained in San Francisco in March 1948 with two children, a boy and a girl, and she claimed that she had left her oldest child, a boy, in China. Under questioning, however, she could not explain discrepancies between her story and that of her husband, and she said that her oldest child was a girl. The INS closed the slot that she tried to create for a boy in China but admitted the woman and the two children, since she was able to establish herself as the wife of a war veteran.[36] Between 1936 and 1941 the INS had deported an annual average of 128 Chinese. The number of Chinese deportees decreased during the war years, as the number admitted also decreased. Between July 1946 and June 1949, thousands of Chinese gained entry each year, but the INS was only able to deport a small fraction of them (see table 4.3).[37]

The Chinese community's campaign to place the actions of the INS under public scrutiny made deporting war brides more and more difficult, as the general public supported efforts of the Chinese American war veterans to bring their wives over. In June 1948, the California branch of the American Veterans Association passed a resolution condemning the poor treatment of Chinese war brides. It accused the INS of violating both the U.S. Constitution and the Bill of Rights and urged the government to treat all immigration applicants equally regardless of race, color, or religion.[38]

The detained war brides worked closely together with the community to put pressure on the INS. On September 21, 1948, the day after Liang Bixia committed suicide, all 104 of the Chinese women detained in San Francisco staged a hunger strike to protest their treatment. That these middle-aged Chinese country women who had never lived in the United States would take group action against an agency of the U.S. government was inconceivable to the INS. Officials in San Francisco, already embarrassed by the death of Liang, refused to admit that the Chinese war brides were capable of organizing a hunger strike. They told reporters that the women did not eat because that was the way Chinese mourned the deceased.[39]

The women would not stay quiet, however. They smuggled out at least two letters, urging the community to take up their cause with the INS.[40] On

TABLE 4.3. *Chinese Immigration Aliens Admitted and Deported,*
July 1936–June 1949

Year	Admitted	Deported	Year	Admitted	Deported
1936	273	75	1943	65	2
1937	293	114	1944	50	11
1938	613	136	1945	71	13
1939	642	158	1946	252	15
1940	643	160	1947	3,191	16
1941	1,003	127	1948	3,987	19
1942	179	11	1949	2,823	19

SOURCES: *Annual Report of the Immigration and Naturalization Service*, 1945, 1949; Helen Chen, "Chinese Immigration into the United States: An Analysis of Changes in Immigration Policies" (Ph.D. diss., Brandeis University, 1980), 174.

September 27, the Chinese War Veterans Association in New York sent telegrams to all Chinese newspapers and community organizations calling for a united protest against the detention of the Chinese war brides. The telegram accused the INS of violating the rights of American war veterans and demanded that the brides be released immediately.[41] During a meeting with representatives of the INS, members of the Chinese Hand Laundry Alliance argued that immigration applicants should not be detained for more than three days. They asserted that more detention constituted an act of racial discrimination, since only Chinese immigrants were being singled out. They also discussed with the INS the possibility of processing immigration papers in China.[42] Under pressure from Chinese Americans, politicians, and the general public, the INS investigated Liang's case. It criticized the conduct of the San Francisco district office and promised future progress.[43] Beginning in 1950, the government changed its procedures. Screening Chinese immigration applications began at the port of departure instead of the port of entry (see chapter seven).[44]

*T*he coming of the war brides excited the Chinese American community. Each time a ship from China arrived in the United States, Chinese-language newspapers reported the number of women it carried. The women were expected to work together with their men to realize their dreams and make the United States their permanent home. The couples were supposed to pick up from where they left off and live happily ever after. At a time of joy, triumph, and high expectations, probably very few thought about the conflicts that were bound to emerge between husbands and wives. Rural China was strikingly different from urban U.S. society, and the lengthy separations marriage partners had endured created social, cultural, and linguistic gaps that would inevitably make adjustment difficult for both men and women. Before a discussion of the problems of Chinese American families in the post-war years, the next chapter will take a look at important changes within the Chinese American community during and after World War II.

CHAPTER 5

Community Institutions
and the Press in Transition

In late 1944 Lew Wah Chew, Lew Chuck Suey's oldest son, bought a house three miles east of Oakland's Chinatown. His children, all born in the United States, settled down nearby after they established their own families. When Lew Chuck Suey's younger sons, Wah Git and Wah Sun, brought their wives from China as war brides after the war, they settled down in east Oakland as well. By 1960, most of Lew Chuck Suey's children and grandchildren had moved farther away from Chinatown.[1] Like the members of the Lew family, the Chinese population spread out from the ghettos after World War II despite the resistance to racial integration found in some residential areas. A number of Chinese Americans eventually moved to Oakland's Lake Shore area, where many Chinese girls had worked as maids before the war.[2] Approximately 96 percent of the 237,292 Chinese in the United States lived in urban areas in 1960, but many of them no longer resided within a Chinatown proper. The San Francisco Department of City Planning listed 22,481 of the 29,000 Chinese in San Francisco in 1960 as Chinatown residents, but it defined census tracts with over a 50 percent Chinese population as Chinatown.[3] In other words, the once fixed boundary lines of Chinatown had become obscure.

The dispersion of the Chinese population in the United States suggests a change in the way Chinese Americans associated with one another and with their community. Before the war a Chinatown was an isolated ethnic enclave with a governing body of its own. As Stanford M. Lyman has demonstrated, San Francisco's Chinatown in the late nineteenth and early twentieth centuries exercised multiple forms of social, economic, and institutional control that dominated the lives of ordinary Chinese immigrants.[4] Chinese Americans depended less on community institutions after the war, as the number of families increased and opportunities outside Chinatowns became available. To many Chinese Americans who lived and worked elsewhere, Chinatown meant a center for Chinese culture, food, and medicine, and a place for social activities.[5]

In addition to the population movement out of the enclaves and the increase in the number of families, political development in China after World War II also worked to divide community groups. New workers and youth organizations that emerged in the late 1930s and 1940s resented the merchants-dominated community establishment, which was backed by the Nationalist government in China. At this time of rapid change, the community press, read by Chinese living in different parts of the United States, inside and outside Chinatowns, played an increasingly important role. As political tension intensified in the late 1940s, independent papers made attempts to break down political and regional factions among different groups and urged community members to form a united front.

The Rise and Decline of the Community Power Structure

The geographical and social isolation of Chinese Americans before World War II necessitated the development of community organizations. Denied naturalization, Chinese immigrants were ignored by American politicians and received little protection from government institutions or law-enforcement agencies. They found comfort and support within their own ethnic enclaves, and they created mutual aid networks based on kinship, native places, and common interests. These networks eventually became the basis of Chinese Americans' own governing bodies.

As Lyman has documented, clan and *huiguan* (district associations) were two of the most important Chinese immigrant organizations in the late nineteenth and early twentieth centuries. Members of a clan or family association were identified by a common surname or lineage, and they shared knowledge of trade, manufacturing, and types of labor. The clan associations were especially important in establishing immigration networks and assisting members in finding jobs, and they were crucial to the development of both ethnic enterprises and Chinatowns. Because new immigrants usually entered occupations in which their fellow clan members had experience or with which they were familiar, each clan developed its own occupational specialties. Some clans became dominant groups in a particular area because of their economic success. The Lees, for example, were most prominent in Philadelphia, as were the Chins and the Toms in New York City. Small Chinatowns sometimes sprang up on the basis of one or two clans.[6] In Santa Barbara, California, for example, a large number of the roughly four hundred Chinese immigrants belonged to either the Gin or Yee family associations.

A huiguan traced its origin to the native place of the immigrants in China and united all the clans and groups from the same region. Members of a huiguan usually spoke a common dialect. Lyman sees a huiguan as a "combined eleemosynary, judicial, representative, and mutual aid society."[7] It provided members with many benefits that were crucial to their survival, and it was important to the immigrant community both economically and socially. The huiguan provided the newcomers with temporary lodging and introduced them to jobs. It arbitrated disputes among its members, ensured the payment of debts, raised funds for projects of common concern, provided medicine, maintained cemeteries, covered burial expenses for the poor, and shipped the exhumed bones of the deceased to their home villages for final burial. Membership dues also provided special funds for the elderly. The Sanyi huiguan (Sam Yup Benevolent Association), for example, had allocated $2,694 to send 188 older members of the association back to China in 1882. Both the clans and the huiguan provided social education for their members as well. They gave immigrants information unavailable elsewhere and taught the newcomers how to deal with the larger society and how to respond to the immigration authorities.[8]

Hierarchically above the clan and the district associations was the Chinese Consolidated Benevolent Association (Zhonghua gongsuo), which was often compared to the ancient Irish Order of Hibernians or the Scandinavian Association. On November 19, 1882, in response to the increasing need of Chinese immigrants for help in dealing with anti-Chinese agitation, Chinese consul general Huang Zunxian pushed for the official establishment of the CCBA in San Francisco to provide community leadership. Commonly known as the Chinese Six Companies, this federation of huiguan was recognized by the larger society as the voice of the community in the United States. The establishment of the CCBA, as Him Mark Lai has pointed out, was especially significant in Chinese American history; it gave individual Chinese living in the United States a sense of community.[9] By 1947 it had thirty branches in Chinatowns throughout the country.[10]

The community power structure was controlled by the merchant class. Exempted from exclusion, the merchants were able to bring in their families and help clan members emigrate. They had the financial resources and often provided employment for others. The merchants were also able to maintain their elite status in the community because there were few scholars at the time. Until the early twentieth century the ranks of government officials in China were awarded according to their performance in a series of imperial examinations. Although this examination system was abolished in 1905, the scholar-gentry continued to be the elite class in China. For several decades, some district associations recruited a small number of scholar-gentry to serve as presidents of huiguan or on the board of directors of the CCBA. Such practice ended in 1925 when the U.S. government tightened immigration restrictions. After that, all the important positions in community establishment were filled by the merchants.[11]

Chinese immigrants also formed organizations based on common interests. One popular organization of this type was called a tong (from *tang*, meaning a meeting hall), which bound its members together through secret initiation rites and sworn brotherhood. The best-known tong among Chinese in the United States was the Zhigongtang (Chee Kung Tong), a secret fraternal society originally formed in China to overthrow the Qing Dynasty and restore the Ming Dynasty. The tongs were famous for their antiestablishment stance. They controlled the immigrant underworld, and they often fought against each other in territorial disputes over gambling, opium smoking, and prostitution.

Chinese who had been born and educated in the United States formed one of the most important organizations in the community. The United Parlor of the Native Sons of the Golden State, the predecessor of the Chinese American Citizens Alliance, was first organized in San Francisco in 1895, despite skepticism from the community elders. In 1904 Walter U. Lum, Joseph K. Lum, and Ng Gunn reorganized the group and led its members to speak out against Chinese exclusion. This action helped the organization expand its membership and gain respect from the community. By 1912 local chapters of the organization had formed in Oakland, San Francisco, and Los Angeles, and Walter U. Lum became the president of the original parlor, the Grand Lodge. A year later, Fresno and San Diego also formed their own local branches. Beginning in the 1920s, the organization played a leading role lobbying Congress to amend immigration laws (see chapter one).[12]

The official voice of the entire community was the CCBA. Beginning in the late nineteenth century, San Francisco's CCBA protested against the treatment of the Chinese in the United States and contested discriminatory laws in court. In addition to voicing grievances for its members when their rights were violated, the mandate of the CCBA, as stated in its 1925 bylaws, was to mediate disputes among the affiliated community organizations, establish Chinese-language schools and other educational programs for children, build hospitals, provide public services, and promote trade with China.[13] In the 1910s, with the support of the consuls general of the new Republic of China, the CCBA had some success in mediating disputes among the tongs and other community groups. The work of the CCBA for the welfare of the community in areas that were neglected by the U.S. system was especially applauded. The association funded many Chinese schools throughout the United States and raised funds for and organized the construction of the Chinese Hospital (Donghua yiyuan) in San Francisco.[14]

The community power structure was strengthened with the support of the Chinese government. Once the Chinese Nationalist Party, the Guomindang, gained control in China in 1927, it began regulating organizations in overseas Chinese communities and expanding its membership to include Chinese living abroad. The party established headquarters in Chinatowns in the United States in the late 1930s and appointed several heads of huiguan and the CCBA as party officials. In exchange for their loyalty to the Nationalist government in China, the Guomindang helped merchants to maintain their control in the community.[15]

The CCBA's income came from exit permits and registration fees, both collected through the huiguan. Steamship companies in the United States agreed not to sell tickets to any Chinese unless the CCBA had cleared the person of debt. A fee was charged for getting an exit permit, and two dollars of that fee would go to the CCBA's headquarters in San Francisco. In 1901 the CCBA also launched its first membership registration drive and collected one dollar from each registered member. In 1926 the CCBA passed a resolution requiring every Chinese American above eighteen to register biennially and pay a one-dollar registration fee to offset the cost of litigation. If an exit permit applicant was not registered, he had to pay a few extra dollars for the permit. If a person who had failed to register wanted to use the CCBA's legal services, he would be charged a fifty-dollar fine. This registration drive was a great success, bringing in a total of 26,676 Chinese American members (the total Chinese population in the United States in 1920 was 61,639, including children).[16] Their dues enabled the association to establish a legal fund to challenge the exclusion laws concerning citizens' wives.[17]

Affiliation with the larger society was so difficult during the exclusion that most Chinese Americans did not object to becoming members of a community organization. Many of them were members of several organizations at the same time. Members of the CACA, for example, were also members of their family or district associations, which were under the regulation of the CCBA. Huang Boyao, who headed the Native Sons of the Golden State in 1908, was also a member of the Zhigongtang.[18] Without support from their community networks, newcomers would face great difficulty in finding jobs and would have no means of voicing their grievances. As more and more immigrants established their own businesses, there was an increasing desire for stability and community building, and most Chinese Americans expected their own organizations, especially the CCBA in San Francisco, to provide leadership.[19]

Beginning in the late 1920s, however, the CCBA in San Francisco found it more and more difficult to consolidate its power and function as the voice of the Chinese American community. Internal struggle within the association presented a major challenge. Of the seven huiguan organized at the time, Ning Yang, composed of immigrants from Taishan County, had the largest membership. It contributed a portion of the CCBA's budget significantly larger than that of any other group—$12,943 of the $26,676 collected by all seven district associations—during the registration drive of 1926.[20] The representation of each huiguan in the CCBA, however, was not commensurate with its membership. In 1907, Ning Yang held eleven out of forty-one positions on the CCBA's board of directors; after 1925, it was entitled to twenty-two positions out of a total of eighty. Still, Ning Yang had more power than other huiguan in the CCBA. In October 1927, *Young China Morning Paper*, a Guomindang-controlled newspaper run by immigrants from Zhongshan and several other districts, published an article criticizing Ning Yang's president for abusing his power within the CCBA. Ning Yang was indignant. It demanded that the newspaper offer a public apology and fire the article writer. To force the paper to give in, Ning Yang organized a nationwide boycott. *Young China* fought back, publishing satires of Ning Yang. The Guomindang's headquarters in San Francisco even threatened to expel from the party anyone who participated in the boycott. As Ning Yang urged its members to protect the interests of the association, *Young China* reported to the Guomindang that the huiguan was controlled by the Communists.[21]

As the battle continued, Ning Yang blamed the CCBA for failing to mediate the situation successfully. It rejected the CCBA's new measures to collect funds, and its president refused to serve his term as the head of the organization. At its first national conference in September 1928, Ning Yang passed a resolution questioning the effectiveness of the CCBA's leadership and expressing its desire for more power:

The slander and defamation of our *ningyang huiguan* by the *Young China Morning Paper* originated from a dispute at the CCBA. Although the CCBA spoke on our behalf, the situation could not be resolved satisfactorily. We have been forced to deal with the newspaper directly. Up to this day, justice has yet to prevail, and our reputation has yet to be cleared. The Ning Yang carried a heavier burden than other members of the CCBA, but we enjoyed very few privileges. For example, we contributed almost half of the CCBA's budgeted revenue from exit permits, but we hold only about a quarter of the board positions. What a loss we have suffered! Instead of getting what we deserve, we have been slandered and defamed. What do they think of our association? Whom do they think we are?[22]

The resolution reasoned that if the CCBA considered itself a federation of huiguan and gave each member the same rights and privileges, its financial burden should be shared equally by the seven participating members. Whatever else was collected should be kept by the huiguan. Otherwise, the CCBA should give each huiguan rights and privileges proportional to its membership. Should the CCBA receive greater financial contributions from Ning Yang than from the other members, it ought to give Ning Yang a greater voice.[23]

Without the participation of Ning Yang, the CCBA found it almost impossible to conduct routine businesses. The vacated presidency was temporarily filled by the presidents of the other six huiguan, who alternated on a monthly basis, but no major decision could be made without Ning Yang's consent. The CCBA finally gave in and agreed to amend its bylaws. Ning Yang, however, insisted that its noncooperative policy would continue until all of its demands were met.[24]

The revised bylaws, passed on April 22, 1930, effectively granted Ning Yang control of the CCBA. A new fifty-five-man board set to work, with Ning Yang members in twenty-seven seats, one less than half of the total. The new bylaws also set the president's term at two months. Ning Yang's president would take every other term; the other huiguan presidents would rotate to fill the remaining terms.[25]

Shortly after the CCBA settled its internal disputes, developments in China came to shape community activities. On September 18, 1931, the Japanese contrived the Shenyang (Mukden) incident and used it as a pretext to occupy three provinces in Northeast China. The Chinese American community quickly responded. The CCBA wired both the Nanjing government and the Guangdong (Communist) government and raised money to send to the Chinese military. Chiang Kai-shek, who was more eager to defeat the Communists, decided not to resist Japan. When Japanese troops attacked Shanghai on January 28, 1932, the Nineteenth Route Army, led by General Cai Tingkai, ignored Chiang's orders and fought back. The bloody battle against the aggressors lasted for thirty-four days and Cai emerged as a national hero. Sentiment in support of Cai's army was especially strong in the Chinese American community because most of the soldiers were from Guangdong, the home province of most Chinese immigrants. Several Chinatowns formed special committees to raise funds for the war effort.[26] On July 7, 1937, the Japanese attacked the Lugou qiao (Marco Polo Bridge) near Beijing and began a full-scale military invasion of China. The Chinese American community responded immediately and urged the Nationalist government to mobilize the nation to resist the aggressors. On August 20, the China War Relief Association (Lümei huaqiao tongyi yijuan jiuguo zonghui) was formed in San Francisco. This association, which included members of many community groups, led the wartime activities of the Chinese Americans for eight years.[27] Meanwhile the agenda of the CCBA was pushed aside.

At the same time many intellectuals, workers, and young people realized that the Guomindang was not as keen to fight the Japanese as it was the Communists. Moreover, they began to see that the merchant-dominated power structure had little interest in providing protection for ordinary Chinese Americans. Disillusioned with the Nationalist government, some found Marxist theories inspiring. They became sympathetic to the Communist cause in China and formed new organizations of their own.

Even before the Lugou qiao attack, some community groups had questioned the leadership of the CCBA. In March 1933, the Council of Aldermen of the City of New York proposed an ordinance to impose a security bond of one thousand dollars and an annual license fee of twenty-five dollars on all public laundries. The proposal also made U.S. citizenship a requirement for every public laundry owner. In his study of the Chinese Hand Laundry Alliance of New York, Renqiu Yu points out that most Chinese laundrymen would not have been able to pay these exorbitant fees. Many of them did not hold U.S. citizenship either, since Chinese immigrants were ineligible for naturalization. If enforced, this ordinance would have put hundreds of Chinese laundrymen out of work. The laundrymen went to the CCBA for help, but the latter wanted them to pay its fees first before taking action.[28]

On April 23, 1933, more than one thousand Chinese laundrymen held a meeting that let to the formation of the Chinese Hand Laundry Alliance

(CHLA), which launched its own campaign against the proposed ordinance. The CCBA, which had long considered itself the spokesperson of the community, had warned against such a step. In May the CHLA's representatives and attorney appeared at a public hearing, and their arguments persuaded the city to revise the proposed ordinance. The security bond was reduced from one thousand to one hundred dollars and the license fee from twenty-five to ten dollars; the citizenship requirement was dropped. This victory encouraged the growth of the CHLA. For nearly two decades it was the major organization confronting the CCBA in New York.[29]

In San Francisco in September 1937, a group of Chinese workers returning from their summer jobs at Alaskan salmon canneries organized the Chinese Workers Mutual Aid Association (CWMAA). Like the CHLA in New York, the CWMAA did not request permission from the CCBA to organize. It maintained strong ties with American trade unions as well as with the American Communist Party. The association held both regular meetings to discuss issues concerning Chinese American workers and seminars to study Marxist theory. It published essays supporting the Communist Revolution in China as well as writings by leaders of the Chinese Communist Party.[30]

Progressive youth organizations also emerged. The largest youth club in New York, the Chinese Youth Club (Niuyue huaqiao qingnian jiuguo tuan), was established in 1938, and it had close ties with the CHLA. In 1942 several youth groups in San Francisco formed the Chinese Youth League, which was the predecessor of Min Qing (Chinese American Democratic Youth League). Both the CPYC and Min Qing sponsored a variety of social and recreational programs. They held classes in Mandarin, music, and photography, and each had a chorus.[31] Unlike the male-dominated and merchant-controlled clans or district associations, these organizations welcomed the participation of young men and women of all social backgrounds. Each group had women among its officers. Min Qing's library provided reading materials for young Chinese Americans who were interested in classical Chinese literature, history, and Marxist theory, and the organization's vocal, dance, and drama groups offered its members opportunities to work together and perform on stage. Young members were also encouraged to write essays for the groups' publications.

The war relief campaign provided an opportunity for a cross-section of Chinese American groups to work together. The workers' organizations and youth groups were especially active in the war effort in China, and women's groups emerged to organize their own fund-raising campaign and other activities. The clans, district associations, and the CCBA, however, still functioned according to the old rules: youngsters were still expected to do as their elders had done and were discouraged from organizing their own groups, and women continued to be excluded from playing major public roles. New ideas and actions were more likely to be ridiculed or condemned than to be encouraged.

But as diverse community activities flourished, the influence of the CCBA declined. The organization had been in trouble financially from the early 1930s. In 1935 the CCBA launched another registration drive, but only 3,925 people, about one-seventh of the 1926 record count, responded, even though the Chinese population in the United States had increased from 61,639 in 1920 to 74,957 in 1930.[32] The money received totaled only about one-ninth of what was collected in 1926. Transportation difficulties during the war also prevented most Chinese Americans from visiting their families in China and therefore generated no exit permit income. In 1947 the CCBA in San Francisco started to issue exit permits again, but this source of income dried up two years later when the United States failed to recognize the People's Republic of China, making it impossible for Chinese Americans to travel to the Chinese mainland. In 1951 the CCBA headquarters in San Francisco began to borrow money from the huiguan to make ends meet.[33]

The official entry of the United States into World War II, on December 7, 1941, profoundly changed the way Chinese Americans associated with one another and with their ethnic community: Chinese Americans could now participate in the war effort or find work without using the resources of their community associations. The war and the end of exclusion two years later also encouraged identification with the United States. As an increasing number of young, educated Chinese American men and women found employment in occupations that were unfamiliar to their clan elders, they became eager to learn about mainstream America's social rules and legal system. They were more likely to consult newspapers for employment information or ask professionals for business advice. Their clans and district associations no longer directly affected their day-to-day lives.[34]

The increase in the number of immigrant women and families also worked to reduce the dependence of Chinese Americans on their community organizations. Huiguan no longer functioned as the first stop for newcomers. The men and women who came after the war were much more likely to be greeted by close family members or relatives at their port of entry. Those who settled in cities and towns where Chinese residents were few did not find it necessary to join a clan or huiguan. Instead of partnerships of male clan members, the family often became the principal small-business unit. Even newcomers who lived in Chinatowns did not have to go to community organizations for employment information.

As Chinese Americans experienced great changes in a rapidly changing world, complex changes in community life also occurred. The political strength of Chinese Americans increased after the repeal of Chinese exclusion, as hundreds of Chinese immigrants became naturalized citizens each year. The participation of Chinese Americans in the war effort also helped redefine the image of the community and brought outside attention. Racial prejudice and discrimination, however, continued to play a major part in American politics, immigration, and social life. It was important for Chinese Americans to act for themselves as a united force for racial equality. Nevertheless, differences among Chinese Americans rooted in class, gender, political views, immigration status, and geographic distribution were far more visible than they had been in the prewar years, making community building a challenging task.

If allegiance to the Chinese Nationalist government had helped the community power structure secure control in the early twentieth century, this political connection also came to tie its hands in terms of community reform. Loyalty to the Guomindang made it almost impossible for community leaders to shift the focus from China's political development to the improvement of the Chinese American community, given the intensified Guomindang–Communist confrontation in the late 1940s. There were new opportunities for reform and new demands by different community groups, but the establishment functioned mostly as a means for the Guomindang to tighten its control over the political lives of community members. In the late 1940s it maneuvered to suppress liberal voices and thereby distanced itself from a cross section of Chinese Americans, especially the second generation, the educated youth, and the new immigrants.

The Emergence of the Chinese American Press

Accompanying the declining reputation of the old community establishment was the rising influence of the community press, although newspapers often argued against each other. The press's role was never the same as that of huiguan and the CCBA, but it was important in representing different views of community members and instrumental in promoting community solidarity.

As Karl Lo and Him Mark Lai have documented, newspapers and periodical magazines had been published in Chinese communities in the United

States since the late nineteenth century. During the exclusion era the press was strongly oriented toward China. Each of the major political factions in China published its own newspaper in the United States in the early decades of the twentieth century. After the Guomingdang established a single-party government in China in 1927, factions within the party developed, and these factions eventually founded their own newspapers in Chinese American communities.[35]

Led by Ng Poon Chew, a group of Christians in 1900 founded the first independent community newspaper, *Chung Sai Yat Po*, in San Francisco. This nonparty-affiliated newspaper aimed at cultivating discussions on community economic and social development, and it enjoyed a large circulation among Chinese in the western part of the United States and Mexico. In 1924 the Chinese American Citizens Alliance started its own news daily, the *Chinese Times*, also in San Francisco. Marxist sympathizers in the community likewise established their own newspapers, the first of which was the *Chinese Vanguard*, founded in San Francisco in the late 1920s.[36]

Most community newspapers were published in Chinese. Although a few American-born Chinese maneuvered to establish English newspapers from time to time, successful attempts were few. The first all-English news weekly, the *Chinese Digest*, was founded in 1935 by a group of second-generation Chinese Americans in San Francisco's Chinatown, but subscribers of the paper never exceeded five hundred and the paper folded in 1940.[37] Another English newspaper, the weekly *Chinese Press* in San Francisco, lasted a little longer, from 1940 to 1952. In contrast, there were more than a dozen Chinese-language newspapers published in San Francisco and New York from 1940 to 1960, and some of these were in publication for several decades.

The dominance of Chinese-language newspapers in the community by no means suggests that only a small number of Chinese Americans could read English. In the early decades of the twentieth century, the number of Chinese born in the United States increased steadily. The population of the Chinese in the United States in 1900 was 89,863, but only 9,010 (about 10 percent) were citizens. By 1940, there were 40,626 citizens out of a population of 77,504 (52 percent).[38] These citizen members of the community were either born in the United States or gained entry through derivative citizenship at a young age. Most of them attended American schools and could read English more fluently than Chinese.

Chinese, however, was the language spoken in immigrant families and the community. Although most second-generation Chinese Americans received education in American public schools, the majority of them also attended community-sponsored Chinese-language schools. Sam Sik Low, president of the CACA in Los Angeles from 1976 to 1977, for example, would not say that his ability to read Chinese is "good"; he attended Chinese schools in San Francisco for only a few years. Nevertheless, Sam grew up reading the *Chinese Times*, the paper that his family had subscribed to for decades. He improved his reading skill by reading Chinese-language newspapers on a daily basis. After Sam established his own family, he continued to subscribe to the *Chinese Times*, because his wife, a war bride who came from Hong Kong in 1947, could not read English until many years later. Besides the *Chinese Times*, the Lows also read other Chinese newspapers at friends' houses or at Chinatown businesses.[39]

Recognizing the importance of the Chinese language among both immigrants and U.S.-born Chinese, the CACA, when it decided to publish its own daily newspaper in 1924, used Chinese instead of English. Walter U. Lum, the founder of the paper, was the president of CACA's Grand Lodge for twelve years. Born in San Francisco in 1882, he had studied Chinese and English with private tutors and was fluent in both languages.[40] Although many members of the CACA had received their formal education in English, Walter wanted to establish a paper that could reach both immigrant and U.S.-born Chinese. The decision to use Chinese for the *Chinese Times* was apparently wise. Despite the existence of several other established Chinese-language newspapers, by 1929 the *Chinese Times* had the largest circulation among Chinese newspapers published in San Francisco. Between 1942 and 1943, its circulation number reached 9,799, four times as high as the *Chinese Press* (2,500), even though the latter was the only English newspaper published in San Francisco's Chinatown at the time.[41]

The independent newspapers tended to be more liberal than those affiliated with the Guomindang, and they were more interested in the welfare of Chinese American groups. Thomas Chinn, one of the founders of the *Chinese Digest*, wanted his paper to facilitate the learning and adaptation processes of second-generation Chinese Americans and help them move out of Chinatown.[42] In the 1930s, the *Chinese Vanguard* and the *Chinese Journal* both sided with the Chinese Hand Laundry Alliance in its struggle against the dominance of the CCBA in New York. The success of the *Chinese Times* had much to do with the paper's devotion to community issues. It was a leading advocate of immigration reform and civil rights for Chinese Americans for several decades, and it is the only nonparty-affiliated Chinese American newspaper that survived the Great Depression, World War II, and the cold war.[43]

As the hostility between the Guomindang and the Communist Party intensified after 1927, the Guomindang tried to increase its influence in overseas Chinese communities through its own newspapers. There were the *Young China Morning Paper* and the *Chinese National* in San Francisco, the *San Min Morning Post* in Chicago, the *Chinese Nationalist Daily* and the *Chinese Journal* in New York, and the *United Chinese News* in Honolulu. These newspapers propagandized the views of the Guomindang and made supporting the Nationalist government their sole responsibility.

In addition to setting up its own propaganda machine, the Guomindang demanded absolute support from other community newspapers. Emulating what the Nationalist government had done in China, the community power structure moved to eliminate its political opponents in the United States. Anyone who dared to criticize or question the authority of the Nationalist government or the CCBA was denounced as unpatriotic or Communist.[44] New York's *Chinese Journal,* because it had openly supported the Chinese Hand Laundry Alliance when that group challenged the leadership of the CCBA, became the target of political accusations in the 1930s. In 1935 the CCBA hired a group of men to harass the paper's staff and disturb its sales.[45] Later in the year the CCBA obtained a court order forbidding the paper to criticize the community power structure for three years and depriving editor Zhu Xia of the right to speak in public.[46] The *Chinese Journal* never recovered from the court defeat. In 1938 another left-wing newspaper, the *Chinese Vanguard*, went out of business.[47] By 1940 pro-Guomindang editors had also gained control of several major independent community newspapers.[48]

The politically biased Guomindang newspapers could hardly meet the needs of all Chinese American readers, and intellectuals and students were especially dissatisfied. Many young Chinese Americans had come from China during the late 1930s, and they had firsthand knowledge of the political and economic deterioration there. People wanted to know what was happening in China, and many did not believe that the Guomindang's propaganda machine would provide them with reliable information. They also wanted to see different views freely expressed in the community press as they were in the mainstream American press.

As some Chinese Americans began to organize their own groups, they also established their own newspapers or magazines. In 1940 members of the Chinese Hand Laundry Alliance in New York funded the *China Daily News;* many laundrymen purchased a few shares each.[49] The newspaper openly expressed its resentment at the Guomindang's control of the Chinese American community through the merchants, and it showed great sympathy toward the

Communist-led revolution in China. Although the paper closely followed events in China, the historian Renqiu Yu sees a link between the paper and the growing "Chinese American consciousness."[50]

In May 1949 the *China Weekly* appeared in San Francisco. Similar to the *China Daily News*, this paper represented the views of leftist community members. Its founder, Cai Fujiu (Henry Tsoi), had attended Japan's Meiji University in the early 1930s and joined the Chinese Communist Party in 1937 in Hong Kong. Cai came to the United States in 1939 on his own initiative, and although he was close to a group of progressive community members, he did not reveal his party affiliation.[51] The paper was financed and operated by members of the community and supported mostly by young readers.

In late 1949 Cai encouraged a group of entrepreneurs in the San Francisco Bay Area to outbid a Guomindang group and purchase the *Chung Sai Yat Po*, the oldest independent newspaper in San Francisco.[52] Actively involved in the new paper were several underground Chinese Communist Party members or sympathizers, including Cai Fujiu, Ma Jiliang, Li Chunhui, and Wang Jue. *Chung Sai Yat Po* was financially independent, however, and it took a rather modest approach to party politics in China.[53]

The political situation in China in the 1940s also led some established newspapermen to ease away from their party. Wu Jingfu, an editor of the *United Journal*, had worked for several Guomindang-funded newspapers. In 1942, however, he started the independent *Chinese American Weekly* and began to offer moderate criticism of the Guomindang. The circulation of the paper reached 11,860 in 1949, which surpassed most of the daily and weekly newspapers in the Chinese American community.[54] Dai Ming Lee, the chief editor of the Guomindang-controlled *United Chinese News* in Honolulu, proposed that a third party be formed in China to challenge the dominance of the Guomindang and reduce hostility between the Guomindang and the Communists. Lee was later hired by the *Chinese World* in San Francisco, and he recruited other independent journalists to work with him.[55] Disputes within the *Chinese Nationalist Daily* also led to the departure of editor Yu Yun Shan, who started the *China Tribune* in 1943.[56] These newspapers appealed to a large number of community members, including conservatives who had been disappointed by the Guomindang.

If some independent newspapers spoke for a particular political or social group, the *Chinese Pacific Weekly*, founded in 1946 in San Francisco, distinguished itself by not taking a partisan position.[57] The paper's founder and editor, Gilbert Woo, was born in Taishan, China, to a Gold Mountain fam-

10. Newspaperman Gilbert Woo. *Courtesy of Nancy Woo.*

ily in 1911. He came to San Francisco in 1932 and went to Hong Kong to get married a few years later. Because of the Chinese exclusion, he could not bring his wife and daughter with him when he returned in 1938. His wife gave birth to a second daughter whom he would not meet for thirty-three years.[58] Before he started his own paper, Gilbert had written for the *Chinese Times* and the *Chinese Nationalist Daily*, and he was close to a group of young Chinese students who had settled in the United States during the Sino-Japanese War.[59]

When the *Chinese Pacific Weekly* was first founded, Gilbert Woo was ridiculed for not having a clear political point of view. Some people predicted that without the financial backing of the Guomindang and community merchants, the paper would not last for more than three months.[60] Nevertheless, the *Chinese Pacific Weekly* enjoyed a wide circulation for over three decades.[61] Within three years it had expanded from sixteen pages to twenty-four pages per issue. It was considered a *jialian wumei* (good value): each issue sold for a dime in 1950, when a daily newspaper usually cost seven cents and a weekly cost a quarter. The paper even offered free overseas delivery.[62] As a self-starter, Gilbert especially encouraged young people who were motivated to write for the community.

World War II and the Press

World War II was seen by some Chinese American journalists as a great opportunity to expand the circulation of the community press. During the war the press, rather than any community organizations, was the first to find ways to reach Chinese Americans beyond the boundaries of Chinatowns.

In March 1943, Gilbert Woo, then an editor with the *Chinese Times,* received a letter from his friend Tinghui Huang, who was serving in the U.S. Army in New Guinea. Huang told Woo that he was lonely, and that he wished his friends would write him often and enclose clippings from community newspapers. Gilbert, who was unable to serve because of poor eyesight, realized that Huang's feelings would be shared by many other Chinese American soldiers, including his own brother Norbert, who was being sent to the Pacific theater. He also felt that the press had a responsibility to keep them informed, so he appointed himself the Chinatown-based correspondent for those who had left to fight.[63]

Gilbert Woo's new column, "I Wish to Inform You," was a combination of news and commentary. It informed Chinese American soldiers of developments on the home front as well as the progress of the war. With a special focus on race relations, the column reported the congressional debate on the repeal of Chinese exclusion, the visit of Madam Chiang Kai-shek to the United States, defense projects in San Francisco's Chinatown, and many other community news events.[64] Most unusually, Gilbert argued in two separate essays that innocent Japanese Americans should not be treated as military aggressors and that the internment of Japanese Americans would not help win the war.[65] In addition, he questioned the position of Chiang Kai-shek in China. Because of these essays, he was accused of being a traitor by the community establishment and was summoned to answer to the China War Relief Association, which caused conflict between him and Walter U. Lum, the managing editor of the *Chinese Times*. Gilbert resigned from his post but was immediately invited to join the staff of the *Chinese Nationalist Daily*.[66] According to Albert Lim, then the manager of the paper, Gilbert's column helped boost sales.[67]

Like other servicemen, Chinese American G.I.s were sometimes transferred from one field of operations to another, and they wanted to find ways to stay in touch with their friends, some of whom were also being relocated. The press provided a way. The *Chinese American Weekly*, for example, let soldiers write to each other in its pages. Among the many letters it published was one from Liang Yingyang to a friend he met at a training center of the U.S. Navy. Fu Shangwei was on his way to the Pacific war zone when the letter was sent, but Liang knew that Fu would get the letter as long as he read the *Chinese American Weekly*.[68]

Serving in racially integrated military units, Chinese American soldiers were further exposed to the racial aspects of American society, and they were frequently reminded that they were considered different. Writing from Texas, Ling Ling told his friends that "Whites Only" signs were displayed outside the day room, and that some of his white fellow soldiers called him "Chink Chong Chinaman."[69] This reality strengthened the emotional ties between Chinese American servicemen and their community. The soldiers felt lonely. They needed friends, and they wanted to talk to people who could understand their frustrations. Several community newspapers therefore created "Self Introduction" sections, where soldiers and civilians could write about themselves in the hope of establishing new friendships.[70]

The press did not have the capacity to send correspondents to follow the armed forces, but it searched for soldiers who had literary talents. The *Chinese Times* and *China Weekly* in San Francisco and the *Chinese American Weekly* and *China Daily News* in New York all created special sections so that people could write about their wartime experiences. The press thus linked the community to members in different parts of the world. It also provided opportunities for young Chinese Americans to contribute to the community.

Community press played an important role in shaping the lives of some young Chinese Americans. When Leong Thick Hing wrote to the *Chinese Times* from the army in search of new friends in 1942, he was encouraged by Ma Siru (Paul Mar), a columnist, and Gilbert Woo to contribute to the paper. Leong later wrote more than a hundred journal entries for the *Chinese*

11. Him Mark Lai, who later became a community historian, and Laura Jung held their wedding reception at Min Qing's clubhouse. *Personal collection of Him Mark Lai.*

12.   Maurice H. Chuck, a self-taught journalist, was imprisoned during the cold war because he published essays in the *China Daily News* and was a member of Min Qing. *Courtesy of Maurice H. Chuck.*

Times's "Junzhong suibi" (Informal Essays from the Military) under the pen name Liang Xiaomai. After the war Leong opened the Oasis Bookstore in San Francisco's Chinatown, which quickly became a gathering place for young Chinese Americans.[71]

Him Mark Lai, who later became a well-known community historian, was also influenced by the community press. Born in San Francisco's Chinatown in 1925, Him Mark received a solid foundation in the Chinese language through early tutoring from his mother and ten years of study in Chinese schools. In 1947, soon after he graduated from the University of California at Berkeley and began working as a mechanical engineer, he discovered the Oasis Bookstore. It was through its owner Leong that Him Mark became acquainted with other Chinese American liberals who had been actively involved in independent newspapers and Min Qing. After *Chung Say Yat Po* reorganized in late 1949, Him Mark volunteered for the paper's weekend pictorial section, and he also spent one hundred dollars each month to purchase shares to support the paper. Through a Min Qing–sponsored English tutoring program he met his future wife, Laura Jung, who had immigrated to the United States in 1949. As Laura remembered, those were the best years of her life. When she and Him Mark married, they held their reception at Min Qing's clubhouse.[72]

Maurice Chuck, later a well-known community journalist, immigrated to the United States in 1947 at age fourteen. Growing up in a village amid war-torn China, Maurice had attended only four years of elementary school. It was at the Oasis Bookstore that he continued his education and met with friends, and he soon became an active member of Min Qing. In 1949 Gilbert Woo hired him as a typesetter for the *Chinese Pacific Weekly*. With Gilbert's encouragement, Maurice began to write, and he eventually became an editor for several newspapers.[73]

Most significant, the press tried to tie the war effort to community reform. In a piece entitled "A Few Words to Chinese American Soldiers," Gilbert Woo reminded those in the military that prejudice against ethnic minorities in the larger society, just like conservative forces against youth and women in the community, would not disappear with the end of the war. He urged young Chinese Americans to work together and fight injustice after they returned to the United States in the same way they had fought against the fascist forces.[74]

In addition to providing news analysis, independent newspapers facilitated the development of a Chinese American literary movement in the late 1930s and the 1940s. The *China Daily News* published short stories, poems, and critical essays in its "Xinsheng" (New Life) section. The paper also sponsored separate publication of works by members of two literary groups, Lüzhou (Oasis) and Qingqi (Light Cavalry). The *Chinese American Weekly* had an "Everyone's Literature Forum," which became a publishing venue for amateur Chinese American writers. Many of these literary works focused on the lives of Chinese Americans and exposed the dark side of the bachelor society. Wen Quan, who wrote in the late 1940s, argued that these works reflected the emergence of the "Chinatown sensibility."[75]

The Chinese community press expanded during World War II. About ten thousand Chinese living on the West Coast had been readers of community newspapers before the war, but less than a quarter of them were subscribers, since Chinese newspapers could be found in Chinatown business offices, schools, and libraries. During the war, however, Chinese American soldiers had no access to community newspapers through their workplace.

According to Gilbert Woo, almost every serviceman who could read Chinese subscribed to one or two Chinese newspapers or magazines.[76]

When Gilbert Woo first came to the United States in 1932, he was dismayed by an environment in which everyone seemed to be interested only in making money. He worked for many years to promote a community consciousness through the press. The wartime increase in subscriptions and newspaper sales was encouraging. Soon after the war Gilbert and his brother decided to start their own paper, and the first issue of the *Chinese Pacific Weekly* appeared on October 5, 1946. From its inception to Gilbert's sudden death in November 1979, the paper served as a leader in the effort to build a Chinese American community.

After many Chinese Americans moved out of Chinatowns during and after the war, they remained connected with their community through the press. Gilbert Woo successfully promoted the distribution of his paper through Chinese grocers in the southern states of the United States.[77] One of the *Chinese Pacific Weekly*'s longtime readers, Harry Wong, recalled that even during the two and a half years when he was stationed in West Germany, he received every single issue of the paper.[78]

The Call for a United and Politically Independent Community

In early 1949 tension mounted between the merchant-dominated community power structure and leftist groups. The Guomindang's influence had been slipping as the collapse of the Nationalist government in China became evident. Within a few months, the People's Liberation Army moved swiftly into Tianjin, Beijing, and Nanjing, the capital of the Nationalists. These sweeping Communist victories generated great excitement among workers, students, and other young Chinese Americans, and some believed that the dominance of the Guomindang-backed community establishment was also about to end.

The Guomindang-controlled newspapers, however, did not hint that the Nationalist government was collapsing, and the CCBA would not tolerate any independent newspaper's attempt to update the coverage of the war in China. Those who dared to report objectively were labeled Communist agents, even if their source was the *New York Times*. Pei Chi Liu, who had been sent to San Francisco's Chinatown by the Central Executive Committee of the Guomindang to assume an editorial position on the *Chinese Nationalist Daily* in 1940, thought that some independent newspapers indirectly supported the

Communists by criticizing the Guomindang.[79] Independent journalists who were familiar with American laws were not scared by the threat of political repression, but many Chinatown business owners were intimidated into withdrawing their advertisements.

In the battle to defend their right of free expression the independent newspapers often stood together. When Dai Ming Lee first came to San Francisco to head the *Chinese World*, he invited Gilbert Woo to join his staff, but the latter declined. A year later, when Gilbert launched the *Chinese Pacific Weekly*, many did not think he would succeed, but Lee went to his office in person to encourage him. When the Guomindang threatened the *Chinese World* with violence and forced Lee to hire Pinkerton guards for protection, Gilbert was there to offer support. Although the two had different political views, they both believed that no one had the right to strangle a free newspaper in the United States.[80]

In April 1949 the word went out that some leftist community members were planning to launch a new paper, the *China Weekly*, in San Francisco to celebrate the coming Communist victory in China. The Guomindang threatened to destroy any printer that dared to print it. Cai Fujiu, the paper's founder, was turned down by several printing houses before he approached Gilbert Woo, whose *Chinese Pacific Weekly* had its own printing facility. Gilbert too was warned against printing the newspaper, but he ignored the threat. The first issue of the *China Weekly* appeared on May 4, 1949, the thirtieth anniversary of the May Fourth Movement in China, with an eye-catching headline: "The Liberation Army Ready for Its Final Attack on Shanghai." Several hoodlums from the Guomindang-controlled Bing Kung Cong soon tried to intimidate the workers at the *Chinese Pacific Weekly*, and they also removed the paper from private mailboxes and student dorms in the Bay Area. But these actions backfired. Several students from the Chinese Central High School volunteered to serve as security, for they liked the new publication. Open support for the paper also came from Suey Sing Tong, an otherwise nonpolitical fraternity organization.[81]

On October 9 and 10, a week after the founding of the People's Republic of China, the Chinese Hand Laundry Alliance, the Chinese Youth Club, the *China Daily News*, and some eighteen other community organizations held two mass meetings in New York to celebrate that historic event. The organizers arranged for a large security contingent to patrol the meeting halls, and the meetings took place without incident.[82]

The peace was broken at a similar mass meeting in San Francisco on the evening of October 9. Among the four hundred people gathered that

13. Celebrating the founding of the People's Republic of China at the auditorium of the Chinese American Citizens Alliance in San Francisco, October 9, 1949. *Personal collection of Him Mark Lai.*

evening at the Chinese American Citizens Alliance auditorium were members of the CWMAA, the Min Qing, student groups from the Bay Area's colleges and universities, and other community liberals. A number of non-Chinese political activists, including members of the California Labor School and dockworkers from the International Longshoremen's Union, were also there as guests. An American flag and the five-starred red flag of the PRC were on display over the speaker's podium, and the front of the stage was covered with floral arrangements. Half an hour after the ceremony began, a group of some forty men suddenly rushed in to break up the meeting. The invaders were armed with lead pipes, eggs, and blue dye. They tore down the red flag, destroyed the flowers, broke chairs and windows, and threw eggs and dye at the participants.[83] William Kerner, the West Coast director of the Committee for a Democratic Far Eastern Policy, was about to speak when the attackers advanced to the speaker's podium. The *San Francisco Chronicle* reported that these men grabbed the microphone from Kerner's hands and "hurled it at the American flag on the wall."[84] According to reports from eyewitnesses, at least two men were injured. Wang Fushi, a college student, was pushed to the floor and beaten by five men. He was later treated for scalp

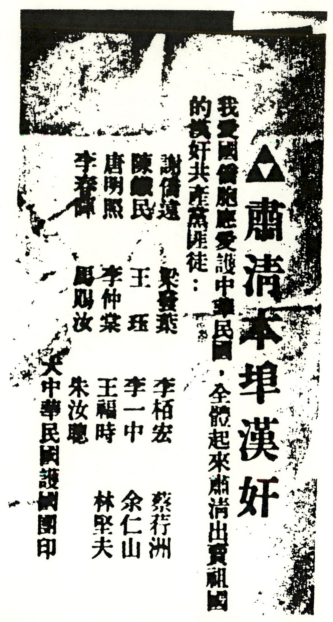

14. The poster "Mop Up Chinatown's Bandits!" appeared in San Francisco's Chinatown on October 10, 1949. Fifteen Chinese Americans, all of them affiliates of leftist groups or newspapers, were named and a five-thousand-dollar reward was offered for each one's death. *Personal collection of Him Mark Lai.*

lacerations at a hospital. Another participant, a white worker, suffered a broken rib. Watching the meeting turn chaotic, the organizer called the members of the California Labor School chorus to the stage to sing the *Yellow River Cantata*, and the meeting continued.[85]

The outbreak was believed to have been planned by the Guomindang. No CCBA leaders were spotted at the scene, but a few were positioned on the streets nearby to give orders. They even persuaded the police to leave the meeting hall before the attack took place.[86] Mr. Liang, a Sonoma chicken farmer, happened to be visiting San Francisco that day with his two young children. When the trio passed the CACA hall at about 11:00 P.M., they ran into a group of men picking fights with those who were leaving the meeting. Liang was indignant and expressed his anger. An older man's voice was heard: "He is also a Communist! Beat him up!" Because policemen were present, several men followed Liang for three blocks and then attacked him. His children screamed for help. The police arrived shortly to find Liang lying on his back; his injuries were severe enough that he was sent to a hospital.[87]

All of San Francisco's Chinatown was in terror the following day as posters calling for the "mop up of Chinatown's bandits" appeared on buildings and walls. Fifteen Chinese Americans were named and a five-thousand-dollar reward was offered for each one's death. Except for two leaders of the CWMAA, Li Zhongtang (Olden Lee) and Lin Jianfu (Happy Lim), and one leader of Min Qing, Zhu Rucong (James Young), all on the list were involved with independent newspapers. They included Francis Leong, Ja Kew Yuen Cai, Chen Tiemin, Li Bohong (Herbert Lee), Li Yizhong, and Wang Fushi, who worked to raise money to purchase the *Chung Sai Yat Po*; Ma Siru (Paul Mar), Cai Fujiu (Henry Tsoi), and Wang Jue of *China Weekly*; Tang Mingzhao (Chu Tong) of the *China Daily News* in New York; Yu Yun Shan, then with the *China Tribune*, also in New York; and Li Chunhui, who later became an editor for *Chung Sai Yat Po*.[88]

Anonymous calls were also made to other independent newspapers warning them against covering the story. Gilbert Woo was not present at the CACA hall that evening, but he was accused of being a planner of the celebration.[89] According to Him Mark Lai, who attended the meeting, Gilbert's name was initially included on the poster, but a Guomindang member who was friendly toward him managed to have it removed.[90] As the accusations led to violence and death threats, some of those singled out went into hiding. Clan associations and church groups were pressed to take a stand, and several announced in newspapers that they were neither Communist nor pro-Communist.[91]

The situation reminded Chinese Americans of the tong wars in the early twentieth century. Many influential community members were shocked by what had been done to their own people. Editor Dai Ming Lee of the *Chinese World* called for police protection of the leftist community members.[92] Several tong leaders also stood up to defend those who had been accused or attacked.[93] Gilbert Woo joined the Ying On Tong and his brother Norbert joined the Suey Sing Tong for protection. Cai Fujiu, editor of the *China Weekly*, was also seen in public with bodyguards from local tongs.[94] It seemed that another tong war was about to be declared.

The use of force, violence, and terror discredited the CCBA, which was dominated by Guomindang members. Chinese American workers and young people strongly believed that they had the right to organize and speak their minds, and they believed their rights should be protected by the government. The CWMAA's statement, released to Bay Area news agencies on October 10, is worth quoting at length:

On Sunday evening, October 9th, a group of hoodlums, led by reactionary elements in the local Kuomintang, attempted to break up a meeting and dance sponsored by the Chinese Workers Mutual Aid Association. At the outset, we want to make it clear that those lawless attempts failed, that the meeting went on as scheduled, and we intend to have similar meetings in the near future. But these hoodlums did destroy property and injured two people who required hospital treatment.

The 400 members and friends of the Chinese Workers Mutual Aid Association at the meeting were there to celebrate the 12th anniversary of the Association and to celebrate the establishment of the new People's Republic of China. It is obvious to many of us that the stormtrooper tactics employed by the hoodlums, tactics familiar to those of us who lived under the Japanese occupation and the terror of the Kuomintang Secret Service, were well planned and not merely the actions of "juvenile delinquents." The finger of blame must be pointed at the local headquarters of the Kuomintang Party.

We want to call attention to the negligence of the police officer who was assigned to protect the people at the meeting. A few minutes before the attack, he left his post and did not return until the guilty parties had fled from the hall.

We call upon our friends, and all people interested in the democratic institutions of free speech and free assembly, to join with us in demanding a complete investigation of this attack that will lead to the arrest of the individuals responsible for this violent disregard of civil liberties.

We call upon the officials of our city to press for an immediate investigation of this attack upon a peaceful meeting by force and violence and to guarantee that the rights of the people will be protected.

We further call upon all candidates for public office to join us in protesting this outrage.[95]

The reactions from the press conflicted sharply. The Guomindang-controlled newspapers declared the October 9 incident a victorious suppressing of "bandits," while the *China Weekly* demanded, "Do we not have freedom in the overseas Chinese society?" Newspapers received many letters from their readers, and many writers expressed their anger toward the Guomindang. The number of Chinese Americans who believed in the Communist ideology was small, but many community members were furious: how could anyone suppress different opinions and use violence against innocent people in the United States?[96]

Gilbert Woo heard about the incident at the CACA hall late in the evening of October 9. He visited the scene the next day, apparently planning to write a report. An official of the CACA showed him the shattered windows, broken chairs, and damaged walls. When Gilbert asked what the organization would do about the loss, the official shook his head and said, "Only Mao Zedong could subdue these people."[97] The CACA later decided not to rent its auditorium for any more political gatherings.

Not a word about this incident could be found in the October 15 issue of the *Chinese Pacific Weekly*, however. The readers must have been surprised and disappointed, and Gilbert Woo was probably asked to explain the omission. The following week, Gilbert acknowledged that his paper had failed to report on an important incident, but he made no attempt to make it up. He did, however, speculate that fifty years later, long after the *Chinese Pacific Weekly* had ceased publication and his name as its editor had disappeared from the memories of community members, researchers would be puzzled about the paper's silence concerning this important event in Chinese American history. They might suspect that the journal had been threatened and the editor had been intimidated. Still, he decided to leave these questions for future scholars, noting that "they could find the answer if they tried hard."[98]

The fact that Gilbert Woo did not report such an important incident seemed to contradict his view of the press's mandate in a democratic society.

Journalistic independence and freedom of expression were his goals. In an editorial celebrating the *Chinese Pacific Weekly*'s first anniversary, he wrote: "The phrase 'Give me liberty or give me death' is most appropriate for newspapers. If a newspaper loses its soul fawning over the powerful, being led on a leash and too afraid to tell the truth . . . it would be better to let it die. We should never give up our heavenly duty in exchange for the survival of our paper."[99] On October 1, 1949, considering *Chinese Pacific Weekly*'s third birthday, he asked, "Have we yielded to pressure from evil forces? Have we dared to voice grievances while outnumbered by the opposition? Have we flinched or fought to the last?"[100] Only a week later, however, Gilbert appeared to have lost the courage to condemn the acts of the Guomindang-backed CCBA.

If Gilbert Woo kept silent to protect his newspaper, it would have been the first occasion he had done so. He had helped print the *China Weekly* against the warnings of the Guomindang, and his sympathy toward the Communist movement in China was never a secret.[101] He was relatively quiet about China politics, however. Essays on developments in China published in the *Chinese Pacific Weekly* were usually translated from major U.S. newspapers. The paper rarely commented on the Guomindang–Communist conflict in China.

A close reading of Gilbert Woo's work published at the time and some twenty years later suggests that while trying to smooth over the growing differences among local groups, he had become increasingly worried about the future of the community. He did not trust the Guomindang-backed establishment to lead community reform. At the same time, he thought those who believed that "a new social order in China would automatically solve the problems for Chinese Americans" were too naive. "What is the new society? What should be done before the new society comes into existence? What should be done afterwards?"[102] What his community needed, he argued, was "peace, democracy, freedom, and tolerance," which would help it gain respect from the larger society.[103] The deteriorating struggle in China only intensified hostilities among community groups, however. What happened in October 1949 confirmed Gilbert's worst fears, which he had stated three months earlier:

> We like to see many different ideas in the Chinese American community, leftist and rightist, opinions that conflicted with one another. Although we do not like to see newspapers fighting a war of words, a war of words is not a big problem. (There is no winner in a war of words. The ordinary readers are the wisest judges. They can tell from

the words who is being deliberately provocative or which group is shifting the blame onto another.) But we are afraid now that a war of words is leading to unnecessarily ugly actions. Some forty or fifty years ago, the Chinese shed their blood fighting over prostitutes, opium, and gambling debts. If we let that tragedy repeat itself because of political disagreement, it will be dreadful to contemplate the future of our community.[104]

When a war of words turned into a riot, and violence and terror were used against the members of his own community, Gilbert was rendered speechless. Perhaps his personal safety was indeed at stake. He later said that he understood why some groups publicly announced that they were not Communists.[105] Perhaps he felt too sad to comment further. Perhaps he could not find words to help ease the growing hostilities among community factions.

Leong Think Hing, a close friend of Gilbert Woo's, suspected that the editor had intentionally avoided commenting on the Guomindang–Communist conflict in China because he so longed for the political and economic reform of the Chinese American community. At a time when many community members, both conservatives and liberals, could not seem to get enough of what was going on in China, Gilbert may have wanted to remind them that they should focus on their own issues. Leong once asked Gilbert why the *Chinese Pacific Weekly* wrote so much about immigration legislation in the United States but so little about the events in China that seemed to fascinate many of its readers. Gilbert replied: "Is there anything more important to our community than the immigration legislation?"[106]

By not writing about the incident, Gilbert Woo may have been making an effort to change the subject. For many years he and several other journalists had been looking for issues that Chinese Americans could focus on as one group. He often suggested to his friends that they should pay more attention to politics in the United States.[107] He encouraged community members to vote, and he believed that participation in elections would effectively eliminate discriminatory practices against Chinese.[108] He advocated a Citizens Alliance for Chinese American Women, and encouraged immigrant women to improve their English skills and become citizens.[109] He wanted his readers to distance themselves from China politics. It was not that he thought events in China were unimportant, but it was clear to him that China politics had carried Chinese Americans away from what he considered their primary struggle and had become a divisive force tearing community groups apart.

As both the leftist and the rightist groups waited for the result of the Guomindang–Communist conflict in China, Gilbert Woo urged them to redefine themselves not only as Chinese but also as Americans. "No matter what type of government China will have . . . we have to think about the interests of our people here first," he wrote. "We should denounce the new government if it exploits us the same way the old government did," he said, "and we should support the government only if it helps us ease our suffering and eliminate our obstacles."[110] Using his newspaper, he urged Chinese Americans to build a community of their own:

> This is the best time for the autonomy of the Chinese American community. Autonomy does not mean isolating Chinatown and placing it outside the laws of the American society, nor cutting off contact with our ancestral homeland. It means to use the space that we have to do things that benefit Chinese Americans. We should not be influenced by [foreign] politics, not be controlled by bureaucrats, not be manipulated by propaganda, not be trapped, and not be blindfolded or cheated. The common interests of all of our community members should be more important than the interests of any political groups.[111]

In November 1950 the Chinese People's Volunteer Army crossed the Yalu River and confronted U.S. soldiers in Korea. Upon learning the news, Gilbert Woo canceled his printing contract with the *China Weekly*. The *San Francisco Chronicle* reported that the *Chinese Pacific Weekly* ceased printing the *China Weekly* because of the latter's left-wing political stand. Gilbert denied that, saying only that the printer was too busy to handle the job in addition to his own paper. With no time to find another publisher, the *China Weekly* went out of business.[112] Many of Gilbert's friends were disappointed and confused, and some protested.[113] It was impossible for him to address the issue frankly. He could not ask his friends to stay quiet, for he believed in freedom of expression. At a time when many Chinese Americans feared that the government would soon put them into internment camps, as it did to Japanese Americans in World War II, the editor may have sensed that a new storm was coming. Not until 1976, twenty-eight years after the incident and three years before his sudden death, did Gilbert publish his long-overdue analysis of what had taken place in San Francisco's Chinatown in October 1949 in the "Reminiscences by the Golden Gate" column of the *Chinese Pacific Weekly*. In his analysis, the incident was the "biggest political riot in the history of Chinatown."[114]

*I*n the late 1940s many of Gilbert Woo's contemporaries had waited for their fate to be decided by the political fate of China. Some groups believed that a Communist victory in China would change the power structure of the community, while leaders of the community establishment were convinced that they would remain in power as long as the Guomindang controlled China. The unexpected outcome of the Chinese Civil War and the onset of the cold war proved that there would be no simple solution. When Mao Zedong declared the founding of the People's Republic of China in Beijing in 1949, he was determined to show the rest of the world that his approach to socialism could succeed on China's mainland. Although Chiang Kai-shek and his surviving followers had to retreat to Taiwan, he spoke of mounting a counterattack on the mainland, backed by the United States and the rest of the West. The struggle between the Guomindang and the Communists was far from over.

It seemed that the cold war provided the community establishment with new ammunition to crush its opponent. This time, the suppression of its political enemies would be supported by American public opinion, the Federal Bureau of Investigation, and the Immigration and Naturalization Service. Whether this turn of events helped the CCBA gain more supporters in the Chinese community, however, is a rather complicated question, as we shall see in chapter seven. Before that, we will look at how the community dealt with the domestic crisis that began to surface in the postwar era.

CHAPTER 6

The Quest for Family Stability

༠ᘓᖇᕚ

$\mathcal{T}$he transformation of the Chinese American community from a bachelor society to a family society was not an easy one. Large numbers of families were united almost overnight. After many years of separation, many Chinese American married couples gradually realized that it was difficult to adjust to each other. Some were disappointed, frustrated, and confused. The unification of their families after the period of Chinese exclusion created unanticipated problems.

Beginning in late 1947, many discussions of marital problems and gender relations appeared in community newspapers. The debate inspired more controversy than most other issues, and it attracted opinions from different groups of Chinese Americans: war veterans and war brides, Americanized men and the new immigrant women, newspaper writers, columnists, and editors, and general readers. Marital problems among Chinese American couples were by no means new, but they had remained largely hidden from public view before World War II. The huiguan, the CCBA, and the CACA provided little support for families once they were united. When young couples needed guidance to sort out their problems, they found it difficult to make their private problems public. Like their mainstream American counterparts, they sought advice through community newspapers, where they could find sympathetic listeners. Writing under pseudonyms, they could also protect their identity.[1]

The importance of the press in analyzing gender relations has been explored by Valerie Matsumoto in her study of second-generation Japanese

Americans, and by Emily Honig and Gail Hershatter in a study of Chinese women.[2] Using newspapers as a forum, the community was presented to itself. Although not every Chinese American man or woman was troubled by the same problems, the debate indicates that many in the community were deeply concerned about these issues, including those who may have had perfectly happy marriages. The debate helps us understand the process of transition from a bachelor to a family society; it illustrates the increasing pressure on the community to take women into more serious account. If marital problems and gender relations were issues of great community concern or controversy during an important period of historical transition, these issues could also be identified with the development of a new set of community values and interests.

Husband versus Wife, American versus Chinese

Issues of marital problems were first raised by male Chinese Americans. Most noticeable was a series of essays written by one Lao Heng (Old Henry), which appeared in the *Chinese Pacific Weekly* in 1947. According to the essays, Lao Heng had been born in the United States. He was educated in American schools and served in the U.S. military. His wife, referred to in the essays as *laopo* (the old woman), had been born and educated in China. She had recently come to the United States under the War Brides Act, and she disagreed with Lao Heng on almost every detail concerning their household affairs. The author was probably a regular contributor to community newspapers, although the pen name was used exclusively for this series. It is unclear whether Lao Heng's account was authentic or fictional, or if he was invited to write by the newspaper, but there is no question that his stories included very realistic details. Most striking was the author's openness in discussing aspects of private life and his ability to shift from a personal story to one that represented a group experience. The issues he wrote about, as he indicated, were often discussed by men who had brought war brides to the United States.[3]

Lao Heng's essays included complaints about his wife that ranged from her relationship with his mother to her appearance in public. The couple's small conflicts over household affairs were often seen as cultural conflicts that developed because of their backgrounds. Lao Heng wanted a modern American wife rather than one who reflected the traditional values and social mores that were still dominant in the Chinese American family.

Lao Heng and his wife were brought together by his mother, who came from China. By age fourteen, he found that he and his mother had little in common. But subsequently his parents insisted that he get a wife from China. When he hesitated, his mother stayed in bed for several days and called him an unfilial son. Under pressure from his mother and his friends, Lao Heng finally gave in:

> My parents (mainly my mother) were willing to pay for my trip to China for two reasons. First, my mother comes from China and does not know any English. She would probably like to have a daughter-in-law who does not speak English either. A chicken gets along with chickens and a duck gets along with ducks. A duck would like to have a few more ducks around to keep her company: that is understandable. Second, my mother thinks that American-born women would not respect her authority or obey her. My brothers all married American-born women, so she has never had a chance to enjoy the power and prestige of a mother-in-law. That is the sorrow of her life. I am the youngest. If my laopo is also a chicken instead of a duck, she will not be able to find peace even after she dies.[4]

After his wife arrived in San Francisco, Lao Heng realized that what his mother wanted was not a good wife for him but a companion for herself. On one occasion he planned to go to see a movie with his wife, but his mother took her to meet friends instead. Lao Heng could not change his mother, but he would not let the old woman control his own family. The two women did not get along well under the same roof in any case, so Lao Heng found a job in Oakland and the couple moved out of his parents' house despite his mother's protest. He hoped that he would be able to exert more influence on his wife and eventually make her his own companion.[5]

Yet Lao Heng found himself losing the competition with his mother for his wife's affection. His wife was not looking for his emotional support, and she made no effort to become like an American. Instead, she became closer to his mother:

> You can't change one's habits. . . . Every weekend that we came to San Francisco she went straight to my mother's room and the two talked for two or three hours. She would go to see a Chinese opera with my mother and let me suffer all by myself in the movie theater.
>
> Whenever we had an argument . . . she would use my mother's words against me. The most unbearable blow to me as a husband is

that she always goes to mother instead of me for advice. Maybe she would like to move back to San Francisco.

This is a triangular tragedy. There should not be such a relationship among a mother, a son, and his wife. A married couple cannot be happy if the wife is too hostile or too close to her mother-in-law.[6]

In one of the essays, Lao Heng described the communication difficulties he and his wife had. In rural China, a husband and wife were referred to in public as *laogong* (the old man) and laopo, but there were no terms for them to use with each other. Lao Heng's friends, he said (himself certainly included), were mostly men who had had "a lot of experience with love affairs" with women in the United States. These men were used to calling their lovers "dear" or "darling," but they did not know what to call their own wives. When his wife first came to the United States, Lao Heng told her that they should call each other "darling" according to American custom, and that the word should be spoken in an affectionate tone. All that he had accomplished, however, was that his wife now addressed him as Henry instead of *Wei!* (Attention!) He realized that he had to live with this: "You can't expect someone who does not speak English to say the word 'darling.' She might manage to say it with an effort, but that would be meaningless." Hence "Darling" was used only when he spoke to his wife.[7]

The trouble came when Lao Heng tried to speak to his wife at a party in front of their friends. She was so unprepared to hear the word "darling" in public that she did not respond even after Lao Heng had called her three times. "Everyone was looking at me. My face was red with shame, but she was standing like a wooden chicken! My God! What an embarrassment!" Lao Heng wrote.[8] After that, the word "darling" disappeared from the couple's conversation. After all, he reasoned, it was awkward to have the word "darling" followed by a conversation in Chinese.

Lao Heng said that he was not the only one facing the problem. Many Chinese couples were in a similar situation, including some staff members of the *Chinese Pacific Weekly*. He was eager to find a solution: "If there is no word that a married man and woman can use to address each other, the couple has to start the conversation without creating an atmosphere of gentleness and softness." He believed that "if we could use words such as 'darling' for each other, maybe the relationship between husband and wife could be improved." Lao Heng suggested two things that could be done to solve the problem. One was to "make the wives read more English until they could understand and use the language so that they could say 'darling' to their husbands naturally." The staff of the *Chinese Pacific Weekly* could also come up with a few Chinese substitutes for "darling": "After all, many of them have wives and children. They should tell us how they and their wives communicate with each other."[9]

Lao Heng was dissatisfied with his wife because she was not intimate with him no matter whether the couple was in the bedroom or in public, and he again spoke for a community group as well as for himself. He said that when the topic of their wives was brought up, some of his friends would sigh: "I would not have gone to China to marry if I had known Chinese women were that cold."[10] His own wife was especially disappointing: "When I sat at home listening to news or music, laopo would either walk away to do things on her own or sit still by herself in a corner like a wooden puppet. She never acted affectionately toward me. When I saw magazine pictures showing a man resting his head on his wife's lap while she combed his hair with her fingers, I would be very disappointed or even get angry. I am not bald yet; my hair is as thick as grass. Why shouldn't it be combed by my wife's fingers?"[11]

Lao Heng understood that the cause of his wife's distance had much to do with the social and cultural environment in which she had been brought up. The problem was that he had no idea how to change her: "I cannot drag her to sit by me every single night or make her touch my hair and face, and I cannot make her hold my hands every time we walk on the street, for intimacy cannot be created by force."[12]

Once, hearing his wife praise a couple for having a loving marriage, Lao Heng jumped at the opportunity: "She is so sweet and affectionate, and they are always seen hugging or holding hands. How could a couple like that not have a loving marriage?" Knowing exactly what he meant, his wife responded, "Then why didn't you marry a prostitute [*laoju*] instead?" Lao Heng was struck speechless. He wrote: "The weakness of a prostitute is that she sells her soul and changes grooms every night. How wrong could it be if she treats her own lover or husband with that sweetness? . . . I believe that laopo should treat her own husband as sweetly as a prostitute treats a client. She should take the initiative, not put herself in a passive position."[13]

Lao Heng was extremely frustrated that his many efforts to modernize his wife were in vain. He did not understand how she could be so easily influenced by his mother but not by him. She did not seem to be interested in improving herself by following his suggestions. For example, when she talked loudly on the bus (the same way his mother did in public) and Lao Heng asked her to lower her voice, she asked why she could not speak freely in a free country. When Lao Heng pointed out that her red jacket and blue skirt did not match and that Americans might think she dressed strangely, she replied, "These are my clothes, and I shall wear whatever I want." Lao Heng once told her that it was improper and ugly to wear slippers without socks on, but she said, "How could I breach etiquette if I had the slippers on? Many Chinese go barefooted because they can't even afford slippers!" She even wanted to quit her English lessons because she was tired of spending her time studying basic English words such as "cow," "dog," "horse," and "sheep" while her Chinese was good enough to teach elementary school children. "I do not want to Americanize her in every aspect," said Lao Heng. "If she cannot be changed . . . the day of blending Chinese culture with American culture will never come!"[14]

Although Lao Heng and his wife often quarreled, he said that he was usually the one to give in. Because of his mild nature, his wife considered him a good husband. The point that his wife had a hard time understanding was that he simply wouldn't let himself get upset at her because he was confident that he was superior. He told her, "I am not afraid of you running away from me. I am not afraid of losing you even if I left you in the parking lot. It is really unnecessary to get angry at you."[15]

Lao Heng was most hurt that his wife did not seem to be open with him. She cried by herself but would not tell him why. Lao Heng was so disturbed that he consulted a psychiatrist in the hope of finding out what might be troubling her, even though he did not think his doctor, who was unfamiliar with Chinese culture and values, would have any idea what might be bothering a Chinese woman.[16]

Lao Heng's stories suggested the important changes that had taken place in the lives of Chinese Americans since World War II. Although he wrote in Chinese for a Chinese audience, he expressed a strong desire that young Chinese Americans should find a lifestyle that was different from the traditional Chinese one. The men he represented were not looking for virtuous wives for themselves or respectful daughters-in-law for their parents. They did not want to subordinate their marital relationship in large households controlled by their parents, and they strongly believed that marriage should provide a variety of satisfactions for the partners. The ideal marriage for Lao Heng emphasized companionship, compatibility, and mutual sexual gratification, terms made current by American family experts in the early decades of the twentieth century.[17] What Lao Heng sought to build was an emotional alliance between a man and a woman.

That Lao Heng did not identify himself and the group he represented simply as Chinese is most striking. He pointed out that the traditional Chinese culture and customs that his wife was unwilling to give up were the major elements hindering the progress of the modern marriage that he desired. The group he represented was American, and it was the Chinese characteristics of their wives that created all of their marital problems.

Lao Heng's stories were both humorous and painful. They exposed the difficulties of Chinese Americans responding to rapid social changes. The men and women were excited by the new prospects families were providing, yet they were also painfully aware of the discomforts that families created. The author's frankness about his private life and his ability to identify himself with a community group may have appealed to many readers.

Lao Heng's sadness about his marriage and his uncertainty about the future, however, raised disturbing questions to which many Chinese Americans had no ready answer. On March 20, 1948, the same day that Lao Heng complained how difficult it was to reform his wife, the *Chinese Pacific Weekly* published an essay by a person using the pen name Shou Yong, which challenged Lao Heng's notions of an ideal marriage and family. Was Lao Heng's mother really an abusive mother-in-law? Wouldn't it be worse if the elderly had to move to senior citizens' homes after their children were married? Was Lao Heng's wife really so stubborn and incapable of improvement, or did Lao Heng push her too hard? Most important, was the American family ideal indeed better than that of the Chinese?[18] Other readers soon joined the debate as well. Huang Wang wrote a short satire making fun of Lao Heng's views.[19] In "I Shall Marry a Country Girl" (*Wo yao qu ge cungu*), Liu Heng wrote that although he had become an urbanite, he was afraid of forgetting his own roots, and he was confident that he could develop a harmonious relationship with a wife from rural China.[20]

Lao Heng apparently did not anticipate such criticism, and he was not ready to respond to the challenges. A week after Shou Yong's essay was published, Lao Heng disappeared. His last essay ran on March 27, and it had probably been submitted before the controversy started.[21]

Those who disagreed with Lao Heng, however, were unable to provide solutions to the problems that he had discussed. They made the point that Lao Heng was Chinese, and noted that it would be strange if a Chinese man could not tolerate a Chinese wife. They also argued that American culture was not necessarily superior to Chinese culture. Their writings were full of ideological and moral jargon, which probably made it difficult for people on Lao Heng's side to defend themselves. The editor of the *Chinese Pacific Weekly*, who must have encouraged Lao Heng to write about these issues, was also not sure what path this discussion might take. In a short essay, editor Gilbert Woo even suggested that it would be better to leave married couples alone to deal with their own problems.[22] The issues raised by Lao Heng were disturbing, but at the time few had answers to his questions.

The Family in Crisis

Lao Heng's marriage was unsatisfactory and disappointing, but the problems revealed in news reports were sometimes far more serious. In the late 1940s and early 1950s, the community was overshadowed by frequent open conflicts, episodes of domestic violence, and cases of disappearance of women. Between April and June 1950, *Chung Sai Yat Po* and the *China Daily News* reported one homicide, two attempted suicides, three missing women, and four incidents of wife battery and abandonment. Most of the women were newcomers.[23] One twenty-year-old woman, Li Ruiling of San Francisco, was beaten by her husband because she did not know how to cook American food.[24] When thirty-four-year-old Zhang Fangshi was reported missing, her husband told the police that she was "tired of living." She had been in the United States for only seven months.[25]

Most shocking was a homicide in San Francisco's Chinatown. On June 3, 1950, an eighteen-month-old boy died after his mother threw him from the roof of a two-story apartment building. That a Chinese woman had killed her son with her own hands was beyond anyone's comprehension. Questions like "How could a mother be so cruel?" and "What kind of woman would take the life of her own son?" from *Chung Sai Yat Po* reflected public sentiment when the story was first reported.[26]

As the incident unfolded and details of the mother's life were released, however, she began to be seen as a victim of unusual circumstances that were unique to the Chinese American family. Zhu Yushi, the alleged murderer, was a twenty-seven-year-old war bride. Her husband, Zhu Rong, a cook at a local hospital, was the first to come to her defense. He maintained that she was a good wife and admitted that his own gambling habit had caused many problems. The couple had an eight-month-old daughter in addition to the eighteen-month-old son. Zhu was often upset with her husband. She took care of the two children by herself during the day, and, not knowing her husband's whereabouts, she could not sleep well at night. On the day the child was killed, the husband returned home from playing mah-jongg at 6:30 A.M. A quarrel erupted, and an upset Zhu locked herself and her son in the kitchen. The husband, who could not persuade her to open the door, called the police. When the officers broke down the door, she ran up the back stairs to the roof and attempted to jump off the building with the toddler in her arms. The officers ran after her, but she screamed and hurled the boy onto the sidewalk thirty-five feet below.[27]

A murder charge was filed. Zhu Yushi's defense lawyer, hired by her husband, pleaded temporary insanity, and the judge ordered a medical evaluation.[28] Dr. Kuang, a Chinese American, was one of the three court-appointed medical specialists. On the witness stand, they testified in Zhu's favor and disputed the prosecutor's theory that the defendant had killed the child to take revenge against her husband. They stated that Zhu showed no sign of hatred toward any member of her family: she only blamed her husband for not spending time with the children. The doctors argued that Zhu was not mentally ill, but that she had acted in fear. They made the point that Zhu had lived in China during the war and witnessed the brutality of the Japanese aggressors. They asserted that her memories of the terror had caused the defendant to act abnormally when the American police arrived.[29]

The community was relieved when the judge found Zhu Yushi not guilty on July 31. In a long *Chung Sai Yat Po* editorial the judge was praised as being "very decent and cautious," and the ruling was said to be "very reasonable, because parents love their children, and mothers especially love their sons." Zhu Yushi was allowed to return home to her daughter and her husband.[30]

Americanizing the War Brides

The intensity of Zhu's conflict with her husband as well as the tragic loss of her son compelled the community to recognize the seriousness of the problems that many families confronted. *Chung Sai Yat Po* was the first newspaper to address the issue, noting that "family conflicts" such as Zhu Yushi's were "common" in the families of war brides. From its point of view, the wives were the ones in difficulty:

> Back in the villages, wives of war veterans would consult with their sisters-in-law when depressed. The parents-in-law or relatives helped care for the children. Every once in a while, they [the wives] could visit their own families and discuss their joys or sorrows with their parents, brothers, and sisters-in-law. With their peers, they could let off their emotions and frustrations. They could go collect firewood

in the hills or work in the vegetable gardens. They had balanced lives. In America, they have no companions but the refrigerator and the stove. They have no relatives, friends, or social life. If they had young children, they wouldn't even have the opportunity to get fresh air or sunshine.

It is interesting to note that the editorial did not mention Zhu Yushi's husband's habitual gambling. Instead, it argued that most men had to "work grueling hours as wage laborers" and therefore "had no time or energy for entertainment and other social activities." The different circumstances of men and women had made it almost impossible to find "mutual understanding and sympathy."[31] The editorial recognized women as human beings with needs and thoughts of their own, but it still left the impression that the wives were responsible for their situation because they had little understanding of their husbands and were selfishly preoccupied with their own pleasure and desires. Instead of urging both husbands and wives to work together to overcome their differences, the editorial considered the women's loneliness to be the cause of tension. They were the ones who needed to be reformed, and the community had to find ways to keep them busy and lead them to a more "balanced" life. That way, argued the editorial, the women would not become bored at home and would develop a better understanding of their hard-working husbands.[32]

The predominantly male perspective on marital problems in the postwar Chinese American family was best articulated in an article entitled "Meihua zhannian," published in *Chung Sai Yat Po* in September 1950. The headline played upon the double meanings of the Chinese character *mei*. The Chinese phrase *meihua* literally means "to beautify." Since the single Chinese character *mei*, "beauty," is also used to form the Chinese bisyllabic compound for "America," *Meiguo*, the title could also be read as "Americanizing War Brides." In the eyes of the men who were born in the United States or had arrived earlier, the presence of these new immigrant Chinese women cast a negative image on the community, and the male author, Wang Shaobi, called for an effort to beautify, civilize, and Americanize them. "The central concern with beautifying/Americanizing war brides," he wrote, "is the matter of their education," for "stupidity would not be tolerated by people in a modern civilization." The war brides had to "get rid of the rural lifestyle and customs that they brought with them from faraway China, and change their typically slow-witted Chinese behavior."[33]

Like Lao Heng, Wang Shaobi framed marital problems between men and women in terms of both knowledge and cultural differences, in a formulation in which Chinese men possessed modern, urban American qualities that Chinese women—portrayed as foreign, rural, and ignorant—lacked. He and many others did not realize or would not admit the challenges that these women had brought to the lifestyles of the Chinese men who were accustomed to their lives in America. They believed that "mutual" understanding between a husband and wife would only be possible if the woman made the adjustments and worked to advance herself.

The Dilemma of the War Brides

Given that a large number of the war brides were middle-aged women with children and that most of their husbands were laborers, few of them enjoyed much leisure in the United States. Oral history interviews suggest that most war brides were busy taking care of their young children, and many began to work immediately after they joined their husbands. Tenley Chin and her husband, David, settled down in South Weymouth, Massachusetts, late in 1948, and opened a laundry. The business generated an income of sixty dollars per week. After paying rent, gas and electric bills and other business expenses, the couple had only ten dollars left, barely enough to buy groceries. There was simply no money for them to hire any extra help, so Tenley worked in the laundry from its first day of operation even though she had just had a baby. For six years, Tenley worked six days a week, and she also gave birth to another three children during that period. All of the children were raised in the laundry, and only on Sundays could she afford the time to bathe herself and them.[34]

Betty Lew, who married a war veteran in 1947, was a graduate of the School of Nursing at China's Peking Union Medical College (sponsored by the Rockefeller Foundation)[35] and a former employee of the American Hospital in Beijing. While waiting for a letter of recommendation from her professor in China that would allow her to apply for a nursing job in the United States, she worked in a cannery in Oakland, California, cutting peaches. Betty had never done such manual labor before: "It was not an easy job. You cut the peach in half on a machine, and you had to cut evenly." She worked at the cannery for three months, then found a job at Alta Bates Hospital in Berkeley.[36]

Tewdy Yee, who smuggled goods between Hong Kong and Japanese-occupied Taishan during the war, joined her husband in Santa Barbara and dreamed of having a business of her own. But first she had to have money.

While taking care of her daughter, who was born shortly after she arrived, Tewdy took odd jobs and saved what she could from her own and her husband's earnings. She eventually opened a gift shop.[37]

Mary Yee, who joined her husband in 1948, worked in her father-in-law's restaurant in Oregon. The work was never done. In addition to cooking and serving the customers, Mary, her husband, Eddy, and her parents-in-law also grew vegetables to supply the restaurant.[38]

Some women were extremely disappointed by their first impressions of the United States. They had not had a clear understanding of their husbands' lives in America. The place that Tenley Chin and her husband had rented for a laundry also served as the family's living quarters. There was neither hot water nor an indoor toilet. What she hated most were the mice, which were "as big as rats."[39] Chiu Chun Ma, who suffered as a child after the death of her mother, had heard many wonderful stories about the Gold Mountain. Her first impression of San Francisco's Chinatown, however, was that it was dirty. Dining in a restaurant her first evening in the United States, she almost became ill when she saw on the table a filthy jar into which customers spit fish bones. While in China, Chiu Chun and her mother had gathered the firewood they needed in the hills. Now, in Burns, Oregon, she was scolded by her husband for using too much firewood for cooking. "How could you make anything boil with so little firewood?" she wondered.[40]

Their hard lives, however, were not the main source of the war brides' frustration. Many had endured long periods of separation from their husbands and suffered great hardships while in China. They had a strong commitment to their families and worked for many years with their husbands to improve the quality of their family lives. Gilbert Woo noted in the *Chinese Pacific Weekly* that women in China lived under harsher conditions than the war brides in the United States, but fewer women in China would commit suicide or leave their families.[41] Jin Xian, who had been exposed to the idea of women's liberation while a high school student in China, joined her father in the United States in the late 1940s. She was surprised by the degree of conservatism of the Chinese community in America. The values and customs of the Chinatown in which she lived were far stricter than those of rural China. For many years Jin Xian felt too sad to think about her future.[42]

Yuen Ock Chu, who arrived in Los Angeles in August 1947, attributed her unhappiness in the United States to her "double burden" of working in the family laundry and maintaining the household. Most of all, she was frustrated by her husband's refusal to cooperate: "It was difficult to work in a laundry and to have a family at the same time. My husband never helped me out by watching the kids while I was busy working and cooking at the same time. Often the food would be burned because I had to do so many things at once. Feeding the children and changing their diapers consumed most of my time, so I almost never had any time to spare for myself."[43]

Most difficult for the women was their husbands' lack of commitment to marriage and family. Having a family in the United States provided a Chinese American man with much-needed comfort, social status, and a sense of fulfillment, but the presence of his wife and children also interfered with the carefree lifestyle to which he had been accustomed for many years. Breaking away from the bachelor past was, for some, easier said than done. A number of women now suddenly found themselves stranded in marriages with compulsive gamblers or frequenters of brothels.

In *Chinese Women of America*, Judy Yung documents the case of Lee Wai Lan. Lee and her children suffered many hardships in China while her husband lived in Cleveland. One of her daughters was killed during a Japanese raid. Overcoming all difficulties, she managed to send the remaining four children to her husband. In 1946 Lee was finally reunited with her family in Ohio, and she thought that her misfortune would become a thing of the past. Only when she arrived in the United States did she find that her husband had a white mistress, and her teenage children were no longer close to her. "I was so disappointed with them and shocked by our home," as Yung recorded, "—a filthy house with a small hole between two bricks for a toilet. I wanted to die." But her hardships in China had made Lee a strong and independent woman. She washed dishes and peeled vegetables in a restaurant, rented a house for her family, and eventually saved money to start her own restaurant.[44]

Adjustment to new family life was difficult for both the newcomers and their husbands. Most war brides and their spouses came from the same region and spoke the same dialect, but they had not shared the same experiences for a long time. A war bride might find her husband no longer resembled the person whom she had married in China many years ago, and he could very well feel the same about her. The fact that their husbands had lived in the United States longer made the situation more difficult for the women. The majority of the war brides came from rural areas of China. In the United States they appeared culturally, socially, and linguistically inept. They were looked down upon by their Americanized husbands and ridiculed by people in the community.[45] They were often the ones to receive the blame when family disputes occurred.

The plight of the war brides was deepened by the possibility of government intervention in the private arena of Chinese American family life. In addition to their lack of linguistic skills and community support, the war brides had yet to establish the legal status that their husbands possessed. A woman who entered the United States as the fiancée of a war veteran would have to leave the country if the marriage did not take place within three months. If a woman ended the marriage that had provided her entry to the United States, she might face an INS investigation that could lead to her deportation.

Some husbands used the specter of the INS to take advantage of their wives. In a case investigated by the service, a woman told investigators that whenever she and her husband got into an argument, he would use deportation as a threat. When the marriage fell apart eight months after she arrived, her husband immediately asked the INS to deport her.[46]

In a letter dated March 24, 1952, another man wrote to the San Francisco INS office: "This is to advise you that I have filed a divorce action against my wife . . . a Chinese national on grounds of desertion and mental cruelty. I expect the divorce to be granted sometime in April 1952. It is my understanding that my wife may have filed for naturalization as wife of a citizen of the United States. Therefore, I am furnishing you this information for your records."[47] It is unclear whether the INS indeed took action against the wife, but the letter writer certainly considered the government agency on his side. The logic was simple: the wife came as his dependent. If the marriage ended, her legal privilege as a citizen's spouse should be revoked. The possibility of government investigation helped consolidate gender hierarchy in the community. It assisted Chinese American men in keeping their wives subordinate. But although it might have made it difficult for some women to challenge their husbands' authority, such intervention could not eradicate the marital problems between a man and his immigrant wife.

The difficulties of living in the United States confused and disturbed many war brides, but these women were a far cry from the stereotypical "traditional Chinese women." Their experiences in war-torn China had given them strength to fight to improve the quality of their lives.[48] Many of them would not submit, even though they were thousands of miles away from their home villages and handicapped by the language barrier.

Mediating Domestic Disputes: The Advice Columns

Few of the confused, frustrated, and in some cases desperate individuals went to their community associations for guidance; most of them turned to advice columns instead. The advice column was an important feature of many community newspapers in the 1940s; it provided free legal advice on immigration issues and opened a forum for discussions about China and U.S. politics. Shortly after the arrival of the war brides, an overwhelmingly large number of the letters focused on marital problems. The issues raised often provoked lengthy replies from the general audience as well as the editorial staff, making private life a subject of public controversy. Among the many forums hosted by the "Readers' Service" (Duzhe fuwu) column in *Chung Sai Yat Po* were "Family Disputes" (Jiating jiufen), "Between Husband and Wife" (Fuqi zhijian), and "Between Men and Women" (Nannü zhijian).

The use of the Chinese language enabled the press to reach a large number of readers from different groups of Chinese Americans, especially the new immigrants. It also helped the community draw its own boundaries. Even though the press made all the discussions public, the publicity was confined within the community. No matter how sensitive the issues might be or how ugly the problems might look, no one would have to worry about bringing shame to the community because he or she disclosed a private situation through newspapers read by Chinese only. The use of Chinese also made editors comfortable in casting their opinions on the basis of a particular set of moral standards and values that would suit the situation of Chinese Americans.

The use of the Chinese language was especially important in the discussion of gender relations, since most of the war brides had been educated in China and could only read Chinese. The advice columns were obviously successful in reaching the female audience: many letters were submitted by women, and sometimes letter writers inquired on behalf of their female friends. Taking advantage of complete anonymity, the letter writers expressed their feelings freely and disclosed their desires and intentions. In addition to sympathy, they looked for approval from the press for the actions that they were about to take. The editors were fully aware of the impact that their advice might have on the lives of the letter writers as well as the social ramifications involved. They were put in the position of defining moral standards for the community. Not only did these columns provide valuable information about marital problems and gender relations, but they also illuminated some of the broader social issues confronting the Chinese American community.

In October 1950 a reader under the pseudonym Zun Ni wrote to *Chung Sai Yat Po* asking for advice. Zun Ni had wed in China before he came to the United States. His marriage was arranged, but he and his wife had made a good start, and they had a son. Then Zun Ni left for the Gold Mountain. His wife and son had to stay in China for ten years before they could join him.

Only when the family reunited did Zun Ni realize how Americanized he had become, and how impossible it was to live with his country wife:

> My ugly Chinese wife [*huanglian bo*] knows nothing. We have noth-
> ing in common. What I like, she doesn't. Where she likes to go, I
> don't. We often fight over things like that. Imagine a man like me,
> working from morning till night for a living and suffering from such
> a wife at home. How can I face the world?
>
> I have thought many times of divorcing her, but my son is still
> young. All sorts of feelings well up in my heart and I suffer so much.
> Please give me guidance.[49]

Zun Ni's query disclosed more than just the cultural gap between a Chinese American man and his immigrant wife. His intention to dissolve the marriage raised a crucial question that the community had to answer: how far should the notion that the newcomers were inferior to their husbands be pushed? The gendered dichotomy of Americanized knowledge versus Chinese backwardness developed in the early discussions presented new problems for the Chinese American community in its struggle for a united front. It was relatively easy to lay the blame on the war brides, yet viewing them simply as a burden to the modern ethnic community would have serious consequences for the recently united families and would legitimize the divorce ideas of men like Zun Ni.

At a time of important community transformation, the press had to relate private issues to the broader sphere of community construction. The impact of World War II on the Chinese American community was "decisive," as Roger Daniels asserts.[50] It changed the way many Chinese Americans saw themselves and encouraged them in their quest for individual freedom and personal happiness. Chinese Americans, however, could not take family life for granted. Immigration restrictions still separated many men from their wives. Recognizing the importance of the family and the challenge that the war brides brought to the community, the press took on the task of examining the values and practices of the old bachelor society and crafting a notion of Chinese Americanness in an attempt to embrace all Chinese in America, regardless of their differences in gender, culture, or immigration status.

Chung Sai Yat Po responded to Zun Ni with a long, carefully phrased essay that offered sympathy for his situation and attributed his problems to the legacy of the Chinese exclusion. The editor pointed out that Zun Ni and his wife had shared a common bond when they formed their family in China;

their differences developed only after they had been separated. If the couple had had a good relationship to begin with, the editor reasoned, it should not be dissolved. To narrow the gap between him and his wife, Zun Ni was advised to view her from a different perspective: "You said that your ugly old bag knows nothing. That is wrong. She may not share your ideas, but she certainly knows her own. Your lifestyle might be too westernized for her; hers might be too Chinese for you. The issue is not how to westernize her or how to accommodate her, but to find a common ground to reconcile your differences."[51]

The editor specifically urged Zun Ni not to denigrate Chinese culture. Instead he suggested Zun Ni try to rebuild his life in such a way that elements of Chinese tradition could be fitted to American modernity. By presenting the idea of a common ground upon which a modern Chinese American family and community could be constructed, the editor, aiming at educating the public, told Zun Ni that his view of the United States versus China was at best unsophisticated because he failed to recognize the merit of a country woman. His wife might not know how to apply makeup or play mah-jongg, and "she may not like to dance or watch cowboy movies, but how beneficial are these things to our life?" Applying community mores instead of those of the larger society, the editor told Zun Ni that forsaking his wife was unacceptable.[52]

The discussion of gender relations pushed the press into the position of defining the identity of the community. The moral standards invoked in the editor's argument were not limited to Confucian ideologies of the past, but mixed the traditional cultural practices with the socialist ideologies that had emerged as orthodox in the People's Republic of China. Marriage and family in this context were not private matters. In a society composed of men and women of different backgrounds, marriage and family tied together public and private interests and attested to individual morals: "In a semifeudal and semicolonial society, tens of thousands of people suffered as your wife did. We should never despise the poor because we are rich, just as we should never look down upon backward and uneducated people because we are more advanced. We should do our utmost to help them to move forward. If you do not have the patience and will to help your own wife, how can you help others?"[53] Zun Ni was not encouraged to pursue individual happiness. Rather, he was advised to make sacrifices for the sake of his family and community.

Although not all newspapers used the ideological jargon of the *Chung Sai Yat Po*, most of them adopted the notion of building on common ground and called for individuals to make sacrifices to preserve family unity. Although they all acknowledged that an individual had the right to take those actions permitted within the American legal system, they advised their readers not to go beyond the moral limits of the community. When a young man fell in love with a married woman who had two children, the *Chinese American Weekly* told him that it would be selfish for him to break up another family and cautioned that even if he was able to marry the woman after she divorced her husband, he might not be happy.[54]

Recognizing that women were likely to become the victims in domestic disputes, the press offered moral support as well as legal advice. In a letter to the *Chinese American Weekly*, Huang Feng, a war bride, wrote: "My husband often told me that he is an American and I am a Chinese. He said that in the United States he could divorce me at any time and I would have no say in the matter. . . . He also told me that I would have to return to China if he divorced me and he would have custody of the children. . . . He said that a woman was nothing but a toy that he could change from time to time."[55] In response, editor Wu Jingfu proclaimed, "A woman is not a toy!" Writing to Huang, he was educating the group her husband belonged to. He said that American divorce laws provided more protection for women than for men, and he wanted every man to consider divorce a "dangerous path." He urged his female readers to be strong, and he told Huang not to be intimidated by the threat of deportation, especially because she had lived in the country for three years and had given birth to children in the United States. Should the INS investigate the case, Wu said, she would have sufficient grounds to defend herself.[56]

Although the editor advised Huang not to submit to her husband, he maintained his role as a mediator. He told Huang that she should take the initiative in making the relationship work because "divorce would be a bad choice." She was advised to "lay bare her husband's threat and make him the one to fear." To control her husband, however, she should "talk to him with reason and persuade him with love," for it was important to win his heart.[57]

Newspaper editors almost never advised anyone to get a divorce. To a woman who described her marriage as a "grave," Wu suggested she find happiness with her husband through their struggle to build a better life.[58] When a wife complained that her husband was a gambling addict, she was encouraged to make their home more attractive than gambling establishments.[59] Fenfang, a war bride, asked if she and her children could stay in the United States should she divorce her husband, another gambler. She was told that having the courage to divorce was not something to be proud of, and that it would be a shame if she could not help her husband to improve. "Staying in

America would be meaningless," said the editor, "if one lost the warmth of the family."[60]

In another case, an immigrant woman using the pseudonym Xiang Yun discovered that her husband, a gambler and a womanizer, had another wife in China. New to the country, Xiang Yun wrote the *Chinese American Weekly* for legal advice. Wu Jingfu assured her that she had enough reason to win a divorce, but he was still reluctant to encourage her. If she could forgive the man, she was told, he might still become a loving and responsible husband.[61] The editor offered no suggestion regarding what the husband should do with his first wife.

The advice columns represented the community's first attempt to engage in a direct dialogue with troubled men and women. The issues that the press were pressured to respond to were complicated and controversial, and the editors did not always have the right answers. It is not clear whether the letter writers followed the advice of the press; some of them probably did not. The expression of values did, however, provide a foundation for the changes that were taking place in the community. The manner in which the press responded to individual inquiries also illustrates the ways in which the community tried to mediate internal conflicts among community members.

Advocating New Gender Relations

The press also helped to set up new moral standards by emphatically denouncing adultery, wife abandonment, and all forms of domestic violence. In May 1950, Chen Zhonghai, president of the CCBA in New York City, left his wife, Tan Shi, and their four young children. When Tan brought charges against Chen for wife beating, the press put him on public trial despite the efforts made by his political allies to keep the matter quiet. Several New York and San Francisco newspapers printed the charges that Tan had brought against Chen.[62] The *China Daily News*, a longtime opponent of the CCBA, disclosed other scandals that Chen had been involved in and questioned his legitimacy as a community leader. It was revealed that Chen had a concubine back in China and had long planned to abandon his wife. Should a man like Chen, who could not even assume the basic social responsibility of taking care of his own wife and children, be given a leadership role in the community?[63]

The embarrassment was almost unbearable for Chen. In a desperate attempt to clear himself, he accused his wife of being a Communist, but even Chen's lawyer brushed him aside. The public's denunciation of Chen helped

Tan Shi get through the ordeal. After the court ordered Chen to move out of the family residence and pay alimony, Tan Shi confronted Chen in front of reporters: "Don't think that I am still afraid of you! Try again and we will see!"[64]

As divorce became an increasing possibility (although it is unclear how many men and women actually divorced), the press called for community acceptance, emphasizing the importance of individual rights in the United States. Newspapers also informed their readers that divorce was no longer a social taboo in China and ran headlines such as "Divorcees are respected in the new Chinese society," and "The liberation of new Chinese women: marriage disputes settled in People's Court in Shanghai." Both the government and the people of China now accepted divorce, so why not those in the Chinese American community?[65]

The public exposure of marital problems had effectively pushed the society toward gender equality. Many Chinese women came to question the social and legal restrictions that limited their freedom in the family and their participation in the society. Their involvement in advice columns eventually led to the creation of new columns on gender relations. The *Chinese American Weekly*, for example, created such columns as "The Art of Life" (Shenghuo de yishu), "Men and Women" (Nannü wenti), and "Marriage Guide" (Hunyin zhidao) to address marriage, family, and gender issues.[66] Such issues were also discussed in *Chung Sai Yat Po*'s "Chinese American Life" (Huaqiao shenhuo). Taking a slightly different approach, the *China Daily News* contributed to the public discourse by providing detailed coverage of land reforms and the marriage law campaign in the People's Republic of China, and it was a leading advocate for gender equality in the Chinese American community.[67]

Most noticeable was the emergence of women's columns. In 1948 the *Chinese Pacific Weekly* invited Tan Ying to host a forum entitled "From the Perspective of Women" (Cong nüxing fangmian kan). Tan pointed out in her first column that the community's reluctance to change was its major problem. She urged all women, regardless of their educational background, to ask questions and pay more attention to the community in order to encourage reform.[68] Similar columns appeared in several other newspapers.

In their attempts to promote democratic marriage, these women's columns openly challenged male superiority in the community. Some essays were written to educate Chinese American men. Chang Xiao, who wrote for the *Chinese American Weekly*, called for husbands to improve themselves. In "To the Husbands" (Xiangei zhangfumen), she wrote,

Gentlemen: have you ever wondered why your wife left with her suit-case and asked for a divorce? Weren't you happily married? What made her decide to divorce you now? What dissatisfied her? I am telling you: don't think that everything is final after the wedding. . . . Don't think that you can lay all the responsibilities upon her once she has married you. She is neither your hired housekeeper nor your paid nurse. She is your wife, your lover, and your companion. . . . A happy marriage can only be assured when the husband shares the responsibilities and joy with his wife. . . . If a husband is not will-ing to change, he will be sure to regret.[69]

Most popular was Wen Ying's "Women's Column" (Funü lan) in the *Chinese Pacific Weekly*, which replaced Tan Ying's in 1953. Before coming to the United States in 1947, Wen had studied at a women's normal school in China. She had attended adult school and then high school in San Francisco's Chinatown, and she had sewed in a garment shop.[70] The charac-ters in her essays were mostly new immigrant women, and many worked in garment shops. One of her reports was about Yan Xin, a young mother of two children who found her own strength after separating from her abusive husband. Yan Xin worked eight hours a day in a factory, leaving her children with a babysitter. "The hard work could not wear her out; it gave her a sense of independence which made her happy." To empower herself, Yan Xin also took English classes in the evenings and planned to write a book about herself.[71]

Almost half of the essays that appeared in Wen Ying's column were submitted by female readers. In "I Was Hurt by an Arranged Marriage," one X.Y. said that she had married a Chinese American man because she and her mother had no means of supporting themselves after her father's death. Life was much harder for her in the United States, however. Her husband often beat her, even during her pregnancy. When she expressed no desire for sex, he suspected that she was having affairs with other men. X.Y. had attempted to kill herself once, and she would not want to live if it were not for her young children. "What could I do?" she asked, "I do not even know enough En-glish to call the police."[72]

Some male readers criticized the "Women's Column" for publishing what they called a "literature of pouring out grievances" (suyuan wenxue), and they protested in writing. They argued that abusive behavior was rare in the "civilized" community, and they thought that "Women's Column" ignored the hardships that men had suffered to establish their families. Two different essays accused the newspaper of creating conflict between married men and women by "giving the wives the chance to tell their side of the story." They warned that such exposure might lead to "family revolution" (jiating geming), and they threatened to boycott the newspaper.[73]

Wen Ying, however, found the criticism amusing. She offered a formal letter of response to her protestors:

> From the way you wrote, I can tell that you gentlemen are both mature and knowledgeable, but what you said is nothing but relics from half a century ago! . . . Today's moral standard is a new one based on the principle of gender equality. No matter how hard a man has worked to establish his family, the law will not allow him to beat up his wife, for that would disturb the peace of the society. . . . If you think that because a man has paid to get married he can treat his wife as his own property and abuse her any way he wishes, alas, you are wrong![74]

Wen Ying argued that letting women pour out their grievances would not create marital problems, and that her column provided therapy for women with unhappy marriages. "When a woman became frustrated, she would want to talk. She wanted sympathy and she wanted to gain strength from her sympathizers. We want to use public force to reform families and reform society. We want to reform what cannot be tolerated by the public and to prevent tragedies."[75]

Like the editors in advice columns, Wen Ying sought to ease tensions between husbands and wives. In an essay entitled "Criticize Yourself" (Jiantao ni ziji), she suggested that every wife should examine her own attitude toward her husband. "If you want to win his heart, you have to approach him appropriately." "The key is to hide negative opinions as much as possible and carry on pleasant conversation as long as you can, for many conflicts are generated by small verbal exchanges."[76] Although Wen Ying denounced arranged marriages, she never encouraged women to walk away from their husbands.[77] Instead she asked women to make their best efforts to repair their marriages, even if they were arranged: "With proper skills, a woman can always change her husband's temper by persuasion."[78]

To help both men and women achieve happy marriages, the press also provided practical advice. Qun, who wrote often for the *Chinese Pacific Weekly*, told married men that they could give sweet comfort to their wives by "putting on aprons to work in the kitchens."[79] Zi Ming, who wrote "The Art of Life" column in the *Chinese American Weekly*, taught women how to take control of their family lives by helping their men to realize their dreams. The wife was to ask herself often, "Am I the one who helps him realize his dreams or who works to destroy them? Am I being considerate or selfish?" Moreover, Zi Ming told the wives that it was their responsibility to provide comfort when their husbands were upset and to help them to get rid of their drinking, smoking, and gambling habits.[80]

Although women were encouraged to work outside the home, they were also advised to show their dependence on their husbands, which was seen as a means of gaining control over their family lives. One essay in "The Art of Life" told the wives that a family could not be happy if the wife was too devoted to her career or if her husband was made into a "female servant." The author also wrote that "a man likes to provide protection for his wife," and "a smart woman should know how to manage the house; she would not let her own career depress her husband."[81]

Model War Brides and *Tangshan taitai*

In addition to helping guide women toward happy marriages, the press also provided role models for married women. In August 1951, the *Chinese Pacific Weekly* published a special report entitled "A Model War Bride" (Mofan de zhanniang). Paradoxically Mariana, who was selected by a female reporter, was neither Chinese nor American; she was German. She and Ah Biao, a Chinese American who remained in the armed forces until 1946, met and married in Germany. According to the report, several of Ah Biao's white colleagues in the military were also interested in dating Mariana, but the then sixteen-year-old decided to go out with Ah Biao. Asked why she married a Chinese instead of a man of her own race, Mariana said that she could see that Ah Biao was more honest and idealistic and would make a more reliable husband. "Whether he is white, yellow, or black had nothing to do with a person's quality."[82]

What made this German woman unusual, according to the report, was her respect for Chinese tradition and the man she was married to. She believed in the "solemn pledge of love" (shanmeng haishi) in marriage. She shouldered all household responsibilities in order to give her husband the opportunity to fulfill his ambitions outside the home, and she adjusted her lifestyle to that of a Chinese wife:

> Five years ago she came from Germany to join Ah Biao. That evening, she used a knife and fork for dinner in a Chinese restau-

rant. The second evening, when the couple went out for dinner with friends, again in a Chinese restaurant, Mariana finished her food with a pair of chopsticks. Since then, she has always used chopsticks. For five years she has enjoyed the food that Ah Biao likes—the Chinese food, not the Western food. . . . Even their children like Chinese food. Mariana likes to cook Chinese food even better. . . . Her cooking skills are as good as those of any Chinese woman with ten years of cooking experience.[83]

The report said that Mariana was both industrious and beautiful. She sewed almost all of her and her children's clothes, and she had never spent a penny on cosmetics. Her natural appearance and radiant smile added extra beauty to her face. In fact, Ah Biao thought his wife was more beautiful than Xishi, an all-time Chinese beauty.[84]

The reporter was especially impressed by Mariana's ability to cope with difficult situations, her efforts to advance herself, and her positive attitude toward life. The life she had chosen was completely different from the one she would have led in Germany. The fact that her husband was from a different culture made her situation more difficult than that of the Chinese war brides, but Mariana had "conquered the newness of the environment." She quickly learned English, and she knew how to make her children and her husband happy. Although she had never attended college, Mariana was intelligent and managed her household well. She understood the Chinese principles of the three obediences (to father before marriage, to husband after marriage, and to son after the death of husband) and the four virtues (morality, proper speech, modest manner, and diligent work). Although she did not think that all Chinese values were applicable to the American environment, she found similarities between the traditional Chinese values and those of her home country. According to the report, Mariana also saw the need to improve the Chinese American community. In the process of the improvement, however, she was very proud of being the wife of a Chinese.[85]

The image of Mariana as a Westerner who had a good understanding of Chinese tradition fit nicely into the mold that the press had been trying to create for different groups of Chinese American women. Several female writers had argued that the modern Chinese American woman should amalgamate aspects of both Chinese and American culture. Xiao Min, who also wrote for the *Chinese Pacific Weekly*, divided Chinese American women into three subgroups. The first group consisted of the women from rural China, commonly known as *tangshan nü* (Chinese girls) or as *tangshan po* (old Chinese women). Brought up according to the feudal values of old China, she said, these women were conservative by nature. They were too dependent on their husbands, and they would have difficulty adjusting to American life. The second group were the *tusheng nü* (U.S.-born Chinese women). These women had received a good Western education and were familiar with U.S. lifestyles, but they were often too "materialistic and individualistic" to be interested in community reform. The third group consisted of American-born Chinese women who had been given education in their native culture either in the United States or in China. These women were grounded in their tradition but were not as conservative as the women from China. They could absorb modern aspects of American culture but were less selfish and individualistic. If all women were organized and a collective effort was made, Xiao Min said, the gaps between these groups would be filled in. The tangshan po should learn English and American lifestyles, and the tusheng nü should study Chinese and appreciate Chinese culture.[86]

In early 1954, a woman who called herself L.Y. wrote to the *Chinese Pacific Weekly*, asking if she would forever remain a tangshan po. No, the editor told her, since the phrase tangshan po only applied to Chinese country women who had no knowledge of American society. "What is the definition of a tangshan po?" one reader asked, excited to learn that her status could be changed. The woman, however, said that she was not ashamed of her past: "We women from China were well educated, and we have thoughts of our own." What she wanted was respect: "Sir, could you please give her a more decent name—*tangshan taitai* [wife from China]?"[87] "If a woman from China no longer believes that the only way to act, think, and talk in the United States is to act, think, and talk as though she were in China, and if she is determined to adjust her life to the new environment," responded the editor, "she might indeed be called a tangshan taitai."[88]

Then how could a tangshan po be transformed into a tangshan taitai? According to Xiao Min, a modern Chinese American woman was one who could "raise her children using scientific methods."[89] "We need to reform ourselves," said another female writer, Qun, "not for the sake of getting rid of the name tangshan po," but to make "our own lives more interesting." Getting an American education was the key. Using her own experience as an example, she told her readers that it was possible for a mother of three young children to find time to study English.[90]

The cultural struggle in which the community was involved in the late 1940s and early 1950s was not simply that of Chinese versus American, traditional versus modern, or rural versus urban. Instead, in Aihwa Ong's words, it was an effort to create "modernity" after its "own fashion," based on the notion that all Chinese in the United States belonged to one group.[91] Wen Ying, the host of the "Women's Column" in the *Chinese American Weekly*, argued that Chinese American women should not simply follow the examples of their European or American counterparts. Being of strong character and strength, "they should rely on themselves for their own liberation."[92]

$\mathcal{A}$s the Chinese American community evolved into a family society, a strong desire for order and control developed. The family was viewed as the primary unit of the community, one that ensured social stability. The effort to bring stability not only emphasized the training of individuals to encourage socially responsible behavior, but also inspired a reevaluation of the old values of the bachelor society. More than anything else, the presence of the war brides called for change, and the community would have to show that it was capable of more than attempts at goodwill mediation. Given the importance of the family to the community after decades of exclusion, advocates for gender equality found the general public responding to their arguments.

Accompanying the changes in the community were the changes in the women themselves. As more and more war brides learned English, obtained driver's licenses, and passed citizenship tests, they began to play more important roles in the community. In early 1951 Gilbert Woo found that the war brides, who had been ridiculed when they first arrived, had become the most visible participants in the community's social activities: "They will probably wield the most influence on Chinatown in another eight or ten years."[93]

CHAPTER 7

In Times of Crisis

THE COLD WAR ERA

⚜

*A*lthough the Chinese American community was hardly a harmonious one, it had acted as a unit in its dealings with the larger society before World War II. In the late 1940s, however, the struggle between rightist and leftist political factions grew into a tense and dangerous rivalry that enabled the U.S. government to intervene in the community's affairs. The consequences were devastating. The INS, supported by other government agencies and acting on leads from individuals who had inside information, finally found a way to break up Chinese immigration networks. In the name of investigating Communist subversive activities, the government went after not only the new arrivals but also those who had successfully gained permanent residence and citizenship in the United States. No leftist groups survived, and thousands of Chinese Americans lived in fear. The cold war had a profound effect on the lives of Chinese Americans and their families. As investigators prowled the streets of Chinatowns and knocked on the doors of Chinese Americans, the community confronted a real threat.

Double Scrutiny of Immigration Applicants

On the surface, the fear that haunted Chinese Americans in the 1950s and early 1960s was the result of decisive steps taken by the U.S. government to end what was described as document fraud. The Chinese exclusion acts had barred all Chinese except merchants, students, diplomats, and tourists from entering the United States. The statutory exclusion, though strictly enforced, did not stop Chinese immigration completely. The INS had long suspected that a large number of Chinese had entered the United States as imposters; many claimed to be family members of exempted classes or descendants of U.S. citizens.

During the first half of the twentieth century, immigration authorities relied on a sometimes lengthy interrogation system to identify those who were applying under false pretenses. Still thousands of Chinese entered the country, established families, and secured legal status, and their immigration records, originally created as they entered the United States, now became a body of evidence that could be rehearsed and memorized by others to gain entry.[1] The situation made it difficult for the government to turn down new applicants. The detention of the Chinese war brides in the late 1940s also generated a public outcry that handicapped the INS's ability to handle immigration cases. In 1949 and early 1950, many Chinese immigrants gained admission without confronting any difficulties at the ports of entry.[2]

In late 1950 the government amended the procedure for handling Chinese immigration cases. Instead of determining an applicant's admissibility after the person landed on American soil, it decreed that a Chinese emigrant first had to obtain travel documents from U.S. diplomatic agencies. This change involved the State Department in Chinese immigration and enabled the government to double-check the identity of each applicant. American diplomats in China would screen each application before a visa or passport was issued, but then those who succeeded in traveling to the United States would still encounter immigration authorities at the ports of entry, where the admissibility of each applicant would be finally determined. After the establishment of the PRC in 1949, the United States withdrew its diplomatic personnel from mainland China, so the Chinese who planned to emigrate had to submit applications through the American consulate in Hong Kong, then a British colony.

Because the 1943 repeal act limited Chinese immigration to an annual quota of 105, regular immigration applicants were subjected to an extremely long wait. In the 1950s the consul in Hong Kong processed fewer than 20 quota applications each year. Relatives of Chinese Americans continued to seek alternate avenues of emigration and ways to circumvent immigration laws. Some applied for nonquota visas under the Chinese Alien Wives of American Citizens Act of 1946. Many more petitioned for American passports as derivative citizens. Like the INS, the consulate staff in Hong Kong suspected that many applicants claimed a paternal relationship that did not exist, and very few Chinese could present public records to prove their identities or their relationship with their alleged fathers.

The problems with Chinese immigration in the early 1950s were further complicated by the practices established during the exclusion era. A large number of Chinese Americans had been documented under false names and had to use their paper identities to bring in family members. Those who failed to establish records for their children had to purchase slots through their own networks. Gaining entry as an imposter, providing false testimony for one's fellow immigrants, or selling paper slots was not considered an immoral act by Chinese Americans because of the difficulty in establishing families in the United States through legal channels.

After World War II, the facilitation of Chinese immigration using false papers became professionalized. Immigration brokers, lawyers, and notaries public gained wealth and power in the community. For two to three thousand dollars, these professionals handled slot trading, prepared *kougong* (family history papers to be used in testimony), recorded affidavits, filed petitions, and provided legal services to individual Chinese.[3]

The American consulate in Hong Kong soon developed a system to deal with the issue of derivative citizenship, which was essentially a question of paternity and identity. In addition to the affidavits and witness testimonies, group blood tests were introduced in 1951 to weed out false paternity applications. The test results brought great satisfaction to Consul General Everett F. Drumright and quickly became the most effective weapon against Chinese imposters.[4] During the first few months the tests were administered, the consul was able to exclude 40 percent of the applicants in Hong Kong. The INS estimated that approximately 50 percent of false relationships could be detected by the tests.[5]

The government also successfully established a number of court cases against Chinese applicants based solely on the results of blood tests. In *Lue Chow Kon et al. v. Brownell*, Lue Don Wing, the alleged father of three plaintiffs, was found to have type N blood. According to the M-N test system, the blood of every one of his children would contain at least one N element regardless the blood type of the mother. One of the plaintiffs, Lue Chow Kon, was found to have blood containing only M elements. Without an N element in his blood, the medical expert who administered the test said that he could not be the son of Lue Don Wing. The other two plaintiffs both had type N blood and therefore were possible sons of Lue Don Wing, but Irving R. Kaufman, a U.S. district court judge, argued that "the blood grouping tests neither proved nor disproved their claims."[6] Because all three plaintiffs "consistently maintained that they are all true brothers," the judge ruled that "Lue Don Wing cannot be the father of any of them, for a father of *all three* would have to have a blood type MN." Thus the judge decided that "by a strange twist, plaintiffs' claim that they are brothers is not scientifically consistent with their claim that they are all sons of Lue Don Wing."[7] This decision was later upheld by the court of appeals. All the brothers were denied entry.[8]

It was difficult for the Chinese to establish paper family relations once the court admitted blood tests as qualified evidence. For the Chinese to conduct preliminary tests would make the process far more complicated.[9] Moreover, the blood-type match of an applicant and his alleged father indicated only the possibility of such a relationship, which was not sufficient to establish paternity. Those who passed the blood tests would still be subjected to the normal interrogation and scrutiny. Even when paternity with the alleged father was established, the government could still reject a petitioner if his sponsor was found to have gained entry under a false identity.

The Hong Kong consulate was more effective than the INS in rejecting Chinese applicants, apparently because its actions and decisions were free from the scrutiny of the American public. Acting on leads from local Chinese informants and discrepancies found through interrogation, investigators sometimes searched the homes of the applicants, seizing letters, kougong, and other materials to be used as evidence to turn down applications.

The INS officials must have felt relief once their battle to exclude the Chinese was supported by the State Department. If a large number of Chinese applicants could be eliminated before they came to the United States, the workload of the INS would be reduced significantly. In any case the INS still had final authority over each new arrival at the port of entry. Most important, the agency was no longer alone in taking the criticism for blocking Chinese entries.

Diaozhi: The Response of the Chinese

The double scrutiny by the government posed new obstacles for Chinese Americans who wanted to bring their family members to the United States. In Hong Kong, the colonial government provided no protection for the rights of Chinese applicants. The consul general rejected many applicants simply because they did not provide sufficient documentary evidence. The would-be immigrants were frustrated that they had no recourse once their applications were turned down.

Chinese Americans looked for a way to *diaozhi*—move the cases out of the hands of the Hong Kong consulate—and they realized that this could only be done through the courts in the United States. In the past Chinese immigrants had used writs of habeas corpus to move their cases to court, but habeas corpus was only applicable to those who had landed on American soil. After their petitions had been turned down in Hong Kong, Chinese applicants learned that diaozhi was only possible under section 503 of the Nationality Act of 1940. The law stipulated that "if any person who claims a right to privilege as a national of the United States is denied such right or privilege by any Department or agency, or executive official thereof . . . such person, regardless of whether he is within the United States or abroad, may institute an action against the head of such Department or agency in the District Court of the United States . . . for a judgment declaring him to be a national of the United States." The same article also provided that "if such person is outside the United States and shall have instituted such an action in court," he may "obtain from a diplomatic or consular officer of the United States in the foreign country in which he is residing a certificate of identity stating that his nationality status is pending before the court, and may be admitted to the United States."[10] In other words, by filing a suit against the secretary of state, an applicant rejected by the Hong Kong consulate might have his case transferred to the United States and be permitted to enter while awaiting trial. If a new arrival was denied admission by immigration authorities at the port of entry, he could still gain temporary admission by filing a 503 action against the attorney general. Diaozhi thus became an important means for the Chinese to bypass immigration regulations in the early 1950s.

Once the rejected applications were transferred to courts in the United States, the INS was called in to assist with the investigations. At first there was little communication between government agencies and the court, and the overburdened judges were often poorly prepared for the trials. The judge who presided over a particular case would sometimes not see the documents until a day or two before the trial began. The information gleaned from the investigations conducted by the Hong Kong consulate or the INS might not even be presented to the judge.[11] The frustrated INS officials felt that under the current law and legal system, it was difficult to defend the government in court. The government simply could not produce sufficient evidence to offset the self-serving testimony of a plaintiff supported by his alleged relatives and witnesses. As early as November 1951, several INS district commissioners requested that their service be withdrawn from participation in court cases.[12]

The court judges soon became frustrated as well. On February 15, 1952, U.S. district judge Louis E. Goodman, who had overseen some of the earlier trials, called a meeting in his chambers attended by lawyers of the represented parties and members of the INS. At the conference the judge admitted that he was loath to try these cases because of the difficulty involved in determining the truth. He suggested the INS take over, since immigration officials were more knowledgeable about the situation.[13]

A lawyer for the Chinese plaintiffs immediately suggested that the INS accept applications for certificates of citizenship for all his clients and make the necessary administrative decisions. If the INS agreed to do so, and if the government agreed not to deport the applicants until the decisions were made, the lawyer said that his clients would withdraw the pending legal actions. Eager to take the burden off the court, Judge Goodman agreed to help the lawyers and the INS reach an agreement so that the Chinese would be induced to drop all pending cases.[14]

At this point, only INS officials who were experienced with problems in Chinese immigration understood what they would be getting into if such an agreement were indeed reached. In a letter to INS Central Office commissioner Argyle R. Mackey, Bruce G. Barber, the San Francisco district director, described the situation as "very grave." "By filing the actions under section 503 following denial of the claims by a consulate officer and thereafter obtaining certificates of identity under that section to proceed to the United States," Barber wrote, "these Chinese have completely bypassed our usual examination at the port of arrival." Moreover, the only material evidence that the INS could now use to determine the identity of an applicant was the immigration records of his alleged relatives. These records, Barber stated, were "limited insofar as tending to prove or disprove the claim of relationship."[15] The issue was simple: if INS inspectors had failed in the past to prevent a paper son from entering the United States, how could they succeed in rejecting a new applicant who claimed to be a relative of that imposter who had already established legal status? Barber argued that the job now was "impossible to handle" given the circumstances. He wrote:

> It must be borne in mind that these persons who have entered the United States on the basis of certificates of identity issued under section 503 have been at large and in contact with their alleged relatives and witnesses for substantial periods of time before the case come [*sic*] to trial. This situation tends to eliminate the possibility of the government being able to develop any substantial discrepancies in the testimony given at the trial. In other words, if the case is a

fraudulent one, by the time it is reached by the Court, the coaching
is well nigh perfect. The same situation would exist if we were to
accept the application on Form N-600 in these cases.[16]

In short, Barber argued that the Chinese who had bypassed the regular
inspection safeguards of the immigration regulations should not be permitted to have their way by "changing their courses," and that his service should
not be required to determine their claims on grounds "chosen" by the
Chinese.[17]

Five days after Barber sent his letter, Commissioner Mackey stated the
position of the INS in a letter to Deputy Attorney General Frank Chambers.
Mackey said that his service was "in no position to accept the jurisdiction in
these cases." "The Government should not enter into an agreement or contrast [*sic*] to withhold deportation of an alien illegally in the United States
merely because he has withdrawn a court proceeding." He wanted the deputy
attorney general to bear in mind the consequences: "the adoption of such a
procedure might well be considered an open invitation for anyone to institute court actions" based on a similar situation. By refusing to enter into an
agreement with the lawyers for the Chinese, which had met with Judge
Goodman's favor, the INS registered a strong protest to a law that, in the opinion of the service, was being taken improper advantage of by the Chinese.[18]

The INS argued that there was a loophole in the Nationality Act of 1940
that allowed petitioners to seek help from the court and therefore gain temporary entry after their applications were denied. Such a loophole was closed
in 1952 by the McCarran-Walter Act, which went into effect on December
24, 1952. The new law set up complicated screening procedures to keep out
subversives and aliens who had associated with totalitarian states, and it au-
thorized the attorney general to deport immigrants affiliated with Communist organizations even if they had been granted citizenship. In addition, the
State Department's Passport Office was given the power to decide who could
enter and leave the United States.[19]

On December 6, 1952, a *Chinese Pacific Weekly* editorial warned Chinese visa applicants that they were running out of time. It pointed out that
the 503 action provided the only chance for Chinese applicants outside the
United States to gain temporary admission. With the effective date of the new
law approaching, they had to proceed immediately. In theory, one could not
file a legal case until a negative administrative decision had been made. Since
there was little time left, the editorial informed its readers that the U.S. sponsors could request a "declaratory judgment" on behalf of the applicants who

were still in China. If they did so, the consul general in Hong Kong would be forced to forward these cases to the U.S. court, and he would also have to issue certificates of identity allowing the petitioners to come to the United States.[20]

Chinese Americans lost no time. By December 24, 1952, 582 applicants had filed suits while still in Hong Kong. An additional 104 cases were filed after that date.[21] Thirty-eight applicants who had arrived in the United States also filed litigation after the INS decided to deport them and after their petitions for a writ of habeas corpus were denied.[22]

The enormous amount of litigation created great difficulties for the court. Confronting the well-prepared Chinese plaintiffs and their witnesses, who had memorized the kougong and had been advised about such inquiries and court proceedings, the government had few advantages. Immigration authorities found that it was more difficult to disprove than prove a false claim of paternal relationship in the absence of certificates or public records.[23] Interrogations in court were hardly ever successful, since the applicants and their alleged fathers had had enough time together to prepare their testimony. Very few plaintiffs and their witnesses volunteered information that was not covered by the kougong, and it was difficult to make the Chinese admit that they had been coached or assisted.

Not only were Chinese Americans prepared to challenge the government, but they also resisted giving the court the authority to exclude them. One of the first cases tried, that of Ly Show, resulted in a decision against the petitioner on January 12, 1953.[24] The case went back to the Ninth Circuit Court of Appeals three times, and it was still pending three years later. In fact, every judgment against Chinese petitioners was reversed and a new trial demanded by the court of appeals.[25] By April 1956 there were still thirty-one cases pending against the attorney general and 512 cases pending against the secretary of state.[26] "This is a sorry record," wrote Ernest J. Hover of the INS, for all these cases would "have to be re-tried." He went on: "[They] should be made a matter of first concern and immediate attention. . . . There has been a final administrative determination of inadmissibility. . . . This issue should have been prosecuted to the Supreme Court, when the first case was filed 6 1/2 years ago." If the government could not find a way to block the imposters, he remonstrated, it would be abetting the creation of another generation of paper fathers and the future operations of more paper sons and daughters.[27]

For several years the INS had been looking for a new way to tackle the problem. Its officials realized that the service needed to develop broader powers and obtain more comprehensive support. The question was how to persuade the government to agree to such a major commitment.

The INS: Making a Case of Subversion and Expanding Power

Scholars have considered Everett F. Drumright, the American consul general in Hong Kong, to be the person behind the government's campaign to associate Chinese immigration with Communist invasion.[28] Beginning his career as a Foreign Service officer in 1930, Drumright had spent many years in China before his posting as the chief of the Office of Chinese Affairs at the State Department in 1945. While in China, Drumright had sought every opportunity to gain access to Chinese Communist leaders such as Zhou Enlai. But because he was more politically conservative than other American China specialists and because he had not been hostile to Chiang Kai-shek, these efforts did not jeopardize his career during the McCarthy era. He in fact was one of the two China-language experts who were able to remain in the field unscathed in the Foreign Service (the other person was Edward E. Rice). Later he became the U.S. ambassador to the Nationalist government on Taiwan.[29] While other well-known China hands, especially Oliver Edmund Clubb, John Paton Davis, John Service, and John Carter Vincent, were either fired or forced to resign from the Foreign Service after their loyalties to the United States were questioned, Drumright was carrying out the government's containment policy with his usual efficiency. On December 9, 1955, Drumright submitted to the State Department a "Report on the Problem of Fraud at Hong Kong," alleging that the PRC was planning "a criminal conspiracy to evade the laws of the United States" through well-organized networks in Hong Kong, New York, and San Francisco, and that these networks had become the main channel for youngsters who had been educated in Communist schools or who had served in the People's Liberation Army to emigrate to the United States.[30] The report was widely circulated and it served to reawaken the fears of Communism that had been so recently instilled by Senator Joseph McCarthy.[31] Even though the Wisconsin senator's career had ended, Drumright's argument that the current immigration laws were incapable of preventing Communist infiltration echoed McCarthy's last Senate speech, in which he accused President Eisenhower of "a shrinking show of weakness" toward Red China.[32] The consul wanted the government to allow him to "place the burden of proof" where it belonged and authorize him to reject any suspicious applications. If this could not be done, he said, there was only one remedy left: to "destroy every claim based on fraud by proving it is fraudulent."[33] Written two months before a federal grand jury probe began in New York, the report seemed to signal the beginning of an all-out crackdown on Chinese immigration networks.

The report revealed nothing new, however. By the time it was made public in March 1956, the INS had already secured enough support from the government to do what the consul had suggested. Immigration authorities had long been acquainted with the dynamics of Chinese immigration, and the INS had spoken on the problems it presented at almost every congressional hearing on immigration issues.

It is not clear that the INS saw the same threat of Communist invasion as the consul. A right-wing China hand, Drumright perhaps believed that some of his colleagues from the Foreign Service were responsible for "losing China" in the late 1940s. He might indeed have seen a connection between Chinese immigration and Communist infiltration. Two months before he sent the report, Drumright warned the State Department that if young Chinese who had served in the Chinese military or had been subjected to Communist indoctrination entered the United States as imposters, and if they later enlisted in the American armed forces, the threat to national internal security would be real.[34] To INS officials, the young people who applied for derivative citizenship in the postwar period did not appear different from the earlier generations of paper children, but the consul's warnings and recommendations were certainly welcome additions to the arguments that they had been accumulating for years.

Beginning in the early 1950s, the INS had been looking for an issue on which to build a political alliance with other government agencies. As tensions between the newly founded PRC and the United States mounted over the Korean conflict, the INS perceived the issue of national security as the key to winning support and increasing its power. On February 15, 1952, when Bruce G. Barber suggested that the INS commissioner not take over the section 503 cases in protest of the rather weak government position, as mentioned earlier, he made the possibility of Communist invasion a special point of importance: "The danger of fraud is perhaps intensified by the Communist seizure of China, with the prospect that the Communists will be seeking every available method of introducing some of their agents into the United States." Barber did not present any evidence of such danger at this time, but his message was delivered to the Justice Department.[35]

The investigation of Communist activities fell under the jurisdiction of the Federal Bureau of Investigation. As the government initiated the prosecution of American Communist Party officials in July 1948, several organizations were placed on the list of the U.S. attorney general for special investigation. No Chinese American leftist organizations ever made the list, but several of them, including the Chinese Hand Laundry Alliance and *China Daily News* in New York and the Chinese Workers Mutual Aid Association and Min Qing (Chinese American Democratic Youth League) in San Francisco, were placed under surveillance by the FBI. Of special interest was these organizations' association with those on the attorney general's list, including the Communist Party of America, the Committee for a Democratic Far Eastern Policy, and the California Labor School.[36] It was not always easy, however, for the FBI to obtain evidence that could bring members of leftist groups to trial. Frustrated, the bureau solicited the cooperation of the INS.

The INS was more than willing to assist the FBI. It was the FBI's interest in illegal Chinese entrants and Chinese American leftist activities that enabled the INS legitimately to link immigration fraud with subversive activities. On October 13, 1951, a copy of the FBI report entitled "Movement of Communist Chinese" had been forwarded to the INS. This and several other reports based on information furnished by the Central Intelligence Agency alleged that the Seamen's Union of Hong Kong was a "Communist-controlled" organization, and that the union was expediting the entry of Chinese into the United States by helping them to jump ship for a fee of two thousand dollars per person. The INS immediately requested that the State Department investigate the nature of the screening process of Chinese seamen, which came under British jurisdiction.[37] The Oriental Fraud Unit of the INS's Investigations Branch in San Francisco was assigned to take charge of the inquiry.[38] Acting upon various leads, its investigators raided living quarters and gathering places in Chinatowns searching for seamen and other illegal immigrants. They also checked the immigration records of leftist Chinese Americans and succeeded in deporting two affiliates of the *China Daily News*, one in 1954 and the other in 1956.[39]

Thus by 1956 the FBI considered the job of the INS closely related to its own, and Director J. Edgar Hoover specifically requested information regarding "any developments of internal security nature resulting from investigations" of Chinese immigration fraud. The support of the FBI cleared the path for the INS. When the grand jury probe in New York began in February, the FBI suggested extending the investigation to Baltimore, Washington, D.C., Boston, and San Francisco. Hoover was especially interested in learning about any Chinese Communist or other subversive connections on the part of applicants, sponsors, brokers, attorneys, or other persons involved in the fraud, and about Chinese attempts to introduce intelligence agents or other subversive elements into the United States.[40]

By the time Drumright's report reached the regional INS chiefs that same month,[41] the INS was ready to launch a joint operation with several government agencies to halt the alleged conspiracy. With the assistance of the U.S. district attorneys' offices, the service met with the Criminal Division of the Justice Department, the FBI, and the Passport Office of the State Department and worked out with them the details of an extensive inquiry into possible fraud by the plaintiffs who had filed the section 503 actions. All of these government agencies were convinced that the investigation of Chinese immigration fraud was of great importance to their own interests.[42] The Passport Office was to handle issues associated with travel documents; the INS, immigration matters; and the FBI, possible cases of subversion.[43]

The State Department's commitment extended the grand jury probe beyond the United States. Secretary of State John Foster Dulles approved the involvement of his staff and indicated that all resources of the department would be made available to investigators. He also specified that he wanted to be informed of any developments.[44] Scores of agents were dispatched to Hong Kong to check the birth claims of every person who had filed a civil suit. Eventually thirty investigative teams worked out of the consulate: each one consisted of an American investigator, two local investigators, and one local clerk-typist.[45]

In the United States, the INS was able to go about its business without being liable for blame by the public, for in theory it was only assisting the district attorneys. James F. Greene, the chief of the INS's General Investigations Division, stated that his office was ready to "investigate for prosecution, denaturalization or deportation any case that . . . is within our investigative jurisdiction." He informed the San Francisco office that it was to give top priority to these cases and assign more experienced officers to them.[46] Investigating illegal entries had always been the job of the INS, but only when it became part of the government's effort to contain Communist infiltration was the service able to act as aggressively as it wished.

The grand jury probe received full support from the media. In New York, U.S. district attorney Paul W. Williams announced on February 14, 1956, that some Chinese young people who had entered the country were probably Communists,[47] while immigration authorities told eager reporters in San Francisco that some newcomers "could become a willing tool for espionage" for Red China.[48] According to INS reports, Chinese were entering the United States from all over. Some Chinese went to other countries in the Western

Hemisphere and came in as citizens of these countries.[49] Others, listed as "transit aliens" on their way to Cuba and other Latin American countries, disappeared in U.S. airports.[50] Since the Communist-dominated Hong Kong Seamen's Union served routes to China, Australia, Great Britain, Indonesia, and Singapore, Chinese crewmen were assumed to pose a major threat at U.S. port cities: the INS reported that 130 jumped ship in 1956.[51]

In addition to playing up the theme of Communist infiltration, INS officials told the press that they were concerned that false citizens might be coerced into slavery by their paper parents. The most publicized case involved Jonathan Yee and his paper father, William Y. Fong. Yee entered the United States in 1940 as the son of a derivative citizen. His paper father, a wealthy dairy products dealer in San Francisco, apparently forced Jonathan to divorce his wife, return to China, and marry another woman, and bring her to America as a war bride so that the paper father could eventually marry her. This case was trumpeted by the INS as a "prize example" of how an illegal entrant could be mistreated, and it implied that such pressure could be applied to any Chinese fraudulently in the country.[52]

The government's campaign to crack down on illegal immigrants, supported by the media, created the impression that every Chinese American was a suspect. When Elizabeth Warner, a New York resident, was referred by an employment agency to a Chinese laundry (she had listed that she could iron garments), she immediately assumed that her real mission, as a white person being sent to work in a Chinese business, was to investigate subversive activities. She soon took action, reporting to the FBI and the INS that the laundry was a "channel by means of which hundreds of Chinese Communists have secured positions of safety for themselves in the United States and by which they would be enabled to sabotage any war effort should the United States become involved in an armed conflict [with China]."[53]

Gerard L. Gouttel, the assistant U.S. attorney in the Southern District of New York, attributed the accomplishments of the grand jury to the work of the INS. At a meeting held at the Department of Justice on June 15, 1956, Gouttel said that INS investigations had proved to be crucial to the grand jury. In addition to documenting all action files, immigration authorities located witnesses and arraigned them for trial, and they pushed Chinese Americans to admit fraud.[54] Investigator Dorris Yarbrough was praised by the district attorney's office as "the most experienced investigator still active" for his "tireless, aggressive and imaginative work," and it was said that Yarbrough's name had become "synonymous with the Immigration Service amongst Chinese." The memo also stated that another investigator, Raymond Atwood, used his personal contacts with the Chinese as a source of "important evidentiary leads."[55]

The INS was so satisfied with its role in the grand jury investigations that it stated there was no need for special handling of the cases outside the district attorneys' offices. James F. Greene assured other government officials that the service would continue to cooperate and maintain a close liaison with the attorneys as well as with other interested agencies.[56] Armed with the power of the grand jury, the INS became intent upon carrying out its investigations to their fullest extent and obtaining "as many confessions as possible."[57]

The Chinese Informants

If the INS succeeded this time, it was not simply because of the political atmosphere of the cold war or because it had the support of other government agencies. During the period of exclusion Chinese Americans had confronted a more aggressive and powerful campaign against them, but they were able to organize among themselves to circumvent the laws. Beginning in the late 1940s, however, a new dynamic had been created in the community. Political rivalries between leftists and rightists not only divided community members but also sent an open invitation to federal authorities to intervene in what had previously been seen as internal affairs.

The FBI files from the period, recently released under the Freedom of Information Act, have all information regarding their sources blacked out.[58] Only a small fraction of the INS's immigration fraud files have been declassified and made available to the public; information concerning informants remains sealed in the National Archives.[59] The limited releases nevertheless reveal a not-so-distant time when many Chinese Americans, from established businessmen, workers, and students to new immigrants, old and young, were scrutinized because of their affiliation with liberal or progressive organizations. It was during the fierce battle against leftist groups in the late 1940s that some Chinese Americans began to work for the government as informants.[60] Their knowledge and assistance enabled investigators to expose the community networks that had been kept secret by Chinese Americans.

In fact, when the FBI began investigating the Chinese Workers Mutual Aid Association in San Francisco in 1943, it accomplished little. The bureau's file was closed within a few months because no subversive activity by the organization could be detected.[61] In 1944, however, the FBI director ordered the bureau to reinvestigate the association because the government had become concerned about the political conflict in China. This time field officers found several Chinese Americans who were willing to cooperate.[62] By the time of the Communist victory in China in October 1949, the FBI's network of Chinese informants was in full operation. The bureau had obtained the CWMAA's membership list and was receiving reports regarding the organization's contacts with other leftist American organizations. Materials published by the CWMAA as well as details of the news coverage in Chinese-language newspapers were forwarded to the bureau on a regular basis. Later, informants identified Min Qing as a "pro–Chinese Communist" organization.[63] In New York, the CCBA and representatives of the Guomindang led the government's surveillance of the Chinese Hand Laundry Alliance and the *China Daily News.* These informants told the FBI that the newspaper continued to provide favorable publicity to Communist causes, and they reported that the Chinese Youth Club in New York was a "pro-Communist organization" controlled by members of the Chinese Hand Laundry Alliance and the *China Daily News.*[64]

As soon as the INS had secured the endorsement of the FBI, it developed its own network of informants in the hope of detecting subversive activity. According to an official policy memorandum sent by Raymond F. Farrell, assistant commissioner of the service's Investigations Division, on May 19, 1955, INS informants included "former or present members of a proscribed or questionable organization," persons who "have not been members of subversive organizations" but "are in possession of information relating to such organizations or members," and "individuals who have knowledge of operations involving smuggling of aliens, document fraud, or other matters within the jurisdiction of the Service."[65]

All FBI and INS informants were recruited by government officials.[66] Given the political nature of the investigations, it was not a secret that the informants were closely associated with the CCBA and the Guomindang.[67] In early 1951, the CCBA in the Washington, D.C., area called an anti-Communist meeting. Because a representative of the Kang Jai Association, Poon Yue-Taat, refused to sign the "Oppose Communism and Resist Russia" resolution, he was accused of being a Communist. In a police raid on the association shortly afterward, eighty-three Chinese were arrested and later were subject to deportation proceedings.[68]

Chinese Americans knew about the community power structure's involvement in the investigation of leftist groups, and the CCBA might have used the government to show that it indeed had the power to make its opponents miserable. Most informants, however, indicated to government agents that they did not wish to disclose their identities.[69] It was one thing to denounce a group as Communist or pro-Communist but quite another to turn in a fellow Chinese for prosecution. Given what Chinese Americans had gone through during the exclusion era, exposing one of their own to the INS for deportation under any circumstances would be considered immoral.

Both the FBI and the INS had their own systems to protect the identity of the informants. The FBI used the letter "T" as a symbol for its informants;[70] the INS assigned each informant a symbol number preceded by the office number and the letter "I."[71] Each INS informant had to fill out a G-169 form that included his name, his organizational affiliations, and the types of information about which he had knowledge. The identity of the informant, however, was never used in written reports.[72] The two informants who provided leads in one INS report, for example, were referred to as "source 1" and "source 2." On a separate administrative page, "source 1" was identified as "Informant SFO-14" and "source 2" as "Informant SFO-22." Informants remained unknown to one another, and each was in contact with only one field officer. Investigators sometimes contacted as many as seven informants to assure themselves of the accuracy of a particular piece of information. On the basis of the information an informant provided, government officials routinely evaluated his or her credibility. Most informants were first approached for tips concerning subversive activities, but once in the system, they were consulted for other information as well. Each time an informant was contacted, he would receive a stipend ($35 to $38) from the government.[73]

The presence of FBI and INS informants in the community created fear among Chinese Americans. Anyone could be a spy, and any community organization could be infiltrated. Informants seemed to be everywhere. The activities of the CWMAA were at one time covered by five FBI informants.[74] In the 1950s, some Min Qing members suspected that there were even spies inside that organization. After Min Qing was dissolved in 1959, a microphone was discovered in the library.[75] Him Mark Lai, who served as Min Qing's president for several years, was reluctant to believe that anyone in the group could have been a spy, and in fact there was no proof, but suspicions created negative feelings among members. If no one inside was spying, however, how could the FBI have gained access to the group's news bulletin, its library records, its mailing lists, and the minutes of every meeting? How could the bureau have taped conversations among group members?[76]

The network of government informants among Chinese Americans made it possible for investigators to keep a close eye on community activities and line up targets. In November 1956 an informant reported that Chinese passports were being forged in Helena, Montana, by one Fred Wong.

Investigators immediately contacted the local post office and without further cause placed a thirty-day check on all mail moving to and from this address.[77]

Informants were sometimes also used to help the government narrow down an investigation. When investigators seized the telephone records of Henry Goon, a Canadian restauranteur who was suspected of smuggling illegal immigrants into the United States, they found that Goon had twice called William Chang, a restaurant accountant in New York.[78] Chang, his employer, and his co-workers were subsequently questioned. After several informants stated that they knew nothing about Chang's involvement in the matter and that as far as they knew he was not a member of any leftist organization, the INS decided to drop this part of the investigation.[79] Another anonymous source led the INS to investigate Albert Chow in San Francisco for the involvement of his law firm in providing fraudulent documents. A former Guomindang deputy chief in the United States, Chow had a reputation as an anti-Communist and was identified as such by informants who watched for subversive activities. The INS thus decided that no investigation was necessary.[80]

The consulate in Hong Kong also hired informants among the Chinese. These people provided background information regarding immigration applicants and furnished the consul with maps of the emigrant areas and information regarding village populations and associated clans. These sources were used to verify each applicant's claims.

As early as 1952, Gilbert Woo had become seriously concerned about the ways the Chinese dealt with immigration issues. "The situation is different now," he said in an editorial in the *Chinese Pacific Weekly*. Under the "systematic investigation" being undertaken with the cooperation of Chinese informants, "trouble" was only "a matter of time."[81]

The Community under Investigation

The collaboration of some Chinese Americans with the government's investigation dealt a deadly blow to leftist organizations. Many Chinese American workers, intellectuals, and young people at first believed that they had the right to organize and express their political views. But although it was difficult for the FBI to obtain sufficient evidence to bring espionage charges against all those who had been blacklisted, immigration authorities could easily intimidate Chinese American liberals and make their lives miserable. Investigators knocked on the doors of Chinese Americans and stopped

15. Officials of the Immigration and Naturalization Service conducting an investigative search on the streets of Seattle's Chinatown during the Chinese Confession Program. *Courtesy of the Immigration and Naturalization Service.*

them on the street, asking about their immigration history and demanding to see their papers. In January 1956 investigator Yarbrough led a special search squad to the Asian Shirt Press Company in Brooklyn, New York, after he learned that the owner of the laundry, a paper son, was a member of the Chinese Hand Laundry Alliance and had advertised in the *China Daily News*.[82]

This investigation and that of many other laundrymen caused the membership of the Chinese Hand Laundry Alliance to drop sharply from two thousand to several hundred in the early 1950s. By May 1956, when U.S. assistant attorney general William F. Thompkins pushed to place the CWMAA in San Francisco on the attorney general's list under Executive Order 10450, the association had already ceased operation.[83]

Many Min Qing members were harassed by the INS officials, and several were arrested. Born in the United States, Him Mark Lai felt that he knew his rights as an American citizen, and he believed that Min Qing did not violate any U.S. law. Immigration authorities, nevertheless, would not leave him alone. They learned that his father-in-law was a paper son, and they went after Him Mark's wife, Laura (Jung) Lai, and members of her family. The couple would never forget the day that INS investigators knocked on their door. Laura's father left the United States under the pressure. As a result of the investigation, she and her brothers lost their citizenship.[84]

The appetite of the INS, however, was for far more than the relatively small number of Chinese Americans who were sympathetic to the Communist movement in China. Under the pretense of searching for possible Communist agents, investigators prowled the streets of Chinatowns in San Francisco, Chicago, Boston, New York, Seattle, and other cities, questioning suspected paper family members and ringleaders. They searched Chinese residences and raided business establishments. On March 1, 1956, police arrested seventeen men and three women in San Francisco's Chinatown on gambling charges. After they were released on bail, immigration agents again took them into custody for interrogation.[85]

A major breakthrough for the INS came after various Chinese were coerced into admitting false claims. On November 28, 1952, Dorris Yarbrough approached Chin Guey Yen, the alleged father of a section 503 plaintiff, Chin Quon Chuck, at a restaurant. Chin Guey Yen was later arrested for attempting to bribe the officer. Frightened, Chin Guey Yen admitted that he had entered the United States as an imposter. His son's real name, he said, was Hom Quon Chuck, and the other two sons whom he had claimed were fictitious.[86] Such confessions exposed a number of professionals who had provided immigrants with legal assistance in the New York area, including lawyers Tom Yuen, Samuel B. Waterman, and Samuel Bernstein; brokers Sing Kee, Wing On Wo, Wilbur Pyn, Eng Bik Shan, and Frank Toy; and notary public Louis S. Treglia.[87] Investigators also suspected that Eng Win On, an INS interpreter in Newark, and several private doctors who administered blood tests for the Chinese were involved in the fraud.[88] It seemed to the immigration authorities that most of the section 503 petitioners had gone to these professionals for false documents.

The INS then organized the section 503 cases into family groups and opened all related immigration files for examination. Reviewing 175 civil action cases filed in the Southern District of New York, the government looked for a pattern in which professionals worked with each other and in which false documents were created.[89] Judge Goodman believed that most of those involved in the fraud claimed to have been born in villages that could not be located on available maps, and that they claimed birth on selected dates that were easy to memorize.[90]

In San Francisco, to prove the government's cases, INS investigators accompanied local law enforcement officers serving subpoenas to family associations.[91] They felt that the Chinese would seek membership in those family associations to which they were linked by true parentage, and they hoped to find suspects in the associations' group pictures. Investigators then planned to check the family associations' records against those who claimed citizenship under different names.[92] Blood-test records of Chinese clients were also subpoenaed from private doctors.[93]

This was a time of despair for Chinese Americans but one of triumph for the INS. The service had never been so successful. Before a Chinese person's case was brought to court, the investigators would already have obtained leads from informants or other sources and pressed individuals into confessing.[94] Once the trial began, the entire paper family would be exposed. The judges had little sympathy toward the Chinese. For the first time, people were convicted because they had given false testimony in court.[95] The investigation of William W. Fong, for example, triggered an investigation of the entire Yee paper clan following the confessions of several family members. Four out of the five indicted were convicted, and deportation proceedings were filed against thirteen members of the paper clan. Another twenty people in China who had been established on paper as part of the clan were no longer eligible to apply for nonquota visas or U.S. passports.[96]

The situation drove Chinese Americans away from Chinatowns. Restaurants, formerly crowded on weekends, were now empty, and family associations canceled their annual New Year's banquets. Most people were afraid of being caught in a raid and being brought in for questioning. At stake was not only their safety but that of their relatives and friends. A curious white reporter visited a business office in New York's Chinatown. As he entered, two Chinese customers who had been waiting to be served got up and left. Later another man walked in. As soon as he saw the reporter, he turned and hurried away.[97] "This is worse than the Exclusion Act of 1882," said one Chinese to a news reporter about the grand jury probe in San Francisco.[98]

As the investigation drew closer to the heart of the community in early 1956, the CCBA became increasingly uneasy over the situation. The government had successfully linked the immigration network to the Communist invasion, but charges were brought against Chinese Americans regardless of their political affiliation. The grand jury summoned more than twenty-six Chinese American civic organizations to San Francisco for hearings, and the CCBA was one of them.[99] At one point even the Nationalist government in Taiwan was suspected of providing documents to agents of the Communist government in China.[100] Alarmed by these sensational stories of Communist infiltration, many Americans were convinced that it was necessary for the government to pursue every Chinese resident in its effort to crack down on immigration fraud.

The leaders of the community power structure perhaps regretted that they had once brought in government forces to oppress their opponents, for allegations were now being made against them as well. Wu Lim Gee, a former secretary of the CCBA, was reported to the INS as a pro-Communist. Several other CCBA officials were alleged to be involved in narcotics dealings as well as immigration fraud.[101] One report to the INS indicated that Chen Ping Ling, president of the Fujian Benevolent Association, was a "habitual gambler, excessive liquor user, and frequenter of brothels."[102] The government also investigated the status of prominent officials of the Nationalist government in the United States and examined the documents of their staff and servants.[103] If the government probe had been pursued further, few Chinese Americans could have survived, for most of them were involved with the immigration networks in one way or another.

Fearful, some organizations tried to create new systems to combat the investigation. In Washington, D.C., the CCBA reportedly held meetings and decided to "create new family associations and other Chinese records" to "conceal" any illegal operations and to destroy records that might be used against the Chinese.[104] The CCBA in Boston was reported to have hired a man who visited Chinese businesses in the area to ask Chinese Americans to remove their names from their true family associations and register in associations corresponding to their paper names. The INS was watching through its informants, however, and any information it received regarding such efforts was immediately forwarded to both the FBI and the CIA.[105] The rapidly changing situation makes clear how awkward and messy the community power structure's bid for control had become.

"We Should Not Act Like 'a Plate of Loose Sand'"

No evidence of espionage was ever used against any of the Chinese who were indicted. All the criminal charges had been founded on false testimony or violation of immigration laws. To the great advantage of the INS, the criminal courts were dealing with illegal entry cases, which did not follow the service's administrative procedures. The criminal courts were more powerful than the INS, and they were more intimidating to the Chinese.

Since the late 1940s, when the political conflict intensified among community groups, Chinese Americans had not had immigration lawyers residing in Washington to work on legislative reform. The grand jury probes of the mid-1950s hit the unprepared community hard, creating an emergency situation that compelled Chinese Americans to rethink their priorities. Community groups were once again urged to work together and build a united front.[106]

Given that most leftist community groups were by then crippled, the CCBA seized the opportunity to reassert its leadership. The CCBA in New York had lost many followers since it had collaborated with the FBI to attack leftist groups in the early 1950s. Responding to the grand jury subpoena of membership lists of family associations in San Francisco, it reemerged as a community voice. On March 3, 1956, the CCBA called a meeting of all Chinese American organizations to pledge support to Chinese Americans in San Francisco. It also established an immigration committee and asked all Chinese Americans to file grievances with the CCBA. Shing-tai Liang, the CCBA's new president, called the grand jury actions discriminatory, and he urged Chinese Americans to fight back and send telegrams of protest to the government. In an open message to all Chinese Americans and their organizations on March 8, the CCBA stated that since the association was the highest authority in the Chinese American community, it had the responsibility for relieving the suffering of all community members and protecting their security.[107]

Within days, the CCBA in New York communicated with Chinese American organizations throughout the United States in an effort to coordinate their actions. Letters in which the government's actions were compared to those of the anti-Chinese movement of earlier decades were sent to members of Congress. In a letter to H. Alexander Smith, a Republican senator from New Jersey, Shing-tai Liang said that "law-abiding Chinese here and in other cities are disturbed over short-noticed, discriminatory and sweeping summonses which are interrupting normal commerce, community well-being and lawful activities of individuals."[108]

Through the media, the CCBA began its negotiations with the government. It argued that a mass inquisition would only give Chinese Communists excuses to spread propaganda about racial discrimination and the anti-Chinese movement in the United States.[109] If its purpose was to weed out Communists, the government should cooperate with Chinese American organizations or allow the community to deal with the problem by itself. Shing-tai Liang said that he felt the people of the Chinatowns could handle any Red agent. "There are few secrets in Chinatown. . . . We are sure that we can straighten out those who have listened too long and too well to Communist authorities."[110]

The CCBA's actions were fully supported by the community press, which saw the notion of Communist infiltration through immigration simply as an excuse for the government to pursue all Chinese Americans. If the Communists indeed wanted to take over the United States, Wu Jingfu of the *Chinese American Weekly* reasoned, why would they invest in a group of youngsters who could speak no English and had no knowledge of America? The editor pointed out that the propaganda machine, which connected Communist subversion to Chinese immigration, was most damaging to the community, for the American people were being led to think that all Chinese were possible Communist spies. Chinese Americans should protest the grand jury's mixing Communist activities with immigration issues. The grand jury should be required to report exactly how many Chinese came as Communist spies after all the cases were closed. "Only in doing so," the editor said, would "democracy be expressed."[111] Gilbert Woo, in the *Chinese Pacific Weekly*, also strongly advocated collective action: "When the entire Chinese community is being illegally targeted and harassed, how could we, as U.S. citizens, not stand up and resist? If we don't, would there be any self-respect left?"[112]

Voices of protest also came from the Nationalist government in Taiwan, the press in Hong Kong, and other overseas Chinese communities. *Hsing Tao Hin Pao*, a pro-Taiwan newspaper in Hong Kong, argued that since the Communists had been in power on the mainland for only five years, their agents could not have been infiltrating the United States for long. It would be enough for the American government to investigate only the new arrivals. "The government of Hong Kong and the government of the Republic of China are only too willing to co-operate with the U.S. and assist in the investigation," said the paper. "There is no need to order a blanket investigation of all Chinese in the United States."[113] Facing a similar investigation, the Chinese Canadian community in Vancouver acknowledged that the harsh immigration regulations were forcing otherwise law-abiding Chinese in Canada to act illegally, and stated that legislative reform was the only way to end this problem.[114]

Responding to the protests, several members of Congress questioned the government's involvement in handling Chinese immigration cases. Democratic congressman John F. Shelley of California, who had been endorsed by San Francisco's Chinatown Voter's League during his campaign in 1952, was among the first to act.[115] Shelley also paid a special visit to the American consulate in Hong Kong and questioned the manner in which the consulate carried out its investigations. He argued that some of the measures taken by the government seemed to smack of Gestapo tactics, citing reports that the Department of Justice had seized rosters of the Chinese associations without proper authorization and that the INS had rounded up Chinese in San Francisco and required them to furnish proper documentation.[116]

The government was thus pressured to justify its behavior to the public. In a press conference held in New York, U.S. district attorney Paul Williams said that the work of his office was not a general investigation of all Chinese, and he stated that his office had no intention of subpoenaing either the Chinese organizations or their files and records.[117] The government stated that it was only trying to catch recent entrants from Red China who were up to no good. To Chinese Americans who had exclusion freshly in mind, such explanations sounded very suspicious. The newcomers might be from Red China, but if the government gave asylum to people who had escaped from behind the Iron Curtain in Europe, why couldn't it extend the same privilege to the Chinese?

At the same time, the CCBA asked Chinese Americans to remain calm and seek solutions within the law. Board members studied the immigration laws, and they told community members that the immigration regulations were so convoluted that violations were not uncommon.[118] Godfrey Schmidt, the CCBA's legal advisor, informed Chinese Americans through the press of their basic constitutional rights. He said that neither a citizen nor an alien had to answer any questions posed by government officials. One could refuse to answer simple questions such as "What is your name?" or "Where do you live?" until an attorney had been consulted.[119]

The CCBA also stated that every necessary step would be taken to fight the court battles, and every victory in court was reported as the result of unity under its leadership.[120] On March 20, 1956, the CCBA in San Francisco won a court motion when district judge Oliver H. Carter ruled that subpoenaing the records of every family association would be "unreasonable."[121] On April

4, 1956, government officials seized photographs from a Chinese photo shop in New York. After the CCBA's lawyers filed a protest at the district attorney's office, all the photographs were returned.[122] Thus the CCBA regained its position as the voice of the community.

Both the INS and the American consul in Hong Kong defended the government investigations. The INS argued that only alleged citizens were investigated and that the purpose of the investigation was to uncover and stop illegal Chinese immigration.[123] Noticing that Chinese Communist or pro-Communist newspapers in Hong Kong paid little attention to the issue, Drumright suggested that the PRC probably feared that its protest might make the American public more concerned with the security aspect of the problem and therefore bring to an end "a system full of present and potential value" to the Communists.[124]

Government officials could not, however, ignore the fact that the initial cause of the widespread fraud in Chinese immigration was a reaction to the Chinese exclusion. Investigator Yarbrough wrote that "they [the Chinese] considered the Act[s] evil, and anything they could do to overcome such evil was proper. In fact, an honest Chinese, otherwise ethical in his personal and business transactions, would not hesitate to use fraudulent means to enable an alien Chinese to enter the United States."[125] The consul in Hong Kong also reported that Chinese applicants felt no "moral twinges" about "gain[ing] documentation illegally since they consider U.S. immigration laws unfair and anti-Chinese."[126] Moreover, so many Chinese had been involved in illegal immigration activities that both the INS and the consul knew that it would be impossible for the government to investigate every case and press charges against all of those involved.

In the early 1950s the INS had pushed some Chinese Americans to confess. Through meetings held in Chinatowns in large cities, investigators had told their subjects that should they be aliens, not citizens as reflected in the records, they might be eligible for an adjustment of status according to the Immigration and Naturalization Act of 1952 if they cooperated.[127] Successful criminal proceedings against some Chinese were often made possible after investigators secured confessions from other members of the Chinese American community, and in exchange for information, the INS sometimes adjusted the status of confessors who subsequently appeared as government witnesses.[128]

Seeking cooperation from Chinese Americans and at the same time making itself look good, the INS began to advertise the so-called Confession Program in mid-1956. No official policy or guidelines were issued at the time; instead, the program was announced through "informal and unwritten publicity" to civic leaders and Chinese Americans. Under this program, Chinese who in the past had fraudulently established U.S. citizenship were advised to come forward, and they were told that the Immigration and Nationality Act of 1952 would allow some of them to adjust their status.[129] Every effort was made to convince Chinese Americans that they were the ones who could gain from the program.

As part of its internal policy, the INS tried to make the Confession Program as ambiguous as possible. The government said in public that it had "no desire to entrap" Chinese Americans, although immigration authorities never promised favorable action to any prospective confessors.[130] The Chinese were told only that they should seriously consider the relief available and secure adjustment of status prior to further proceedings, which gave the impression that confessors would have more to gain than to lose. In a memo to the regional chief of investigations, the service's assistant commissioner of the Investigations Division pointed out that a "wider application" of the program would be "beneficial to the Service." The commissioner was particularly satisfied, noting with "approval" that his staff had not made "promises of immunity from prosecution or commitments that discretionary relief will be granted," and he reiterated "every medium is used to advise Chinese in the United States regarding the possibilities of adjustment under the law."[131]

Because there was no written policy, the INS was able to decide arbitrarily whom it would allow to stay and whom it would deport. Ralph E. Stanley, an INS investigator in San Francisco, wrote in late 1956, "It must be admitted that there have been cases wherein this Service has ultimately found it necessary to institute deportation proceedings against Chinese, even though they had appeared as government witnesses in criminal proceedings involved other Chinese."[132]

The INS used grand jury investigation as a threat to press Chinese to participate in the program. The agents approached individuals based on leads from informants, anonymous sources, and letters and coaching materials seized by government agencies.[133] Should they persist in the fraudulent pattern, the Chinese were told that they might ultimately involve themselves and their family members in criminal charges.[134]

Chinese American veterans from the U.S. armed forces, who were eligible for relief under the law, were seen by the INS as easy prey. One lead from the consulate in Hong Kong, for example, indicated that Lew Bok Yin, who had established himself as a native-born U.S. citizen by means of a habeas corpus proceeding in 1902, had been born in China. The INS records revealed that seventeen persons had gained entry as Lew's sons and grand-sons and their wives. In addition, the family had claimed another seventeen members in China and Hong Kong as being eligible for nonquota status. Immigration authorities suspected that some members of the family were not Lew's descendants. To prove their cases, investigators approached several family members who had served in World War II or the Korean War. The veterans were told that they were eligible for relief according to the law and would not be in danger of deportation if they told the truth. The entire family eventually went to the INS office and made full confessions.[135]

The group confession of the Lew family could hardly be seen as voluntary, for the family members could no longer conceal their identities. Chinese Americans well understood the disturbing and terrifying experiences that the veteran members of the Lew family had gone through. They not only had to reverse their own early sworn testimonies, but also had to provide information that would put relatives and friends in jeopardy. Two members of the Lew family were faced with deportation proceedings as the result. The process to receive relief was also convoluted. The veterans were naturalized first, but their wives had to wait until the husbands' status was adjusted before they could attempt to adjust their legal status under 8 CFR 235 of the act. Other family members had to seek relief under section 244.[136] Most damaging to the family was that once the members admitted their fraud, they gave up the hope of bringing in family members who were still in China. All the slots that they had created on paper would be closed.

The INS gave considerable publicity to the war veterans of the Lew family when they were naturalized in 1956 under the provisions of section 329 of the 1952 Immigration and Naturalization Act. Each time a group of Chinese veterans was naturalized, the INS would furnish a press release to the Chinese American community.[137] The government tried to advertise what it called the humanitarian aspect of the program, that is, to free those otherwise law-abiding persons from the constant pressure of living with a lie, while its obvious purpose was to "terminate permanently the machinery which facilitated a steady influx of illegal aliens."[138] The Chinese community press printed these news releases verbatim, but no attempt was made to elaborate upon the Confession Program, and neither the CCBA nor the press called upon Chinese Americans to participate in it.

Chinese Americans soon came to realize that they could not trust the INS despite its honeyed words and oblique promises. The Immigration and Naturalization Act of 1952 subjected aliens who entered the United States by fraud to deportation, and even though an amendment passed on September 11, 1957, provided that such a person might be granted permanent U.S. residency if he or she admitted the commission of such a perjury, this required the consent of the attorney general.[139] Although the Chinese were pushed to admit perjury and fraud, the INS would not promise its forgiveness for such criminal offenses, which were prerequisite for the Chinese to receive the discretionary relief.[140]

As it turned out, some confessors brought disaster upon their own families. In late 1955, acting on an FBI request, the INS investigated Lee Ying, the co-owner of the World Theater in San Francisco. The FBI had received information that the theater was an outlet for Artkino, a company that imported movies from Russia and China, and that it had sponsored benefits for newspapers and organizations that were listed as Communist or pro-Communist. Lee Ying had entered the United States as a paper son of Hui Suey (Fong Suey). Under pressure, Hui Suey admitted that Lee Ying was really his son-in-law. The confession implicated other family members who had made false claims, including Hui Suey's wife, his two sons, and his daughter. Although Hui Suey had cooperated fully with the investigators, he could not protect his family. A week after his father-in-law testified, Lee Ying was arrested and his home searched. The arrest warrant charged that he did not possess a valid immigration visa. On January 30, 1957, the grand jury in San Francisco filed four criminal indictments against him for document fraud and giving false testimony.[141] Lee Ying admitted his guilt and left the United States.[142]

The case of Lee Ying reflected another internal INS policy, which held that no relief would be granted to a person who had been investigated by another government agency.[143] While this policy was especially effective in punishing leftist Chinese Americans, it did not guarantee that other members of the community would not be targeted.

The fear of prosecution haunted Chinese Americans who had never violated any laws other than those related to immigration. On September 24, 1956, Poon Bok Shing of San Francisco wrote a confession for INS officials, admitting that he and Poon Gon On had gained entry as sons of natives, although they were in fact sons of citizens of China. The circumstances under which Poon Bok Shing confessed are unclear, but the humiliation, the realization that he had committed perjury and some fraud, and the guilt over betraying a friend were so overwhelming that Poon Bok Shing took his own life that same day. Agents later requested full relief for Poon Gon On.[144]

To escape any contact with INS investigators, many Chinese changed their addresses and telephone numbers, and some closed down their businesses.

Shirley Wong, born in San Francisco in 1949, recalled years of living in fear while her parents and relatives tried to hide from immigration authorities. Investigators eventually found her father in 1962 and pressed him and his wife to confess.[145] According to Shirley's mother-in-law, Mary Yee, everyone was scared at the time. Mary's husband, Eddie, was a paper son, and although he was a World War II veteran and therefore eligible for relief, he knew that telling the truth might result in the deportation of his relatives. Eddie confessed when his paper family was exposed in 1962.[146]

Even for those who were confident of getting relief, confessing would make their lives more complicated. In a letter to the *Chinese American Weekly* in 1960, a woman expressed fear upon learning that immigration authorities had obtained her name and her whereabouts from her paper father. "I am so scared," she said. "Should I go confess?"[147] The woman had been in the United States for more than twenty years, but because her husband, the son of a merchant, was not a citizen when they married and was therefore not qualified to buy property, all family assets had been purchased under her name. Even if relief were granted, it would take at least three years for her to be naturalized. What would happen to her family property then? What could the government do if she did not cooperate with the INS?[148]

Editor Wu Jingfu encouraged the woman to go forward. He said that since she had lived in the United States for twenty years and her husband and children were all citizens, deportation would be unlikely. Given that she had come as a minor, she might also be able to demonstrate that she had not understood what she had done.[149] Once a family was under investigation, cooperating with the government seemed to be the only solution. Many slots would be closed, but it was hoped that the individuals already in the United States would be able to stay; people simply had to make the best of the grave situation. If there was an unwritten internal principle among the Chinese Americans faced with the Confession Program, it was to go forward only when they could no longer hide.

The Confession Program, which encouraged Chinese Americans to testify against one another, had a mixed impact on many families. The program led to mistrust among family members, tearing some families apart. Jat Fang Lew, a member of the Lew clan who entered as a paper grandson of Lew Chuck Suey (see chapter two), confessed in 1962, pointing INS investigators to his paper father and brothers. To this day, members of the Lew family consider Jat Fang Lew's confession unwise and unnecessary, and he declined to be interviewed.[150] But to some extent, the investigation also brought family members together. Few individuals acted alone. Once there was any indication that the INS was after a certain person, the person would immediately notify everyone in his family. The entire family would then consult a lawyer and go to confess together. In 1962 Maurice Chuck, the Min Qing member who had written for the *China Daily News*, was indicted for making a false statement to obtain a certificate of citizenship in 1954. The INS brought Hwong Jack Hong, Chuck's father, to court to testify against him. They shared a hotel room during the trial. For the first time, father and son had long, emotional talks. After Chuck was sent to jail, it was Hwong Jack Hong who helped Chuck's wife get through the difficult time.[151]

As the INS used court charges to intimidate Chinese Americans and tried to force them to leave the country, it confronted persistent resistance.[152] In 1961, following a lead from a relative's confession, the INS filed criminal charges against Dear Kai Gay, a member of Min Qing who had entered the United States in 1933 as a paper son. Dear Kai Gay was convicted on three charges, including knowingly making a false representation of a matter within the jurisdiction of a U.S. agency. After his jail sentence was set, the INS reduced it to six months on the condition that he would leave the United States.[153] Using what were described as "voluntary" departure cases, the service tried to demonstrate that it was sending Chinese people back to China to be with their families.[154]

By then, however, many of those who were on the deportation list had already established families in the United States. Leaving the country meant that a married man like Dear Kai Gay would have to part from his wife and children and gave up the right to return. In an effort to block or delay forced deportations, lawyers for the Chinese deportees pooled information, evidence, and witnesses to claim that their clients would be physically threatened and persecuted if they were deported to China. Even though the INS believed that only those who had been affiliated with the Nationalist government or who had opposed the Communist regime would face such dangers, it failed to establish a case in court to prove it was safe for most Chinese to go back to China.[155] The INS then tried to deport some Chinese to Taiwan, but since many of those targeted were sympathizers of the PRC, it was difficult to prove they would not face persecution by the Nationalist government.[156] Dear Kai Gay appealed. A year later, the judge for the Ninth Circuit Court of Appeals declared the sentence "cruel and unusual." Such a punishment, the judge ruled, was unconstitutional, and the district court was ordered to resentence him according to the law.[157]

*W*hen Gilbert Woo called for an end to the community's preoccupation with China politics and asked Chinese Americans to get involved in political reform in the United States in the late 1940s, not many people listened. His friends thought that he was being intimidated; supporters of the Nationalist government accused him of being pro-Communist. In 1951, after the Kang Jai Association was raided by the police, one reader wrote to the *China Daily News*, urging a "united action of all of the Chinese."[158] At that time, however, the Guomindang-controlled CCBA was still eager to exterminate all leftist groups. In the midst of the government's investigation into immigration fraud, the CCBA finally called for united action. The Guomindang's mouthpiece, the *Chinese Journal*, told Chinese Americans that they "should not act like 'a plate of loose sand' [*yipan sansha*]," for everyone's life would be affected if the government were able to use the investigation to further restrict Chinese immigration.[159]

The investigation of immigration fraud in the 1950s also compelled the Chinese American community to find new ways to deal with discriminatory government policies: their old strategy of circumventing immigration laws was no longer working. During the exclusion era, many Chinese Americans believed that making China strong would be the key to improving their status in the United States. Now it was clear that neither the PRC nor the government on Taiwan could protect them.

In March 1957 the CCBA in New York called a national conference. One hundred and twenty-four Chinese American representatives from thirty-four cities throughout the United States gathered in Washington, D.C.[160] A few participants proposed that the thrust of the conference should be anti-Communist and pro-Taiwan, but it soon became clear that such an agenda would go nowhere. Chinese American journalists put pressure on the conference organizers. Gilbert Woo wrote:

> If some people enjoy a conference on [China] politics, let them go. I strongly advise all citizens of the United States not to be involved. . . . For decades, involvement in China's political struggle has caused endless conflict in the Chinese American community and brought about zero benefit. . . . If the primary purpose of this conference is a political power struggle rather than an attempt to benefit the entire community, our delegation should withdraw and hold a conference of its own. If they are too myopic to see the harm, why should we follow them down this path?[161]

Seeing that they had few followers, the organizers shifted the focus of the conference and passed resolutions to lobby Congress for immigration reform.[162] This meant not that the CCBA had finally decided to relinquish its involvement in the political struggle between the PRC and Taiwan, but that the majority of Chinese Americans had decided that they did not want to be manipulated by a few community leaders, and that they wanted to exercise their political power to secure the protections provided by the U.S. Constitution.

Once again, legislative reform on immigration brought Chinese Americans together, and the Chinese American Citizens Alliance again played an active role working together with CCBA and other community organizations. Throughout the late 1950s and early 1960s, the Chinese American community had its lobbyists stationed in Washington, D.C., working together with other Asian American groups. A great effort was made to amend the McCarran-Walter Act of 1952, which retained the national origins quota system of 1924. Both the CCBA and the CACA especially urged their members to vote and write to their representatives in Congress to draw attention to the interests of the Chinese American community.[163]

Although relatively few deportation proceedings went through, the INS viewed the Confession Program as one of its greatest accomplishments. Paper families were rooted out one after another, and the number of slots closed was featured in the service's annual report between 1957 and 1965.[164] It was indeed an impressive record for the INS: 13,895 Chinese participated in the program, leading to the exposure of 22,083 persons and the closing of 11,294 slots.[165]

The success of legislative reform in the late 1950s and early 1960s would require a reevaluation of the Confession Program. The 1965 Immigration Act, signed into law by President Lyndon B. Johnson in front of the Statue of Liberty on October 3, repealed the Asian-Pacific triangle provisions of the 1924 Immigration Act. Instead of requiring quotas based on racial ancestry, as was provided by the 1943 repeal act, the new law used place of birth to determine an immigrant's country of origin, and a new system was established to grant each country the same immigration quota. The act also provided special protection for the family unit, allowing American citizens' immediate relatives, including their children, spouses, and parents, to come outside the quota limit, and gave quota preference to their other relatives.[166] The new law changed the outlook of Chinese immigration entirely. Many Chinese Americans, paradoxically, now found that their participation in the Confession Program enabled them to claim immediate family members and other relatives in China using their true identities.

On February 2, 1966, the INS decided that it would no longer solicit confessions. The service could not, however, reject Chinese Americans who wanted to confess voluntarily in order to take full advantage of the new immigration act.[167] Under the new domestic and international political climate of the late 1960s, the government finally decided that "no special treatment is to be given to aliens of that nationality [the Chinese] not accorded to all others."[168]

Epilogue

꙯ꙮ꙯

*I*n 1951, after the founding of the People's Republic of China, Him Mark Lai quit his job at the Utilities Engineering Bureau in San Francisco and made plans to go to China, the ancestral land he had never set foot on. Young, energetic, and idealistic, he wished to devote his future to the building of a new China. He even removed his name from the deeds of his family property, which he would have been entitled to inherit. He could not get a visa, however. Instead, Him Mark went on to graduate school and continued his career as an engineer in the United States.[1]

Some Chinese American liberals did manage to go to China. Among them were Tang Mingzhao of the *China Daily News*; Cai Fujiu, editor of the *China Weekly*; Tan Lian'ai, a former English secretary for New York's Chinese Hand Laundry Alliance, and several of his fellow members; and seventeen members of Min Qing.[2] Some young Chinese Americans who had been attending college or training programs in China also decided to stay. Few realized at the time that they would not be able to see their families and friends in the United States again until some twenty years later.

For several generations, the Chinese community in America had been longing for a strong, independent, and prosperous China, a country that for the past century had been humiliated, divided, and exploited by foreign powers and suffered from wars, famine, and corrupt governments. Many Chinese Americans believed that the discriminatory treatment against Chinese in the United States was a reflection of a weak China, and some found the ideals of the new Chinese government, such as gender equality and Mao's philosophy "to serve the people," refreshing and inspiring. Some developments in China were in fact encouraging: early period land reform gave land to poor peasants, and more educational and employment opportunities were opened to both men and women. There were disturbing developments in China as well, however. Between 1950 and 1953 the land reform movement was often carried out harshly in rural areas, and the government confiscated land and other property from landowners. Because of China's limited investment opportunities in the late 1940s, many family members of those who had immigrated to the United States had saved a considerable portion of the money sent by their U.S. relatives toward the purchase of land and real estate. Now they were among the landlords who were publicly humiliated and physically abused in the land reform; some were executed.[3] Investment from the Chinese living in the United States was no longer welcome in their ancestral homeland.

Beginning in the early 1950s and for more than two decades afterward, the China policy of the United States favored the Republic of China and opposed the People's Republic of China. The Guomindang exerted great effort in seeking American support and aid for Taiwan. Well-financed Nationalist Chinese officials and lobbyists were active in Washington, and a well-organized informal network of allies was formed to recruit sympathizers. Supporters of the Taiwan government worked together in a loosely organized confederation known as the China lobby. Wealthy and influential Americans, including textile importer Alfred Kohlberg, Time-Life publisher Henry Luce, and Pittsburgh industrialist Frederick McKee, were members of the group. With the support of senators and congressmen like Joseph McCarthy, Patrick McCarran, and Walter Judd (according to one scholar, Judd became "practically an honorary member" of the Guomindang),[4] the China lobby was able to secure U.S. assistance to Taiwan in an effort to overthrow Communism in China. At a time when support of Chiang Kai-shek's government was associated with loyalty to the United States, the Guomindang-backed Chinese American community establishment also mounted anti-Communist campaigns in Chinatowns throughout the United States.[5]

The United States recognized many Communist countries, including the Soviet Union, but not the People's Republic of China. China thus was no longer accessible to Americans. Chinese Americans lost touch with their family members in the villages. Trade with China stopped; products that were suspected to be of PRC origin were all intercepted. Many Chinese American businesses were forced to close down, especially those owned by people who were thought to be pro-PRC. U.S. customs agents cut off the supply of Chinese books of the Oasis Bookstore in San Francisco and forced it out of business in 1957. Some import/export companies had to shift to alternate routes via other Asian countries for Chinese goods.

For a few years after the outbreak of Korea War, the Chinese Workers Mutual Aid Association and other labor and youth groups, none connected with Chinese Communists, continued to meet and celebrate the anniversary of the founding of the PRC.[6] But under relentless harassment and threats by U.S. government agencies and pro-Guomindang forces, the membership of the CWMAA had dropped to about twenty by the time it disbanded in 1956.[7] Although Min Qing was still able to recruit some new immigrants by shifting to community-oriented programs, it too was forced to shut down in 1959 when the landlord refused to renew its lease. During this period of anti-Communist hysteria, nearly all alternative political voices were suppressed in the Chinese American community.[8]

After the dissolution of Min Qing, former members of the group set up the less formal Haiyan (Petrel) Club to study Chinese literature and organized a Chinese folk dance group. The Haiyan members met often in Him Mark and Laura Lai's garage, where books and materials from Min Qing were stored. Such community-oriented efforts to preserve Chinese culture and identity encouraged Chinese Americans to cultivate the notion that all Chinese living in the United States belonged to one social group.

Disengagement with China compelled many Chinese Americans to devote more energy toward the improvement of their own community. Their efforts became part of liberal and radical activism in the 1960. Inspired by the civil rights movement in the United States and by China's Great Proletarian Cultural Revolution that was sporadically reported in the American press, young rebellious Chinese American activists, along with their fellow Asian, black, Chicano, and white peers, participated in demonstrations for civil rights and against the Vietnam War. Many went to Chinatowns, where they strongly opposed the involvement of the Republic of China in community activities. When these young revolutionaries, Red Guards, erected the PRC's red national flag in San Francisco's Chinatown, leaders of the old community establishment did not dare to challenge them. Activists also engaged in debate over other issues facing the community. They demanded more allocation of government and community resources for social services to improve living and working conditions, and they opposed excessive promotion of commercial interests in the community. Many social agencies, health clinics, and bilingual educational programs for immigrants were established during this period, and many Chinese Americans from different persuasions participated in community reform. In 1968, a group of Chinese Americans formed the San Francisco Chinese Community Citizen's Survey and Fact Finding Committee. It identified areas for improvement, such as social services, health, housing, education, employment, and youth and cultural programs. Eventually more than three hundred Chinese Americans served as members of the committee or its subcommittees.[9]

Meanwhile some Chinese Americans began to research and write the history of their community. In 1963 the Chinese Historical Society of America was founded in San Francisco. A few years later, when Maurice Chuck, now the editor of a bilingual weekly newspaper, *East/West*, invited Him Mark Lai to write articles on Chinese American history, Him Mark began devoting himself to researching Chinese American history while still working full time as an engineer. His essays for *East/West* became part of one of the very first books on Chinese America.[10] Later, Him Mark Lai, Gilbert Woo, and several other intellectuals also taught classes and produced radio and television programs on the history of Chinese America. These activities laid the foundation for the field of Chinese American Studies.

The announcement of President Richard M. Nixon's visit to China in 1971 sent shock waves around the globe, and it was felt deeply in the Chinese American community.[11] In the early 1970s, after Nixon's visit to Beijing, many Chinese Americans traveled to China as soon as they were permitted to do so, at a time when the Cultural Revolution was far from over. Under the watchful eye of Chinese government officials, Him Mark Lai and other new visitors from the United States met with their relatives and old friends and saw Communist China firsthand. In Beijing, Gilbert Woo's daughters, Lucy and Nancy, had to get permission from their work units before meeting with him; they had not seen him for more than thirty years.[12] It took Jade Snow Wong and her husband a few weeks during their visit to locate her brother-in-law, Norman Ong, a World War II veteran who went to China in 1947 to study and who stayed there to train Chinese athletes. To her surprise, Norman, who was a physical education instructor at the Beijing University, had been working for years in rural Gansu Province with the peasants, hundreds of miles from his wife and children.[13] At least two Chinese Americans who returned to China after the founding of the PRC had committed suicide. Tan Lian'ai, the former English secretary for the Chinese Hand Laundry Alliance, killed himself during China's antirightist campaign in 1957, and a former Min Qing member also took his own life during the Cultural Revolution.[14] Archie Lee, a decorated U.S. pilot whose heroic actions during World War II in North China were well publicized and praised in both the United States and China, had a successful career as a Chinese civilian pilot in the 1950s and early 1960s. During the Cultural Revolution, however, both Archie and his wife were tortured in public and he was later sent to the desert of Inner Mongolia for reeducation.[15] The cruel reality of the period painfully shattered many Chinese Americans' long-held romantic notions about the new China.

In 1979 the United States and China established formal diplomatic relations, and after the Cultural Revolution China underwent radical political and economic reforms. Visits and exchanges between the two countries became more common and frequent. As China expanded its market economy, financial investments became more welcome than political support or sympathy. Many well-to-do Chinese American businessmen, who had once been staunch members of the anti-Communist camp, cut lucrative business deals with the PRC.

The enactment of the 1965 Immigration Act had brought to the United States a large number of new Chinese immigrants from the PRC, Taiwan, Hong Kong, and Southeast Asia. These new immigrants and their children became increasingly visible in colleges and universities and in business and professional ranks, both inside and outside Chinatowns. New Chinatowns were erected in the suburbs of large cities to meet the increasing demand for ethnic foods and services. In old Chinatowns in San Francisco, New York, and Los Angeles, one could still find buildings of traditional Chinese American family associations, district associations, the CCBA, and the CACA. The memberships of these organizations now included many post-1965 immigrants, some of whom served in important posts.

Today the annual celebration of the founding of the People's Republic of China is still a big event in the Chinese American community. In 1994, the organizing committee in San Francisco invited Cai Fujiu, the founder of the *China Weekly*, who had been living in Hong Kong since 1950. Forty-five years earlier, because of Cai's involvement in the celebration of the founding of the PRC, the Guomindang had offered a five-thousand-dollar reward for his death. Now he could walk on the streets of San Francisco without a bodyguard.[16]

Some participants in the PRC celebration parties on October 1, however, also go to the celebration of the founding of the Republic of China on the tenth of the same month. Flags of both the PRC and the ROC can be seen in Chinatowns these days, and many Chinese American enterprises conduct business with both mainland China and Taiwan. Most community newspapers have maintained a critical distance from the official government lines of both the PRC and the ROC, and they are now comfortable forming their own opinions without appealing to any governments in China. Over the decades, Chinese Americans across the political spectrum have realized that they are, before all else, Americans.

NOTES

Introduction

1. 59 Stat. 659, Act of Dec. 28, 1945; 60 Stat. 339, Act of June 29, 1946; 60 Stat. 975, Act of Aug. 9, 1946.
2. U.S. Bureau of the Census, *Sixteenth Census of the United States,* Population, 1940; U.S. Bureau of the Census, *United States Census of Population,* 1960: Nonwhite Population by Race, 4.
3. In the late nineteenth century, a large number of Chinese in the United States lived in agricultural regions and earned their living by farming. The urbanization of Chinese America, to a large extent, is the result of the anti-Chinese movement that swept the rural areas of western states. See Sucheng Chan, *This Bittersweet Soil: The Chinese in California Agriculture, 1860–1910* (Berkeley: University of California Press, 1986).
4. Roger Daniels, *Asian America: Chinese and Japanese in the United States since 1850* (Seattle: University of Washington Press, 1988), 68–69.
5. Stanford M. Lyman, "Conflict and the Web of Group Affiliation in San Francisco's Chinatown, 1850–1910," *Pacific Historical Review* 43:4 (November 1974): 473–499; idem, "The Structure of Chinese Society in Nineteenth Century America" (Ph.D. diss., University of California, Berkeley, 1961).
6. Sandy Lydon, *Chinese Gold: The Chinese in the Monterey Bay Region* (Capitola, Calif.: Capitola Book Company, 1985).
7. Victor G. Nee and Brett de Bary Nee, *Longtime Californ': A Documentary Study of an American Chinatown* (New York: Pantheon Books, 1972); Peter Kwong, *Chinatown, New York: Labor and Politics, 1930–1950* (New York: Monthly Review Press, 1979); Clarence E. Glick, *Sojourners and Settlers: Chinese Migrants in Hawaii* (Honolulu: University of Hawaii Press, 1980); Paul C. P. Sui, *The Chinese Laundryman: A Study of Social Isolation* (New York: New York University Press, 1987); Renqiu Yu, *To Save China, to Save Ourselves: The Chinese Hand Laundry Alliance of New York* (Philadelphia: Temple University Press, 1992); Judy Yung, *Unbound Feet: A Social History of Chinese Women in San Francisco* (Berkeley: University of California Press, 1995); idem, *Unbound Voices: A Documentary History of Chinese Women in San Francisco* (Berkeley:

University of California Press, 1999); Yong Chen, *Chinese San Francisco, 1850–1943: A Trans-Pacific Community* (Stanford: Stanford University Press, 2000).

8. See, for example, Peter Kwong, *The New Chinatown* (New York: Hill & Wang, 1987); Min Zhou, *Chinatown: The Socioeconomic Potential of an Urban Enclave* (Philadelphia: Temple University Press, 1992); Timothy P. Fong, *The First Suburban Chinatown: The Remaking of Monterey Park, California* (Philadelphia: Temple University Press, 1994); John Horton, *The Politics of Diversity: Immigration, Resistance, and Change in Monterey Park, California* (Philadelphia: Temple University Press, 1995).

9. On the concept of community, see Lyman, "Conflict and the Web of Group Affiliation"; William T. Rowe, *Hankow: Conflict and Community in a Chinese City, 1796–1895* (Stanford: Stanford University Press, 1989); Benedict Anderson, *Imagined Communities: Reflections on the Origin and Spread of Nationalism* (New York: Verso, 1991).

10. See Khachig Tölöyan, "The Nation State and Others: In Lieu of a Preface," *Diaspora* 1 (1991): 3–7. See also Madeline Yuan-yin Hsu, " 'Living Abroad and Faring Well': Migration and Transnationalism in Taishan County, Guangdong, 1904–1939" (Ph.D. diss., Yale University, 1996).

11. George Anthony Peffer, *If They Don't Bring Their Women Here: Chinese Female Immigration before Exclusion* (Urbana: University of Illinois Press, 1999).

12. Works by Charles J. McClain and Lucy E. Salyer provide examples of the importance of legal documents in the study of Chinese history. See McClain, *In Search of Equality: The Chinese Struggle against Discrimination in Nineteenth-Century America* (Berkeley: University of California Press, 1994); Salyer, *Laws Harsh as Tigers: Chinese Immigrants and the Shaping of Modern Immigration Law* (Chapel Hill: University of North Carolina Press, 1995).

13. Yung, *Unbound Feet*; idem, *Unbound Voices*. For other studies on Chinese women, see Peggy Pascoe, *Relations of Rescue: The Search for Female Moral Authority in the American West, 1874–1939* (New York: Oxford University Press, 1990); Benson Tong, *Unsubmissive Women: Chinese Prostitutes in Nineteenth-Century San Francisco* (Norman: University of Oklahoma Press, 1994). See also Lucie Cheng Hirata, "Free, Indentured, Enslaved: Chinese Prostitutes in Nineteenth-Century America," *Signs* 5: (Autumn 1979): 3–29; Xiaojian Zhao, "Chinese American Women Defense Workers in World War II," *California History* 75:2 (Summer 1996): 138–153, 182–184.

14. See, for example, Jenel Virden, *Good-bye, Piccadilly: British War Brides in America* (Urbana: University of Illinois Press, 1996); Bok Lim Kim, "Asian Wives of American Servicemen: Women in Shadows," *Amerasia Journal* 4:1 (1977): 91–95; Evelyn Nakano Glenn, *Issei, Nisei, War Bride: Three Generations of Japanese American Women in Domestic Service* (Philadelphia: Temple University Press, 1986). See also Regina Frances Lark, "They Challenged Two Notions: Marriage between Japanese Women and American GIs, 1945 to present" (Ph.D. diss., University of Southern California, 1999).

15. Anderson, *Imagined Communities*, 47–65.

16. These files were declassified on November 24, 1998. See chapter seven for details.

17. Serena Chen, "Special Report: A Look Back at the Chinese Confession Program," *East/West* 21:16 (Apr. 23, 1987).

CHAPTER 1 *The Struggle for Family Unification*

1. 43 Stat. 153, Act of May 26, 1924.
2. U.S. House of Representatives, *Admission of Wives of American Citizens of Oriental Ancestry: Hearings before the Committee on Immigration and Naturalization on H.R. 6544*, 69th Cong., 1st sess., 1926, 37, 42.
3. Before the Supreme Court handed down its decision in *Chang Chan et al. v. John Nagle* (268 U.S. 346) in 1925, the admissibility of Chinese wives of American citizens was determined by district court judges; their interpretations of the law sometimes contradicted one another. The court judges in California and Seattle denied entry to all Chinese wives of citizens, but a district court judge in Massachusetts ordered Chiu Shee, a citizen's Chinese wife, to be released to her husband. See *Ex parte Chiu Shee* (D.C.D. Mass.), 1 F. 798, 1924.
4. U.S. House of Representatives, *Admission of Wives of American Citizens of Oriental Ancestry*, 42.
5. 46 Stat. 581, Act of June 13, 1930.
6. Evelyn Nakano Glenn, "Split Household, Small Producer, and Dual Wage Earner: An Analysis of Chinese-American Family Strategies," *Journal of Marriage and the Family* 45:1 (Feb. 1983): 38; Peter S. Li, "Fictive Kinship, Conjugal Tie, and Kinship Chain among Chinese Immigrants in the United States," *Journal of Comparative Family Studies* 8:1 (Spring 1997): 47–63; Adam McKeown, "Transnational Chinese Families and Chinese Exclusion, 1875–1943," *Journal of American Ethnic History* 18 (Winter 1999): 73–110.
7. Judy Yung, *Unbound Feet: A Social History of Chinese Women in San Francisco* (Berkeley: University of California Press, 1995), 2; Madeline Yuan-yin Hsu, " 'Living Abroad and Faring Well': Migration and Transnationalism in Taishan County, Guangdong, 1904–1939" (Ph.D. diss., Yale University, 1996), 147; Erika Lee, "At America's Gates: Chinese Immigration during the Exclusion Era, 1882–1943" (Ph. D. diss., University of California, Berkeley, 1998), chap. 2.
8. Glenn, "Split Household," 38; Sucheng Chan, "The Exclusion of Chinese Women, 1870–1943," in *Entry Denied: Exclusion and the Chinese Community in America, 1882–1943*, ed. Sucheng Chan (Philadelphia: Temple University Press, 1991), 94–95.
9. George Anthony Peffer, *If They Don't Bring Their Women Here: Chinese Female Immigration before Exclusion* (Urbana: University of Illinois Press, 1999); idem, "Forbidden Families: Emigration Experiences of Chinese Women under the Page Law, 1875–1882," *Journal of American Ethnic History* 6:1 (Fall 1986), 28–47; Chan, "The Exclusion of Chinese Women," 105–109.
10. Elaine Kim, *Asian American Literature: An Introduction to the Writings and Their Social Context* (Philadelphia: Temple University Press, 1982), 119.
11. Chan, "The Exclusion of Chinese Women," 97–105.
12. 18 Stat. 477, Act of March 3, 1875.

13. Peffer, *If They Don't Bring Their Women Here*; idem, "The Forces Without: The Regulation of Chinese Female Immigration to America, 1852–1882" (Ph.D. diss., Carnegie-Mellon University, 1988); idem, "Forbidden Families," 28–47; Chan, "The Exclusion of Chinese Women," 105–109. Some historians have argued that the Page Law had only limited impact on Chinese immigration. See Mary Coolidge, *Chinese Immigration* (New York: Henry Holt, 1909), 498; Elmer Sandmeyer, *The Anti-Chinese Movement in California* (1939; repr. Chicago: University of Illinois Press, 1973), 52–53; Stanford M. Lyman, *Chinese Americans* (New York: Random House, 1974), 87; Lucie Cheng Hirata, "Free, Indentured, Enslaved: Chinese Prostitutes in Nineteenth-Century America," *Signs* 5:1 (Autumn 1979): 10; Benson Tong, *Unsubmissive Women: Chinese Prostitutes in Nineteenth-Century San Francisco* (Norman: University of Oklahoma Press, 1994), 47.

14. Peffer, *If They Don't Bring Their Women Here*, 43–56.

15. Helen Chen, "Chinese Immigration into the United States: An Analysis of Changes in Immigration Policies" (Ph.D. diss., Brandeis University, 1980), 201.

16. Chan, "The Exclusion of Chinese Women," 108.

17. 22 Stat. 58, Act of May 6, 1882.

18. Both immigration records and legal grievances filed by the Chinese suggest that laborers' wives were not barred until 1884.

19. 23 Stat. 115, Act of July 5, 1884.

20. *In re Ah Quan*, 21 F. 182 (C.C.D. Cal. 1884).

21. *Case of the Chinese Wife*, In re *Ah Moy*, 21 F. 785 (D. C. D. Cal. 1884). See also Chan "The Exclusion of Chinese Women," 110–112.

22. According to Chan, no case involving the wife of a Chinese laborer appeared in published legal documents after 1884. See Chan, "The Exclusion of Chinese Women," 112.

23. 22 Stat. 58, Act of May 6, 1882.

24. 25 Stat. 504, Act of Oct. 1, 1888.

25. 27 Stat. 25, Act of May 5, 1892.

26. 32 Stat. 176, Act of April 29, 1902.

27. 33 Stat. 428, Act of April 27, 1904.

28. One exclusionist report said it point-blank that such laws were necessary to stop the influx of Chinese immigration so that "gradually, by voluntary departures, death from sickness, accident, or old age, . . . [the Chinese] race may be eliminated from this country"; quoted in Charles J. McClain, *In Search of Equality: The Chinese Struggle against Discrimination in Nineteenth-Century America* (Berkeley: University of California Press, 1994), 202.

29. *Chinese Times*, Feb. 8, 1929.

30. 23 Stat. 115, Act of July 5, 1884.

31. Chan, "The Exclusion of Chinese Women," 114–118.

32. *United States v. Mrs. Gue Lim*, 176 U.S. 459, 1900.

33. Lucy E. Salyer, *Laws Harsh as Tigers: Chinese Immigrants and the Shaping of Modern Immigration Law* (Chapel Hill: University of North Carolina Press, 1995), 45–53.

34. *Fong Yue Ting v. United States*, 149 U.S. 698 (1893), 713; Salyer, *Laws Harsh as Tigers*, 45–48.
35. *Tsoi Sim v. United States,* 116 F. 738 (1902), 920–927, quote at 926.
36. Department of Labor, Bureau of Immigration, *Annual Report of the Commissioner General of Immigration to the Secretary of Labor* (Washington, D.C.: Government Printing Office, 1924).
37. 43 Stat. 153, Act of May 24, 1924, section 13 (c).
38. Roger Daniels, *Asian America: Chinese and Japanese in the United States since 1850* (Seattle: University of Washington Press, 1988), 150–151.
39. *Ex parte Chan Shee et al.,* 2 F. 2d 995 (1924).
40. Pei Chi Liu, *Meiguo huaqiaoshi xubian* [A history of the Chinese in the United States of America, II] (Taipei: Limin wenhua qiye gongsi, 1981), 93–94.
41. Ibid., 94, 98.
42. *Cheung Sum Shee v. Nagle*, 268 U.S. 336 (1925). Chan argues that under the general antagonism, American laws provided differential degrees of discriminatory treatment to Chinese immigrants according to class. Chan, "The Immigration of Chinese Women," 138.
43. *Chang Chan et al. v. John Nagle*, 268 U.S. 346 (1925).
44. Hsu, " 'Living Abroad and Faring Well,' " 157.
45. Chan, "The Exclusion of Chinese Women," 110; McKeown, "Transnational Chinese Families and Chinese Exclusion," 84.
46. For the involvement of CACA in the lobby, see Y. C. Hong, *A Brief History of the Chinese American Citizens Alliance* (San Francisco: Chinese American Citizens Alliance, Nov. 1955), 2–3; idem, "Milestones of the Chinese-American Citizens Alliance," 1963, reprinted in *Chinese American Citizens Alliance 38th Biennial National Convention, August 7–10, 1985* (Los Angeles: Chinese American Citizens Alliance, 1985), 32–39; Sue Fawn Chung, "Fighting for Their American Rights: A History of the Chinese American Citizens Alliance," in *Claiming America: Constructing Chinese American Identities during the Exclusion Era*, ed. Scott Wong and Sucheng Chan (Philadelphia: Temple University Press, 1998), 108–110.
47. "A Second Plea for Relief," in U.S. Senate, *Admission as Nonquota Immigrants of Certain Alien Wives and Children of United States Citizens: Hearing before a Subcommittee on Immigration on S. 2271,* 70th Cong., 1st sess., 1928.
48. *Chang Chan et al. v. John Nagle*, 346.
49. U.S. House of Representatives, *Admission of Wives of American Citizens of Oriental Ancestry*, 19.
50. Ibid., 2–4, 31–32.
51. Ibid., 8, 13–14, 16–17, 38.
52. Ibid., 17.
53. Ibid., 10–11; U.S. Department of Labor, Bureau of Immigration, *Annual Report of the Commissioner General of Immigration to the Secretary of Labor* (Washington, D.C.: Government Printing Office, 1925), 22.
54. "A Second Plea for Relief," 19.
55. U.S. Senate, *Admission as Nonquota Immigrants of Certain Alien Wives and*

Children of United States Citizens; E. P. Hutchinson, *Legislative History of American Immigration Policy, 1798–1965* (Philadelphia: University of Pennsylvania Press, 1981), 202–203.

56. Ibid., 95.
57. *Chinese Times*, July 23, 24, Aug. 15, 25, 1930.
58. U.S. House of Representatives, *Hearing before the Committee on Immigration and Naturalization on H.R. 2404, H.R. 5654, H.R. 10524*, 71st Cong. 2nd sess., 1930; Hutchinson, *Legislative History of American Immigration Policy*, 218.
59. Hutchinson, *Legislative History of American Immigration Policy*, 218.
60. U.S. House of Representatives, *Hearing before the Committee on Immigration and Naturalization on H.R. 2404, H.R. 5654, H.R. 10524*; 46 Stat. 581, Act of June 13, 1930.
61. Liu, *A History of the Chinese in the United States of America*, II, 98.
62. Wen-Hsien Chen, "Chinese under Both Exclusion and Immigration Laws" (Ph.D. diss., University of Chicago, 1940), 28.
63. Hutchinson, *Legislative History of American Immigration Policy*, 237–238.
64. Ibid., 246.
65. Liu, *A History of the Chinese in the United States of America*, II, 98.
66. Hutchinson, *Legislative History of American Immigration Policy*, 264.
67. Active members of the committee included Donald Dunham, who had worked for years at the American consulate in Hong Kong; Pearl Buck, a Nobel laureate in literature and the author of *The Good Earth*; and Buck's husband, Richard J. Walsh, editor of *Asia and the Americans* and president of the John Day Company.
68. Several Chinese American community organizations worked closely with the Citizens Committee to Repeal Chinese Exclusion and voluntarily made financial contributions. See Fred W. Riggs, *Pressures on Congress: A Study of the Repeal of Chinese Exclusion* (New York: Columbia University Press, 1950), 56, 111–118; Renqiu Yu, "Little Heard Voices: The Chinese Hand Laundry Alliance and the *China Daily News'* Appeal for Repeal of the Chinese Exclusion Act in 1943," *Chinese America: History and Perspectives* (1990): 21–35. Among the many American organizations that took actions to support the repeal were the Women's International League for Peace and Freedom and the California League of Women Voters. The latter passed a resolution unanimously at its annual convention in 1942 urging revision of the exclusion laws. See *Hawaii Chinese Journal*, June 18, 1942. See also Him Mark Lai, *Cong huaqiao dao huaren: ershi shiji meiguo huaren shehui fazhan shi* [From overseas Chinese to ethnic Chinese: A history of the social development of America's Chinese in the twentieth century] (Hong Kong: Sanlian shudian, 1992), 330.
69. Chen, "Chinese Immigration into the United States," 111–112.
70. "Repeal Exclusion Laws Now," *Asia and the Americas*, June 1943, 322.
71. Ibid., 322.
72. "Repeal of the Chinese Exclusion Acts," in U.S. House of Representatives, *Hearings before the Committee on Immigration and Naturalization*, 78th Congress, 1st sess., 1943, 249.

73. "Repeal of the Chinese Exclusion Act," *Monthly Review*, Immigration and Natu-ralization Service, Aug. 1943, 16.

74. *Chinese Times,* Sept. 7, 1943; *Chinese American Weekly*, May 27, 1943.

75. Warren G. Magnuson to William Green, Sept. 28, 1943, Warren G. Magnuson Papers, B58 F21, Manuscripts and University Archives Division, University of Washington Libraries.

76. Message of the President, October 11, 1943, in Riggs, *Pressures on Congress*, 211.

77. Him Mark Lai, "Unfinished Business: The Chinese Confession Program," in *The Repeal and Its Legacy: Proceedings of the Conference on the 50th Anni-versary of the Repeal of the Exclusion Act, Nov 12–14, 1993* (San Francisco: Chinese Historical Society of America, 1994), 47.

78. Riggs, *Pressures on Congress*, 40.

79. The new 212a section was similar to section 213, but it excluded section 4(a)—a clause that permitted alien wives and children of citizens to enter without a quota limit. The Chinese quota is established on a different basis than quotas for other countries. See 57 Stat. 600, Act of Dec. 17, 1943; 43 Stat. 153, Act of May 24, 1924, sect. 13(3) at 162; Riggs, *Pressures on Congress*, 223–224.

80. Riggs, *Pressures on Congress*, 40, 125.

81. Gilbert Woo, "Feichu paihua lü" [On repeal of the Chinese exclusion acts], *Chi-nese Times*, Dec. 1, 1943, in Hu Jingnan jinian weiyuan hui, *Hu Jingnan wenji* [Selected works of Gilbert Woo] (Hong Kong: Xiangjiang chuban youxian gongsi, 1991), 41–42.

82. Numbers of Chinese aliens naturalized: 1937, 44; 1938, 30; 1939, 30; 1940, 20; 1941, 57; 1942, 45; 1943, 497; 1944, 731; 1945, 739; 1946, 599; 1947, 851; 1948, 763; 1949, 927. *Annual Report of the Immigration and Naturalization Ser-vice*, 1946 and 1949. Many Chinese gained naturalization through military ser-vice.

83. S. 412, 580, Downey, Calif.; H.R. 3976, Havenner, Calif.; H. R. 4109, Dou-glas, Calif.; H.R. 4179, 4844, Miller, Calif.; H.R. 4531, Patterson, Calif. See Hutchinson, *Legislative History of American Immigration*, 270.

84. 59 Stat. 659, Act of Dec. 28, 1945.

85. The exclusion of Asian Indians and Filipinos ended in 1946. An amendment of the War Brides Act in 1947 made it possible for World War II veterans to bring in Asian wives who were otherwise inadmissible.

86. 60 Stat. 339, Act of June 29, 1946.

87. 60 Stat. 975, Act of Aug. 9, 1946. The admission of unmarried alien Chinese minors continued to be subject to the quota after 1946, even though American citizens could bring their non-Asian minor children in as nonquota immigrants. On August 29, the CCBA allocated $4,300 to commission gold plaques for Miller and two other congressmen in recognition of their efforts to push the bill through Congress. See Liu, *A History of the Chinese in the United States of America*, II, 98.

88. H.R. 65, Feb. 10, 1949; Hutchinson, *Legislative History of American Immigra-tion Policy*, 286–287.

89. Riggs, *Pressures on Congress*, 39, 110.
90. U.S. House, *Hearings before Subcommittee on Immigration and Naturalization of the Committee on the Judiciary, House of Representatives, on H.R. 5004, a Bill to Provide the Privilege of Becoming a Naturalized Citizen of the United States to All Immigrants Having a Legal Right to Permanent Residence, to Make Immigration Quotas Available to Asiatic and Pacific People.*, 80th Congress, 2nd session., Apr. 19 and 21, 1948.
91. *Chinese American Weekly*, March 10, 1949; *Chinese Pacific Weekly*, Mar. 12, 26, 1949; Hutchinson, *Legislative History of American Immigration Policy*, 287.
92. *Chung Sai Yat Po*, Feb. 24, 1949.
93. *Chinese American Weekly*, Mar. 10, 1949.
94. *Chung Sai Yat Po*, Mar. 11, 1949.
95. Ibid., Mar. 24, 28, 30, 1949.
96. Ibid., Mar. 8, 18, 1949.
97. Ibid., Mar. 21, 1949.
98. Ibid., Mar. 28, 1949.
99. Ibid., Mar. 9, 1949.
100. Ibid., Mar. 22, July 26, 1946; Hutchinson, *Legislative History of American Immigration Policy*, 286; Hong, "Milestones of the Chinese American Citizens' Alliance," 35.

CHAPTER 2   *Gender and Immigration*

1. *Annual Report of the Commissioner General of Immigration to the Secretary of Labor*, 1925, 22–23.
2. Four children's sex was not recorded in the database.
3. This issue is discussed in many studies dealing with the early immigration of the Chinese. See especially Evelyn Nakano Glenn, "Split Household, Small Producer, and Dual Wage Earner: An Analysis of Chinese-American Family Strategies," *Journal of Marriage and the Family* 45: 1 (Feb. 1983), 35–48; Peter S. Li, "Fictive Kinship, Conjugal Tie, and Kinship Chain among Chinese Immigrants in the United States," *Journal of Comparative Family Studies* 8, no. 1 (Spring 1997): 47–63; Erika Lee, "At America's Gates: Chinese Immigration during the Exclusion Era, 1882–1943" (Ph.D. diss., University of California, Berkeley, 1998), chap. two; Adam McKeown, "Transnational Chinese Families and Chinese Exclusion, 1975–1943," *Journal of American Ethnic History* 18 (Winter 1999): 75–77.
4. Peter Lew, "The Family Immigration History and Genealogy of Lew Chuck Suey (Lew Hawk Yee)," unpublished manuscript, 1997 (in author's possession).
5. Ibid., 2; Lew Chuck Suey immigration file 12017/8518, in ibid.
6. Lew Chuck Suey immigration file 12017/8518, in Lew, "The Family Immigration History."
7. Paper sons (or paper daughters) are individuals who entered the United States using false kinship ties, often as children of American citizens or merchants. See Li, "Fictive Kinship, Conjugal Tie, and Kinship Chain" 55; Victor G. Nee

and Brett de Bary Nee, *Longtime Californ': A Documentary Study of an American Chinatown* (New York: Pantheon Books, 1972), 62–63.

8. Lew, "The Family Immigration History," 2–3.

9. The date of Gay Heung's marriage is not recorded. According to Chinese custom, she was most likely married by the time she turned twenty.

10. Lew, "The Family Immigration History," 4; interview with Peter Lew by the author.

11. George Anthony Peffer, *If They Don't Bring Their Women Here: Chinese Female Immigration before Exclusion* (Urbana: University of Illinois Press, 1999), 12–27.

12. McKeown, "Transnational Chinese Families and Chinese Exclusion," 100–101.

13. Bryna Goodman, *Native Place, City, and Nation: Regional Networks and Identities in Shanghai, 1853–1937* (Berkeley: University of California Press, 1995), 5.

14. Haiming Liu, "Between China and America: The Trans-Pacific History of the Chang Family" (Ph.D. diss., University of California, Irvine, 1996), 3.

15. Lew, "The Family Immigration History," 5.

16. Ibid., 6, 8.

17. Ibid., 2–5.

18. Lisa See, *On Gold Mountain: The One-Hundred-Year Odyssey of My Chinese-American Family* (New York: Vintage Books, 1995). See also May Wong; "My Journey: In Search of Roots," *Chinese America: History and Perspectives*, 2000, 54–61.

19. Huang Yunji (Maurice Chuck), *Benliu—Yixiangqu diyibu* (Shengyang: Shengyang chuban she, 1996), 1–11. Maurice's sister and her family came to the United States in 1984. Interview with Maurice Chuck by the author, Feb. 22, 1998.

20. 10 Stat. 604, Act of Feb. 10, 1855; Cyril D. Hill, "Citizenship of Married Women," *American Journal of International Law*, 18 (1924): 720–736. See also Nancy F. Cott, *Public Vows: A History of Marriage and the Nation* (Cambridge, Mass.: Harvard University Press, 2000).

21. 34 Stat. 1228, Act of March 2, 1907.

22. *Mackenzie v. Hare*, 239 U.S. 299 (1915).

23. Hill, "Citizenship of Married Women," 722–723.

24. For a discussion of party politics over women's rights and justice to Asian immigrants, see Dale Baum, "Woman Suffrage and the 'Chinese Question': The Limits of Radical Republicanism in Massachusetts, 1865–1876," *New England Quarterly*, 56:1 (March 1983): 60–77.

25. 42 Stat. 1021, Act of Sept. 22, 1922. The Cable Act affected mostly U.S.-born Chinese and Japanese women.

26. *Ex parte (NG) Fung Sing*, 6 F. 2d, 670–671 (1925).

27. 34 Stat. 898, Act of Feb. 20, 1907; *Ex parte (NG) Fung Sing*, 6 F. 2d, 670–671 (1925); Candice Lewis Bredbenner, *A Nationality of Her Own: Women, Marriage, and the Law of Citizenship* (Berkeley: University of California Press, 1980), 136.

28. *Chinese Times*, July 27, 31, 1931.

29. 2 Stat. 153, Act of April 14, 1802; 10 Stat. 604, Act of Feb. 10, 1855; Rev. Stat. sect. 1993, 1878.

30. In 1922 Lew Chuck Suey took his children from his second marriage, all of them born in the United States, to China to attend school. He died a year later, and the children continued their education in China. Lew, "The Family Immigration History," 2–3.

31. Lew Wah Chuck visa petition file A 13–695–425 and confession file A 12–996–004, in Lew, " The Family Immigration History."

32. 46 Stat. 849, Act of July 3, 1930; 46 Stat. 1551, Act of Mar. 3, 1931.

33. As Bredbenner records, at the hearing of the House Committee on Immigration and Naturalization of the 72nd Congress, the Labor Department's commissioner of naturalization, Raymond Crist, argued that if women were given the opportunity to bring their children into the country as citizens, they, especially the Chinese, could make false claims for the admission of children who were not their offspring. During a discussion among House committee members at a hearing of the 73rd Congress, Charles Kramer of California asked a female advocate of the reform how she would feel if her daughter had to sit next to Asian boys in school: "Don't you feel that we are increasing the probability of bringing in more of the Chinese and Japanese, and what have you, from those nations over there, by reason of this bill?" Bredbenner, *A Nationality of Her Own*, 227–228, 230–231.

34. 48 Stat. 797, Act of May 24, 1934. The Nationality Act of 1940, however, provided that a child born outside the United States could not gain citizenship automatically unless the citizen parent had resided in the U.S. for ten years prior to the birth of the child (Nationality Act of 1940, sec. 201).

35. 59 Stat. 659, Act of Dec. 28, 1945. The term "war brides" is not used in the act, but the INS nicknamed it the "War Brides Act" (*Annual Report of the Immigration and Naturalization Service*, 1950); 60 Stat. 975, Act of Aug. 9, 1946.

36. Fang Di, "Cong renkou pucha ziliao zhong fanying chulai de qiaoxiang laonian nuqiaoshu tedian" [Characteristics of elderly women among the overseas families as reflected in the census], in *Huaqiao huaren shi yanjiu ji* [A history of overseas Chinese], ed. Zheng Min and Lian Cumin (Beijing: Haiyang chuban she, 1989), 304–314. See also Sandra M. J. Wong, "For the Sake of Kinship: The Overseas Chinese Family" (Ph.D. diss., Stanford University, 1987), 51; Madeline Yuan-yin Hsu, "'Living Abroad and Faring Well': Migration and Transnationalism in Taishan County, Guangdong, 1904–1939" (Ph.D. diss., Yale University, 1996), 146.

37. This is the endeavor of a number of Asian American scholars in recent years. See Haiming Liu, "The Trans-Pacific Family: A Case Study of Sam Chang's Family History," *Amerasia* 18:2 (1992): 1–34; Hsu, "'Living Abroad and Faring Well'"; Glenn, "Split Household"; Sylvia Yanagisako, "Transforming Orientalism: Gender, Nationality, and Class in Asian American Studies," in *Naturalizing Power: Essays in Feminist Cultural Analysis*, ed. Sylvia Yanagisako and Carol Delaney (New York: Routledge, 1995), 275–300.

38. McKeown, "Transnational Chinese Families," 103.

39. Hsu, "'Living Abroad and Faring Well,'" 141–144.

40. Interview with Mary Yee by Denise Yee, directed by the author, Mar. 9, 1998.
41. See, *On Gold Mountain*, 15.
42. There were many such incidents reported in community newspapers published in the United States in the 1930s and 1940s.
43. Interview with Mary Yee.
44. Lew, "The Family Immigration History," 2.
45. Interview with Way Shew Gin by Britton Yee and the author, May 8, 1998.
46. Wong, "For the Sake of Kinship," 41–45.
47. Interview with Way Shew Gin by Britton Yee and the author.
48. Lew Wah Chuck visa petition, file A 13–695–425, and confession file, A 12–996–004, in Lew, " The Family Immigration History."
49. Toward the end of the 1940s, *Chung Sai Yat Po* changed "Benfu xinwen" to "Gefu xinwen [News of the cities]," covering news of Chinatowns throughout the United States, Canada, and South and Central America. The home village news mostly covered four home counties, Taishan, Xinhui, Kaiping, and Enping, but later it was expanded to include a larger geographical area in Guangdong Province and Hong Kong. Similar changes occurred in other newspapers.
50. Renqiu Yu, *To Save China, to Save Ourselves: The Chinese Hand Laundry Alliance of New York* (Philadelphia: Temple University Press, 1992), 118, 124–129.
51. *Annual Report of Immigration and Naturalization Service*, 1948.
52. This puzzlement was expressed in the congressional hearings on Chinese immigration in 1926, 1928, and 1930.
53. For immigration network and tactics used to circumvent exclusion laws, see Erika Lee, "Enforcing and Challenging Exclusion in San Francisco: U.S. Immigration Officials and Chinese Immigrants, 1882–1905," *Chinese America: History and Perspectives*, 1997, 1–15; idem, "At America's Gates," chaps. 5–6; Madeline Hsu, "Gold Mountain Dreams and Paper Son Schemes: Chinese Immigration under Exclusion," *Chinese America: History and Perspectives*, 1997, 46–60.
54. Yitang Chang, as documented in Haiming Liu's study, sponsored more than forty relatives to the United States. See Liu, "Between China and America," 32; idem, "The Trans-Pacific Family."
55. Interview with Chiu Chun Wong by Denise Yee, directed by the author, Jan. 30, 1998.
56. Zheng Yijun, *Chuanqi rensheng: ji Cai Fujiu zouguo de lu* [A legendary life: The path of Cai Fujiu] (Hong Kong: Haifeng chubanshe, 1997), 58–59.
57. Ibid., 112, 137–139.
58. Based on the author's reading of 1,035 immigration case files. See chapter four for more details.
59. However, Jennie's younger son, Quan Hing Fay, who was born in 1941, after the Nationality Act 1940 went into effect, could not enter with his mother since the new law stipulated that derivative citizenship would be given only to a child whose citizen parent lived in the United States ten years prior to the birth of the child. Quan Hing Fay entered in 1952 as the beneficiary of Private Bill H.R. 6415. Quan Jennie immigration file 1303/6272, in Lew, "The Family Immigration History."
60. *Chung Sai Yat Po*, Dec. 8, 1948; *China Daily News*, Dec. 17, 1948.

CHAPTER 3   ***Women and World War II***

1. Jade Snow Wong, *Fifth Chinese Daughter*, 2nd ed. (1950; Seattle: University of Washington Press, 1990), 194–198.
2. See *San Francisco Chronicle*, Apr. 17, 1943; *Chinese Times*, Apr. 19, 20, 1943.
3. There are a number of books on American women workers in World War II, but none mention Chinese Rosie the Riveters. See, for example, Ruth Milkman, *Gender at Work: The Dynamics of Job Segregation by Sex during World War II* (Urbana: University of Illinois Press, 1987); Sherna Berger Gluck, *Rosie the Riveter Revisited: Women, the War, and Social Change* (Boston: Twayne Publishers, 1987). Only Charles Wollenberg has noticed that many of Bechtel's Marinship workers came from local Chinese American communities. See Charles Wollenberg, *Marinship at War: Shipbuilding and Social Change in Wartime Sausalito* (Berkeley: Western Heritage Press, 1990), 72.
4. Judy Yung, *Chinese Women of America: A Pictorial History* (Seattle: University of Washington Press, 1986), 66–77; idem, *Unbound Feet: A Social History of Chinese Women in San Francisco* (Berkeley: University of California Press, 1995), chap. 5; idem, *Unbound Voices: A Documentary History of Chinese Women in San Francisco* (Berkeley: University of California Press, 1999), 409–510; Xiaojian Zhao, "Chinese American Women Defense Workers in World War II," *California History* 75:2 (Summer 1996): 138–153, 182–184.
5. Chinese American women's work is not apparent in the published U.S. Census. The census of 1940 shows that only 25.7 percent of Chinese women fourteen years and older were in the labor force in San Francisco and Oakland, lower than the proportions of both white and black working women (32.4 and 41.3 percent, respectively). The Chinese figure is low because the census did not count those who took piecework home and those who worked in their family-owned shops.
6. California State Emergency Relief Administration, "Survey of Social Work Needs of the Chinese Population of San Francisco, California" (1935), 1, 35–36, Bancroft Library, University of California, Berkeley; Wong, *Fifth Chinese Daughter*, 165.
7. Lucy Jen Huang, "The Chinese American Family," in *Ethnic Families in America,* ed. Charles H. Mindel and Robert W. Habenstein (New York: Elsevier, 1982), 124. In the early 1940s, the idea of using public daycare was new to the majority of American working women. Childcare facilities in Richmond, California, for example, could not get full enrollment. See *Fore 'n' Aft*, Sept. 3, 1943.
8. "Survey of Social Work Needs of the Chinese Population of San Francisco," 35.
9. Roger Daniels, *Asian America: Chinese and Japanese in the United States since 1850* (Seattle: University of Washington Press, 1988), 69.
10. Sandy Lydon, *Chinese Gold: The Chinese in the Monterey Bay Region* (Capitola, Calif.: Capitola Book Company, 1985), 34.
11. Interview with Maggie Gee by the author, Feb. 20, Mar. 27, 1994, June 20, 1998; interview with Florence Gee Tom by the author, July 15, 1994.
12. Charles J. McClain, *In Search of Equality: The Chinese Struggle against Discrimination in Nineteenth-Century America* (Berkeley: University of California

Press, 1994), 133–144; Charles M. Wollenberg, *All Deliberate Speed: Segregation and Exclusion in California Schools, 1855–1975* (Berkeley: University of California Press, 1976), 8–44; Victor Low, *The Unimpressible Race: A Century of Educational Struggle by the Chinese in San Francisco* (San Francisco: East/West), 50–123.

13. Interview with Maggie Gee. Of the seventy-nine Chinese students graduated from the University of California, Berkeley, between 1940 and 1942, twenty-seven (29 percent) were females. See Yung, *Unbound Feet*, 305.

14. Interview with Aimei Chen by the author, July 11, 1994.

15. Wong, *Fifth Chinese Daughter*, 109, 134–135, 168.

16. Interview with Luella (Chinn) Louie by Andrea L. Chow and the author, Oct. 21, 1998.

17. Richard Kock Dare, "The Economic and Social Adjustment of the San Francisco Chinese for the Past Fifty Years" (M.A. thesis, University of California, Berkeley, 1959), 20; interview with Jane F. Lee by Ben Tong and Kathleen Chin, 6, Bancroft Library, University of California, Berkeley; interview with Maggie Gee; Wong, *Fifth Chinese Daughter*, 189.

18. *The Chinese Youth*, (New York) 3 (Oct. 1940), 2, 5, 9.

19. The 1940 census recorded 14,560 American-born Chinese women and 5,555 China-born women in the United States. U.S. Bureau of the Census, *Sixteenth Census of the United States*, Population, 1940. Yung, *Unbound Feet*, 303.

20. Wong, *Fifth Chinese Daughter*, 53, 90.

21. Interview with Elizabeth Lew Anderson by the author, Nov. 14, 15, 1997.

22. Interview with Aimei Chen.

23. Interview with Yulan Liu by the author, Jan. 8, 1993.

24. Interview with Maggie Gee.

25. *Time*, December 22, 1941.

26. *Chinese Times*, July 4, 5, 1942.

27. Ibid., Apr. 22, May 11, 20, 24, 30, June 20, 23, 24, Aug. 22, 1942, Mar. 1, 2, 17, Apr. 13, Aug. 12, Nov. 16, 1943.

28. Ibid., Apr. 28, 1942, Mar. 17, 1943.

29. Few defense industries recorded the number of Chinese American employees, and the existing literature tends either to overlook them or to give inaccurate estimates of them. In *The Chinese Experience in America*, Shih-shan Henry Tsai estimated that in 1943, Chinese Americans "made up some 15 percent of the shipyard workforce in the San Francisco Bay area." In that year, the Bay Area had about 100,000 shipyard workers. Tsai's estimation therefore suggests that 15,000 of them were Chinese. Given that the entire Bay Area's Chinese American population, including all age groups, was only about 22,000 in 1940, and only a small number of Chinese Americans migrated to the West Coast during the war, it is very unlikely that 15,000 of them (over 68 percent) were defense workers. On August 21, 1942, the *Chinese Press*, a San Francisco Chinatown-based English-language newspaper, reported that 1,600 Chinese Americans worked in Bay Area defense industries. This was one year before the peak of the war. The number would have increased significantly a few months later, after Kaiser's Shipyard Number Three in Richmond and Bechtel's Marinship in

Sausalito began their production work and major defense establishments ran their ads in Chinese community newspapers. Marinship alone, according to the *Chinese Times*, employed 400 Chinese Americans by March 1943. See Shih-shan Henry Tsai, *The Chinese Experience in America* (Bloomington: Indiana University Press, 1986), 116; Marshall Maslin, ed., *Western Shipbuilders in World War II* (Oakland, Calif., 1954), 59; *Chinese Press*, Aug. 21, 1942; *Chinese Times*, Mar. 21, 1943.

30. *Chinese Press*, May 29, 1942.
31. Including interviews with family members.
32. Ah Yoke Gee lost her citizenship after she married her husband, a Chinese national. She regained it through naturalization in the early 1950s. Interview with Maggie Gee.
33. Interview with Elizabeth Lew Anderson.
34. Interview with Aimei Chen.
35. Interview with Yulan Liu.
36. Interview with Maggie Gee.
37. Jane Jeong dreamed of being a pilot flying for China against the Japanese and had accumulated 200 flying hours by the end of 1941. After America officially entered the war, Jane realized that she could serve both the United States and China by working in the defense industry. See *Chinese Times*, June 7, 1942.
38. *Fore 'n' Aft*, Apr. 16, 1943, Apr. 14, 1944.
39. *Chinese Press*, Dec. 18, 1942.
40. *Fore 'n' Aft*, July 2, 1943.
41. Interview with Elizabeth Lew Anderson and Peter Lew by the author.
42. *Chinese Times*, Nov. 29, 1942.
43. Interview with Maggie Gee.
44. *Fore 'n' Aft*, Nov. 19, 1942.
45. Interview with Jade Snow Wong by the author, Nov. 25, 1991; Wong, *Fifth Chinese Daughter*, 188–190.
46. Interview with Elizabeth Lew Anderson.
47. Interview with Aimei Chen.
48. Interview with Joy Yee by the author, Aug. 18, 23, 1994.
49. Interview with Yulan Liu.
50. Interview with Luella Louie.
51. Interview with Maggie Gee and Florence Gee Tom.
52. Him Mark Lai, *Cong huaqiao dao huaren: ershi shiji meiguo huaren shehui fazhan shi* [From overseas Chinese to ethnic Chinese: A history of the social development of America's Chinese in the twentieth century] (Hong Kong: Sanlian shudian, 1992), 320–324; idem, "Roles Played by Chinese in America during China's Resistance to Japanese Aggression during World War II," *Chinese America: History and Perspectives*, 1997, 79–81.
53. She paid five dollars an hour for the lessons. See Cicillia Rasmussen, "China's Amelia Earhart Got Her Wings Here," *Los Angeles Times*, Apr. 12, 1998; Lai, *Cong huaqiao dao huaren*, 326.
54. See ibid.
55. Lai, "Roles Played by Chinese in America," 81; Marianne Verges, *On Silver*

Wings: The Women Airforce Service Pilots of World War II, 1942–1944 (New York: Ballantine Books, 1991), 106, 197.

56. Verges, *On Silver Wings*, 103–105.
57. Ibid., 106–107, 196–197.
58. Interview with Maggie Gee.
59. Verges, *On Silver Wings*, 214, 216–217, 227.
60. Daniels, *Asian America*, 299–300; Yung, *Unbound Feet*, 253. See also Lai, *Cong huoqiao dao huaren*, 336; idem, "Roles Played by Chinese in America," 99.
61. Daniels, *Asian America*, 68–69.
62. Charles S. Johnson, *The Negro War Workers in San Francisco: A Local Survey* (San Francisco, 1944), 3.
63. Ping Chiu, *Chinese Labor in California, 1850–1880: An Economic Study* (Madison: State Historical Society of Wisconsin for the Department of History, University of Wisconsin, 1967), 89–128; Thomas W. Chinn, Him Mark Lai, and Philip P. Choy, *A History of the Chinese in California: A Syllabus* (San Francisco: Chinese Historical Society of America, 1969), 49–55.
64. David Roedinger, *The Wages of Whiteness* (New York: Verso, 1991), 179. See also Alexander Saxton, *The Indispensable Enemy: Labor and the Anti-Chinese Movement in California* (Berkeley: University of California Press, 1971); Elmer Clarence Sandmeyer, *The Anti-Chinese Movement in California* (1939; repr. Urbana: University of Illinois Press, 1973).
65. Chiu, *Chinese Labor in California*, 94, 97–98, 110, 115, 117–119, 122–123; Sucheng Chan, "Chinese Livelihood in Rural California: The Impact of Economic Change, 1860–1880," in *Working People of California*, ed. Daniel Cornford (Berkeley: University of California Press, 1995), 67.
66. Wong, *Fifth Chinese Daughter*, 182–183; interview with Maggie Gee.
67. Wong, *Fifth Chinese Daughter*, 170.
68. *Marin-er*, June 26, 1943, 2, 3, 4.
69. Katherine Archibald, *Wartime Shipyard: A Study in Social Disunity* (Berkeley: University of California Press, 1947), 59–74, 100–109.
70. During the war African Americans vowed to win double victory—against fascism abroad and racism at home. They challenged racial discrimination in housing, employment, and union membership through strikes, political campaigns, and litigation. See Charles Wollenberg, "James v. Marinship: Trouble on the New Black Frontier," *California History* 60 (Fall 1981); idem, *Marinship at War*, 70–84; Marilynn S. Johnson, *The Second Gold Rush: Oakland and the East Bay in World War II* (Berkeley: University of California Press, 1993), 67–76.
71. *Marin-er*, June 26, 1943, 1–2.
72. *Chinese Times*, Sept. 9, 1943; *Chinese Press*, Sept. 29, 1943.
73. Interview with Aimei Chen; *Fore 'n' Aft*, Apr. 7, 1944.
74. "Richmond Took a Beating," *Fortune* magazine, Feb. 1945, 267.
75. *Fore 'n' Aft*, Apr. 20, 1945.
76. Wong, *Fifth Chinese Daughter*, 192–195.
77. Ibid., 125–130.
78. Ibid., 196–198.
79. Interview with Yulan Liu.

80. Constance Wong, "Marinship Chinese Workers Are Building Ships to Free Their Home Land," *Marin-er*, June 26, 1943, 3.
81. Interview with Elizabeth Lew Anderson.
82. Ibid.
83. Interview with Maggie Gee.
84. Wong, *Fifth Chinese Daughter*, 109–110.
85. Hua Liang, "Fighting for a New Life: Social and Patriotic Activism of Chinese American Women in New York City, 1900 to 1945," *Journal of American Ethnic History* 17:2 (Winter 1998): 22–38.
86. *Chinese Press*, Oct. 9, 1942.
87. *Chinese Times*, Feb. 9, 22, Apr. 11, 1942; *Chinese Press*, Jan. 30, 1942.
88. Interview with Yulan Liu.
89. Interview with Maggie Gee and Florence Gee Tom.
90. Interview with Joy Yee.
91. Interview with Luella Louie.
92. Interview with Maggie Gee.
93. Mary P. Ryan, *Womanhood in America: From Colonial Times to the Present*, 3rd ed. (New York: Franklin Watts, 1983), 257.
94. Xiaojian Zhao, "Women and Defense Industries in World War II" (Ph.D. diss., University of California, Berkeley, 1993); Wollenberg, *Marinship at War*, 28–39, 46.
95. Eugene Danaher, *Apprenticeship Practice in the United States* (Stanford: Graduate School of Business, 1945), 15.
96. Ethel McCarthy, "Shipbuilder and Seaman Training: A Clearing House for Ideas on the War-Winning Job of Wholesale Production of Skill in the Maritime Crafts," *Pacific Marine Review* 51 (February 1943); U.S. Department of Labor, Bureau of Apprenticeship, *Apprenticeship Statistics: A Summary of National Data on Registered Apprentices and Apprenticeship Systems in the United States, 1949–1952*, Technical Bulletin, no. T-137 (Washington, D.C., 1953), 10; Danaher, *Apprenticeship Practice in the United States*, 17.
97. Terms such as "skill" and "skilled workers" were often misused during the war. As one woman pointed out to the author, a mistake was made by a news reporter who addressed her as a "journeyman." She was not a journeyman, or a welder, but a tacker. "Tacking in welding," she explained, "was like basting in sewing." On a big welding job, a tacker would roughly fasten two plates together and then a welder would weld them to the desired standard. Interview with Janet Doyle by the author, July 26, 1990.
98. For more discussions on women's work, training programs, and the structure of defense industries in World War II, see Zhao, "Women and Defense Industries in World War II."
99. Interview with Maggie Gee.
100. Ibid.
101. Verges, *On Silver Wings*, 206–207; interview with Maggie Gee.
102. Interview with Maggie Gee; Vera S. Williams, *WASPs: Women Airforce Service Pilots of World War II* (Osceola, Wisc.: Motorbooks International Publishers & Wholesalers, 1994), 24, 31, 54, 69, 76, 77, 115, 126, 129, 140, 144.

103. Wong, *Fifth Chinese Daughter*, 194, 233–234, 237.
104. Interview with Jade Snow Wong; Wong, *Fifth Chinese Daughter*, 236.
105. Interview with Lanfang Wong by the author, Aug. 20, 1994.
106. Interview with Maggie Gee; Berkeley Historical Society, *Looking Back at Berkeley: A Pictorial History of a Diverse City* (Berkeley: Book Committee of the Berkeley Historical Society, 1984), 28.
107. Interview with Joy Yee.
108. Interview with Lihua Zhou by the author, Aug. 10, 1994.
109. Interview with Yuk Wah Fu by the author, Aug. 19, 1994.
110. Interview with Aimei Chen.
111. Interview with Aimei Chen; interview with Lili Wong by the author, Aug. 10, 1994.
112. Interview with Maggie Gee.
113. Interview with Jade Snow Wong; Wong, *Fifth Chinese Daughter*, 234, 235.
114. Interview with Maggie Gee.
115. Verges, *On Silver Wings*, 231–236.

CHAPTER 4   *The Family Reunited*

1. In 1948 the husbands of citizens, if their marriage had occurred on or after January 1, 1948, also gained nonquota status (47 Stat. 656, Act of May 19, 1948). *China Daily News*, July 19, 1948; E. P. Hutchinson, *Legislative History of American Immigration Policy, 1798–1965* (Philadelphia: University of Pennsylvania Press, 1981), 282.
2. *I Was a Male War Bride*, film directed by Howard Hawks, 1949.
3. Judy Yung, *Unbound Feet: A Social History of Chinese Women in San Francisco* (Berkeley: University of California Press, 1995), 253; Him Mark Lai, *Cong huaqiao dao huaren: ershi shiji meiguo huaren shehui fazhan shi* [From overseas Chinese to ethnic Chinese: A history of the social development of America's Chinese in the twentieth century] (Hong Kong: Sanlian shudian, 1992), 336; idem, "Roles Played by Chinese in America during China's Resistance to Japanese Aggression during World War II," *Chinese America: History and Perspectives*, 1997, 99.
4. *Annual Report of the Commissioner General of Immigration to the Secretary of Labor*, 1940–1950.
5. *Annual Report of the Immigration and Naturalization Service*, 1947–1950.
6. Much of the secondary work on postwar Chinese immigrant women is based on Rose Hum Lee's study. See Lee, "The Recent Immigrant Chinese Families of the San Francisco–Oakland Area," *Journal of Marriage and Family Living* 18 (1956): 14–24. See also Roger Daniels, *Asian America: Chinese and Japanese in the United States since 1850* (Seattle: University of Washington Press, 1988), 306; Judy Yung, *Chinese Women of America: A Pictorial History* (Seattle: University of Washington Press, 1986), 80–87. Using oral history interviews, Xiaolan Bao allows women to tell their own stories, although her research focuses mostly on post-1965 immigrants. See Bao, "When Women Arrived: The Transformation of New York's Chinatown," in *Not June Cleaver: Women and*

Gender in Postwar America, 1945–1960, ed. Joanne Meyerowitz (Philadelphia: Temple University Press, 1994), 19–39; idem, "Holding Up More than Half the Sky: A History of Women Garment Workers in New York's Chinatown, 1948–1991" (Ph.D. diss., New York University, 1991). In her literary critiques of a set of short stories published in postwar Chinatown in New York, Sau-Ling C. Wong draws the connection between the postwar transformation of the Chinese American community and women's intrusion into the bachelor society. See Wong, "Tales of Postwar Chinatown: Short Stories of *The Bud,* 1947–1948," *Amerasia* 14:2 (1988): 61–79. I find Wen Quan's essay on Chinatown literature between 1939 and 1949 and Marlon K. Hom's introduction to its English translation especially helpful. See Wen Quan, "Chinatown Literature during the Last Ten Years (1939–1949)," trans. Marlon K. Hom, *Amerasia* 9:1 (1982): 75–100. Also see Elaine H. Kim, *Asian American Literature: An Introduction to the Writings and Their Social Context* (Philadelphia: Temple University Press, 1982), 109–121.

7. Lee, "The Recent Immigrant Chinese Families of the San Francisco–Oakland Area"; *Sewing Women,* film directed by Arthur Dong, 1982; Yung, *Chinese Women of America,* 80–87.

8. Lee, "The Recent Immigrant Chinese Families of the San Francisco–Oakland Area," 14. Chinese American G.I.s marrying young, "mercenary" and "scatter-brained" Chinese women who used marriage as a stepping-stone to come to America is also a common theme in several postwar short stories. See Wong, "Tales of Postwar Chinatown," 65, 74–79.

9. Louis Chu, *Eat a Bowl of Tea* (New Jersey: Lyle Stuart, 1961).

10. Not included are students, merchants' wives, tourists, government officials, re-entries, and quota immigrants.

11. The Chinese General Immigration Case Files, 1944 to 1955, RG 85, Records of the U.S. Immigration and Naturalization Service, National Archives, Pacific Sierra Regional Facility, San Bruno, California, include documents from both the San Francisco district office and the Honolulu district office. The collection contains 252 boxes of case files of noncitizen passengers arriving mostly at the port of San Francisco from China. Most of these case files were created in the investigation process of the Immigration and Naturalization Service to determine the eligibility of each applicant to enter the United States. My goal was to collect data from 1,000 randomly selected women's case files for statistical analysis. After I went through 238 of the 252 boxes and examined tens of thousands of files, 1,035 complete files were found and recorded. For immigration case files at the National Archives, see Waverly B. Lowell, *Chinese Immigration and Chinese in the United States: Records in the Regional Archives of the National Archives and Records Administration* (Washington, D.C.: National Archives and Records Administration, 1996).

12. Women who entered as fiancées of the war veterans are not included.

13. Jenel Virden, *Good-bye, Piccadilly: British War Brides in America* (Urbana: University of Illinois Press, 1996), 11.

14. Ibid., 62.

15. Ibid., 54–62.

16. *Annual Report of the Immigration and Naturalization Service,* 1946, 13.

17. Virden, *Good-bye, Piccadilly*, 80–88.
18. Because of the special relationship between the United States and the Philippines, Filipinos were "nationals" and free to come and go until the mid-1930s, but several naturalization petitions by Filipinos were turned down in the first two decades of the twentieth century.
19. Zheng Yijun, *Chuanqi rensheng: ji Cai Fujiu zouguo de lu* [A legendary life: the path of Cai Fujiu] (Hong Kong: Haifeng chubanshe, 1997), 157.
20. Interview with Tenley Chin by Kristen Martin, directed by the author, May 29, 1997.
21. *Sewing Women* (film by Arthur Dong); Yung, *Chinese Women of America*, 81.
22. *Chung Sai Yat Po*, June 2, 9, 1948; Pei Chi Liu, *Meiguo huaqiaoshi xubian* [A history of the Chinese in the United States of America, II] (Taipei: Limin wenhua qiye gongsi, 1981), 107.
23. Chinese General Immigration Case Files, 1944 to 1955, RG 85, Records of the U.S. Immigration and Naturalization Service, National Archives, San Bruno, California, file, 603. To protect individual confidentiality, access to the case files is restricted by the National Archives. The author obtained permission to review the collection in 1996, but agreed not to record original case numbers and applicants' names. Case numbers used here were added by the author in the order of the files selected. The original name is used only if the author has the permission to do so or if the person's case is discussed in published sources. *Chung Sai Yat Po*, Sept. 21, Oct. 1, 22, Nov. 24, 1948. See also Yung, *Chinese Women of America*, 80–81.
24. *Annual Report of the Immigration and Naturalization Service*, 1950.
25. Interview with Mary Yee by Denise Yee, directed by the author, Mar. 9, 1998.
26. Chinese General Immigration Case Files, 1944 to 1955, RG 85, Records of the U.S. Immigration and Naturalization Service, National Archives, San Bruno, California, file 990.
27. Officially commenced in 1956, the Chinese Confession Program was terminated on February 2, 1966. After that the INS ceased to solicit confessions but continued to accept volunteer confessions. "News release of the Department of Justice," Dec. 27, 1959. See chapter seven for more details.
28. On interrogation and deportation of Chinese immigrants during the exclusion, see Him Mark Lai, Genny Lim, and Judy Yung, *Island: Poetry and History of Chinese Immigrants on Angel Island, 1910–1940* (San Francisco: HOCDOI Project, 1980), 19.
29. Chinese General Immigration Case Files, 1944 to 1955, RG 85, Records of the U.S. Immigration and Naturalization Service, National Archives, San Bruno, California, file 501.
30. Ibid.
31. It is unclear exactly when the woman was deported, probably a year after she made the attempt to enter in 1931. The photos on file were taken by the immigration authorities before her departure.
32. Chinese General Immigration Case Files, 1944 to 1955, RG 85, Records of the U.S. Immigration and Naturalization Service, National Archives, San Bruno, California, file 138.

33. Ibid. The photos on file show that the faces match closely.
34. The 1930 law granted admission to Chinese wives of citizens who married before 1924. See chapter one.
35. *Chinese Pacific Weekly*, Oct. 23, 1948.
36. Chinese General Immigration Case Files, 1944 to 1955, RG 85, Records of the U.S. Immigration and Naturalization Service, National Archives, San Bruno, California, file 684.
37. *Chinese Pacific Weekly*, Oct. 23, 1948; *Annual Report of the Immigration and Naturalization Service*, 1945, 1949.
38. *Chinese Pacific Weekly*, June 26, 1948.
39. *Chinese American Weekly*, Sept. 30, 1948; *Chung Sai Yat Po*, Sept. 22, 1948.
40. One letter regarding the death of Liang Bixia and the actions of women, and the second reported an attempted suicide by Li Jingtang, the son of a war veteran; *China Daily News*, Nov. 2, 1948.
41. *Chung Sai Yat Po*, Sept. 21, Oct. 1, 22, Nov. 24, 1948. Other newspapers and journals quickly responded. See *Chinese American Weekly* (New York), Sept. 30, 1948; *Chinese Pacific Weekly*, Oct. 9, 1948; *China Daily News*, Oct. 22, 1948.
42. *China Daily News*, Oct. 10, 1948.
43. *Chung Sai Yat Po*, Sept. 22, 1948; *China Daily News*, Oct. 10, 1948.
44. Yung, *Chinese Women of America*, 81.

CHAPTER 5   *Community Institutions and the Press in Transition*

1. Peter Lew, "The Family Immigration History and Genealogy of Lew Chuck Suey (Lew Hawk Yee)," unpublished manuscript, 1997, 3; interview with Peter Lew by the author, Nov. 14, 15, 1997. By 1960 only one of Lew Chuck Suey's sons, Wah Sing, still resided in Oakland's Chinatown.
2. Interview with Peter Lew by the author.
3. San Francisco Chinese Community Citizens' Survey and Fact Finding Committee, *Report of the San Francisco Chinese Community Citizens' Survey and Fact Finding Committee* (San Francisco: H. J. Carle & Sons, 1969), 4.
4. Stanford M. Lyman, "Conflict and the Web of Group Affiliation in San Francisco's Chinatown, 1850–1910," *Pacific Historical Review* 43:4 (Nov. 1974): 473–499.
5. Richard Reinhardt, *Chinatown, San Francisco* (Berkeley: Lancaster-Miller Publishers, 1981), 8.
6. Lyman, "Conflict and the Web of Group Affiliation," 478–479. The author thanks Him Mark Lai for information regarding regional family associations.
7. Ibid., 479.
8. Ibid., 477–479; Him Mark Lai, "Historical Development of the Chinese Consolidated Benevolent Association/Huiguan System," *Chinese America: History and Perspectives*, 1987, 19–20; Sam Yup Benevolent Association History Editorial Committee, *A History of the Sam Yup Benevolent Association in the United States* (San Francisco: Sam Yup Benevolent Association, 2000), 53.
9. Lai, "Historical Development of the Chinese Consolidated Benevolent Association," 24.

10. Pei Chi Liu, *Meiguo huaqiaoshi xubian* [A history of the Chinese in the United States of America, II] (Taipei: Limin wenhua qiye gongsi, 1981), 191–195. Hawaii is not included.

11. These scholars entered as Chinese diplomats, and they served as a link between the community and the Chinese government. Because the U.S. government questioned the legitimacy of these scholars as diplomats, the Chinese government stopped issuing passports to them in 1925. Him Mark Lai, *Cong huaqiao dao huaren: ershi shiji meiguo huaren shehui fazhan shi* [From overseas Chinese to ethnic Chinese: A history of the social development of America's Chinese in the twentieth century] (Hong Kong: Sanlian shudian, 1992), 157.

12. Y. C. Hong, *A Brief History of the Chinese American Citizens Alliance* (San Francisco: Chinese American Citizens Alliance, Nov. 1955), 1; Sue Fawn Chung, "Fighting for Their American Rights: A History of the Chinese American Citizens Alliance," in *Claiming America: Constructing Chinese American Identities during the Exclusion Era*, ed. K. Scott Wong and Sucheng Chan (Philadelphia: Temple University Press, 1998), 100–101.

13. Lai, "Historical Development of the Chinese Consolidated Benevolent Association," 20; idem, *Cong huaqiao dao huaren*, 39.

14. Lai, *Cong huaqiao dao huaren*, 43, 55–56.

15. Ibid., 342–343; Victor G. Nee and Brett de Bary Nee, *Longtime Californ': A Documentary Study of an American Chinatown* (New York: Pantheon Books, 1972), 200–201, 207–208.

16. U.S. Bureau of the Census, *The Fourteenth Census of the United States*, 1922.

17. Liu, *A History of the Chinese in the United States of America*, II, 171–174, 178.

18. Chung, "Fighting for Their American Rights," 101.

19. Lai, *Cong huaqiao dao huaren*, 43.

20. Liu, *A History of the Chinese in the United States of America,* II, 167, 174. More than half of the CCBA's income from exit permits also came from Ning Yang. Liu, *A History of the Chinese in the United States of America*, I, 173–174.

21. Lai, *Cong huaqiao dao huaren*, 26; Liu, *A History of the Chinese in the United States of America*, II, 174–175, 380–381.

22. Liu, *A History of the Chinese in the United States of America,* II, 175.

23. Ibid.

24. Ibid., 176–177.

25. Ibid., 177; Lai, *Cong huaqiao dao huaren*, 26.

26. Him Mark Lai, "Roles Played by Chinese in America during China's Resistance to Japanese Aggression during World War II," *Chinese America: History and Perspectives,* 78.

27. Ibid., 89.

28. Renqiu Yu, *To Save China, to Save Ourselves: The Chinese Hand Laundry Alliance of New York* (Philadelphia: Temple University Press, 1992), 32.

29. Ibid., 32–43.

30. Federal Bureau of Investigation, file 100–197835, "Chinese Workers Mutual Aid Association" (FBI-CWMAA); Nee and Nee, *Longtime Californ'*, 206.

31. Nee and Nee, *Longtime Californ'*, 206–207; Yu, *To Save China, to Save Ourselves*, 124.

32. U.S. Bureau of the Census, *Sixteenth Census of the United States*, Population, 1940.

33. Liu, *A History of the Chinese in the United States of America*, II, 180–181.

34. Stanford M. Lyman, "The Structure of Chinese Society in Nineteenth Century America" (Ph.D. diss., University of California, Berkeley, 1961); idem, "Conflict and the Web of Group Affiliation in San Francisco's Chinatown," 473–499; idem, *Chinese Americans* (New York: Random House, 1974), 29–53.

35. For bibliographical information on Chinese community newspapers, see Karl Lo and H. M. Lai, *Chinese Newspapers Published in North America, 1854–1975* (Washington, D.C.: Center for Chinese Research Materials, Association of Research Libraries, 1977). See also Him Mark Lai, "The Chinese Press in the United States and Canada since World War II: A Diversity of Voices," *Chinese America: History and Perspectives*, 1990, 107.

36. Lo and Lai, *Chinese Newspapers Published in North America*, 10, 11, 14; Yung, *Unbound Feet*, 10–11; Chung, "Fighting for Their American Rights," 105, 113.

37. Julie Shuk-yee Lam, "The *Chinese Digest*, 1935–1940," *Chinese America: History and Perspectives*, 1987, 120–121.

38. U.S. Bureau of the Census, *Sixteenth Census of the United States*, Population, 1940.

39. Interview with Sam Sik Low by the author, Aug. 5, 2000.

40. Munson Kwok, "Walter Urian Lum, Founder of the *Chinese Times* (Interview with Mable Lum Lew)," *Gum Saan Journal* 1:1 (Aug. 1977), 2–3; Chung, "Fighting for Their American Rights," 112–114.

41. See J. Percy H. Johnson, ed., *Ayer Directory of Newspapers and Periodicals* (Philadelphia: N.W. Ayer & Son, Inc., 1925–1943).

42. Lam, "The *Chinese Digest*," 120.

43. Lo and Lai, *Chinese Newspapers Published in North America*, 11; Chung, "Fighting for Their American Rights," 113–114.

44. Lai, "The Chinese Press in the United States," 109.

45. Yu, *To Save China, to Save Ourselves*.

46. Liu, *A History of the Chinese in the United States of America*, II, 388–389.

47. Yu, *To Save China, to Save Ourselves*, 66–67, 95.

48. Lai, *Cong huaqiao dao huaren*, 340; idem, "The Chinese Press in the United States," 108–109.

49. Lo and Lai, *Chinese Newspapers Published in North America*, 10; Yu, *To Save China, to Save Ourselves*, 95.

50. Yu, *To Save China, to Save Ourselves*, 96.

51. Zheng Yijun, *Chuanqi rensheng: ji Cai Fujiu zouguo de lu* (A legendary life: The path of Cai Fujiu) (Hong Kong: Haifeng chubanshe, 1997), 38–50, 57–59.

52. Zhou Sen (Sam Wah You), the main shareholder of the paper, was a prominent merchant in Stockton, California; *Chinese Pacific Weekly*, Nov. 21, 1949.

53. It is unclear whether Ma Jiliang ever joined the Chinese Communist Party, but before coming to the United States in the late 1940s, he had served as the chief editor of the *Wenhui Bao* in Shanghai and Hong Kong, a post usually held by an underground party member. The journalist was better known in China for

his earlier acting career in Shanghai, especially because of his brief marriage to Lan Pin (Jiang Qing), who later became Madame Mao Zedong. *Chung Sai Yat Po* ceased operation in early 1951. See Zheng, *Chuanqi rensheng*, 177–179; Lo and Lai, *Chinese Newspapers Published in North America,* 10–11; Lai, "The Chinese Press in the United States," 107–155.

54. Johnson, *Ayer Directory of Newspapers and Periodicals*, 1949.
55. Gilbert Woo, "Baoren Li Daming" [Newspaperman Dai Ming Lee], *Chinese Pacific Weekly*, Mar. 23, 1961, in Hu Jingnan jinian weiyuan hui, *Hu Jingnan wenji* [Selected works of Gilbert Woo] (Hong Kong: Xiangjiang chuban youxian gongsi, 1991), 163.
56. Liu, *A History of the Chinese in the United States of America*, II, 391.
57. Lo and Lai, *Chinese Newspapers Published in North America*, 13; *Chinese Pacific Weekly*, Oct. 1, 1949.
58. Him Mark Lai and Betty Lim, "Gilbert Woo, Chinese American Journalist," in *Hu Jingnan wenji*, 34–41.
59. Ibid.
60. *Chinese Pacific Weekly*, Oct. 4, 1947, Oct. 1, 1949.
61. *Chinese Pacific Weekly*, Oct. 8, 1949. Circulation of the paper was 3,325 in 1957, 4,230 a decade later, and 4,263 in 1975. See Johnson, *Ayer Directory of Newspapers and Periodicals*, 1957–1965 (no numbers for the paper were listed in the earlier issues); *Encyclopedic Directory of Ethnic Newspapers and Periodicals in the United States*, ed. Lubomyr R. Wynar and Anna T. Wynar, 2nd ed. (Littleton, Colo.: Libraries Unlimited, 1976), 57.
62. Zhong Guoren, "Jialian wumei de Taipingyang zhoubao" [A well-priced, high-quality *Chinese Pacific Weekly*], *Chinese Pacific Weekly*, Oct. 8, 1949.
63. *Chinese Times*, March 9, 1943.
64. *Hu Jingnan wenji*, 25–97.
65. *Chinese Times*, Apr. 8, 1943, Feb. 1, 1944, in *Hu Jingnan wenji*, 31–32, 43–44.
66. Lai and Lim, "Gilbert Woo," 39–40.
67. Albert Lim, "Baoren Hu Jingnan yu wo" [My friendship with Gilbert Woo the journalist]," in *Hu Jingnan wenji*, 64.
68. *Chinese American Weekly*, May 24, 1945.
69. Ibid., Oct. 5, 1944.
70. The section was available in a number of community newspapers.
71. Leong Think Hing, "Nanwang de ta—dao Jing Nan" [The unforgettable Jing Nan], in *Hu Jingnan wenji*, 67–68.
72. Lorraine Dong, *Him Mark Lai: Historian* (San Francisco: Chinese American Historical Society, 1995); interview with Laura Jung Lai by the author, May 20, 1997; interview with Him Mark Lai with the author, July 27, 2000.
73. Interview with Maurice Chuck by the author, Feb. 20, 1998.
74. *Chinese Times*, July 6, 1943.
75. Wen Quan, "Chinatown Literature during the Last Ten Years (1939–1949)," trans. Marlon K. Hom, *Amerasia* 9:1 (1982): 82–84, 95.
76. *Chinese Pacific Weekly*, Jan. 14, 1950.
77. Wong Tik Wah, "Dao Hu Jingnan jun" [Mourning Gilbert Woo], in *Hu Jingnan wenji*, 60.

78. Harry Wong, "Zhuiyi Hu Jingnan xiansheng" [Reminiscing of Mr. Gilbert Woo], in *Hu Jingna wenji*, 76.

79. Nee and Nee, *Longtime Californ'*, 219.

80. Gilbert Woo, "Baoren Li Daming," 163–164.

81. Zheng, *Chuanqi renshen*, 166–168; Lai, *Cong huaqiao dao huaren*, 342.

82. Lai, *Cong huaqiao dao huaren*, 343–344; idem, "The Chinese Press in the United States," 111; Yu, *To Save China, to Save Ourselves*, 183; Zheng, *Chuanqi renshen*, 178. On Nov. 9, 1948, a group of eighty Chinese students held a seminar on "War and politics in China" in New York. Participants arrived at the auditorium to find that the walls, chairs, and piano had been covered with feces. See *China Daily News*, Nov. 10, 1948.

83. *China Weekly*, Oct. 22, 1949; Nee and Nee, *Longtime Californ'*, 210–211, 214–215; Lai, *Cong huaqiao dao huaren*, 343; Him Mark Lai, "A Historical Survey of the Chinese Left in America," in *Counterpoint: Perspectives on Asia America*, edited by Emma Gee et al. (Los Angeles: Asian American Studies Center, University of California, Los Angeles, 1976), 72; Zheng, *Chuanqi rensheng*, 184–185.

84. *San Francisco Chronicle*, Oct. 10, 1949.

85. *China Weekly*, Oct. 22, 1949; Nee and Nee, *Longtime Californ'*, 210–211, 214–215; Lai, *Cong huaqiao dao huaren*, 343; idem, "A Historical Survey," 72; Zheng, *Chuanqi rensheng*, 184–185; *San Francisco Chronicle*, Oct. 10, 1949. The *San Francisco Examiner* also reported the incident on Oct. 11, 1949. See FBI file 100–197835, CWMAA, memo of Oct. 11, 1949.

86. Gilbert Woo, "Tongyuanhui shijian" [The CACA incident], *Chinese Pacific Weekly*, July 1 to Aug. 5, 1971.

87. *China Weekly*, Oct. 22, 1949.

88. Ibid.; Nee and Nee, *Longtime Californ'*, 210–211; Lai, *Cong huaqiao dao huaren*, 343; idem, "A Historical Survey," 72; Zheng, *Chuanqi rensheng*, 184–185.

89. Lai and Lim, "Gilbert Woo," 43–44.

90. Lai, "The Chinese Press in the United States," 137.

91. Gilbert Woo, "Tongyuanhui shijian," Aug. 5, 1976.

92. Him Mark Lai, "China Politics and the U.S. Chinese Communities," in *Counterpoint*, ed. Gee et al., 158.

93. *China Weekly*, Oct. 22, 1949; Lai, *Cong huaqiao dao huaren*, 344; Zheng, *Chuanqi rensheng*, 185–186.

94. Nee and Nee, *Longtime Californ'* 211; Lai and Lim, "Gilbert Woo," 44; Zheng, *Chuanqi rensheng*, 185–186.

95. FBI-CWMAA.

96. Zheng, *Chuanqi rensheng*, 185; *China Weekly*, Oct. 22, 1949.

97. Gilbert Woo, "Tongyuanhui shijian," July 22, 1976.

98. *Chinese Pacific Weekly*, Oct. 22, 1949.

99. Ibid., Oct. 4, 1947.

100. Ibid., Oct. 1, 1949.

101. Even in the late 1950s Woo would try to arrange to send his daughter from Hong Kong to study in Beijing. See Leong, "Nanwang de ta," 68.

102. *Chinese Pacific Weekly*, July 4, 1953.
103. *Chinese Pacific Weekly*, Sept. 3, 1949.
104. Ibid.
105. *Chinese Pacific Weekly*, Aug. 5, 1976.
106. Leong, "Nanwang de ta," 68.
107. Wong, "Zhuiyi Hu Jingnan xiansheng," 77.
108. *Chinese Nationalist Daily,* April 16, 1946, in *Hu Jingnan wenji*, 82–83.
109. *Chinese Nationalist Daily*, April 19, 1946, in *Hu Jingnan wenji*, 84–85.
110. *Chinese Pacific Weekly*, Feb. 5, 1948.
111. Ibid., Sept. 3, 1949.
112. *China Weekly*, Dec. 13, 1950.
113. Maurice Chuck considered Gilbert Woo his mentor. Chuck protested when Woo canceled the contract with the *China Weekly*. Maurice Chuck, *Huang Yunji xuanji* [Selected works of Maurice H. Chuck], vol. 2 (San Francisco: Chinese Journal Corporation), 219.
114. Gilbert Woo, "Tongyuanhui shijian," July 1, 1976.

CHAPTER 6   *The Quest for Family Stability*

1. In the summer of 1947, *Life* magazine published a thirteen-page report on the "American Woman's Dilemma." See William H. Chafe, *The American Women: Her Changing Social, Economic, and Political Roles, 1920–1970* (New York: Oxford University Press, 1972), 199–225.
2. Valerie Matsumoto, "Desperately Seeking 'Deirdre': Gender Roles, Multicultural Relations, and Nisei Women Writers of the 1930s," in *Frontiers: A Journal of Women Studies* 12: 1 (1991): 19–32; Emily Honig and Gail Hershatter, *Personal Voices: Chinese Women in the 1980s* (Stanford: Stanford University Press, 1988).
3. Nine of Lao Heng's essays appeared in the *Chinese Pacific Weekly*: "Songli" [Gifts], Sept. 13, 1947; "Zhangfu fa piqi" [Husband's temperament], Oct. 18, 1947; "Lengnuan fuqi" [Cold or warm couples], Nov. 15, 1945; "Youmo gan" [A sense of humor], Nov. 22, 1947; "Daling" [Darling], Feb. 28, 1948; "Guxi zhijian" [Between mother- and daughter-in-law], Mar. 6, 1948; "Maipiao" [Buying lottery tickets], Mar. 13, 1948; "Ziman" [Complacency], Mar. 20, 1948; "Hanxu" [Reserving], Mar. 27, 1948.
4. *Chinese Pacific Weekly*, Mar. 6, 1948.
5. Ibid.
6. Ibid.
7. Ibid.
8. Lao Heng, "Daling."
9. Ibid.
10. Lao Heng, "Lengnuan fuqi."
11. Ibid.
12. Ibid.
13. Ibid.
14. Lao Heng, "Ziman."
15. Lao Heng, "Zhangfu fa piqi."

16. Lao Heng, "Hanxu."
17. Paula Fass, *The Damned and the Beautiful: American Youth in the 1920s* (New York: Oxford University Press, 1977), 71.
18. Shou Yong, "Xiezai guxi zhijian hou" [Some afterthoughts about Lao Heng's "mother- and daughter-in-law"], *Chinese Pacific Weekly*, Mar. 20, 1948.
19. Huang Wang, "Xiangei Lao Heng xiansheng fuzheng" [A debate with Mr. Lao Heng]," *Chinese Pacific Weekly*, May 22, 1948.
20. Liu Heng, "Wo yao qu ge cungu" [I shall marry a Chinese country girl], *Chinese Pacific Weekly*, Nov. 13, 1948.
21. Huang, "Xiangei Lao Heng xianshen fuzheng."
22. Gilbert Woo, "Zagan" [Some afterthoughts], *Chinese Pacific Weekly*, July 1, 1948.
23. *Chung Sai Yat Po*, Apr. 12, 15, 22, May 18, 19, 30, June 5, 14, 16, Oct. 25, 1950; *China Daily News*, May 24, June 10, 12, 1950.
24. *Chung Sai Yat Po*, Oct. 25, 1950.
25. Ibid., Apr. 22, 1950.
26. Ibid., June 5, 1950; *San Francisco Chronicle*, June 4, 1950; *China Daily News*, June 10, 1950.
27. *Chung Sai Yat Po*, June 14, 1950; *San Francisco Chronicle*, June 4, 1950.
28. Ibid., June 15, 16, 17, 23, 1950; *China Daily News*, June 28, 1950.
29. *Chung Sai Yat Po*, June 27, July 11, 22, Aug. 1, 2, 1950.
30. Ibid., Aug. 9, 1950.
31. Ibid.
32. Ibid.
33. Ibid., Sept. 22, 1950.
34. Interview with Tenley Chin by Kristen Martin, directed by the author, May 29, 1997.
35. On the medical school, see Mary Brown Bullock, *An American Transplant: The Rockefeller Foundation and Peking Union Medical College* (Berkeley: University of California Press, 1980).
36. Interview with Betty Lew by the author, Dec. 2, 1997.
37. Interview with Danny Gin by Britton Yee, directed by the author, May 8, 1998.
38. Interview with Mary Yee by Denise Yee, directed by the author, Mar. 9, 1998.
39. Interview with Tenley Chin.
40. Interview with Chiu Chun Ma Wong by Denise Yee directed by the author, Jan. 30, 1998.
41. *Chinese Pacific Weekly*, June 24, 1950.
42. Ibid., Jan. 17, 1953.
43. Interview with Tuen Ock Chu by Jeff Wong directed by the author, Nov. 20, 1995 and Feb. 27, 1996.
44. Judy Yung, *Chinese Women of America: A Pictorial History* (Seattle: University of Washington Press, 1986), 81.
45. Gilbert Woo, "Huafu Tuanti" [Chinese American Community Organizations] *Chinese Pacific Weekly*, Jan. 27, 1951, in Hu Jingnan jinian weiyuan hui, *Hu Jingnan wenji* [Selected works of Gilbert Woo] (Hong Kong: Xiangjiang chuban youxian gongsi, 1991), 279.

46. The investigators concluded that the couple had a bad marriage and the woman was allowed to stay. Chinese General Immigration Case Files, 1944 to 1955, RG 85, Records of the U.S. Immigration and Naturalization Service, National Archives, San Bruno, Calif., file 207. There are a few cases of deportation. One French woman who married a Chinese American man while he was stationed in Paris was ordered to leave the country after she filed for a divorce. An investigation was conducted to determine if the husband should return to her what she claimed to be her personal property (Immigration case file 69).

47. Chinese General Immigration Case Files, 1944 to 1955, RG 85, Records of the U.S. Immigration and Naturalization Service, National Archives, San Bruno, Calif., file 589.

48. Mirjana Morokvasic's work is helpful in understanding immigrant women in the United States. See Morokvasic, "Women in Migration: Beyond the Reductionist Outlook," in *One Way Ticket: Migration and Female Labor,* ed. Annie Phizacklea (Boston: Routledge & Kegan Paul, 1983), 13–32.

49. *Chung Sai Yat Po,* Oct. 23, 1950.

50. Roger Daniels, *Asian America: Chinese and Japanese in the United States since 1850* (Seattle: University of Washington Press, 1988), 187.

51. *Chung Sai Yat Po,* Oct. 23, 1950

52. Ibid.

53. Ibid.

54. *Chinese American Weekly,* Feb. 8, 1951, 32.

55. Ibid., Jan. 25, 1950

56. Ibid.

57. Ibid.

58. Ibid., July 21, 1950.

59. Ibid., May 1, 1947.

60. Ibid., July 1, 1948.

61. Xiangyun's marriage took place after she came to the United States, but she was a postwar immigrant. *Chinese American Weekly,* Oct. 27, 1949.

62. *China Daily News,* May 24, 1950; *Chung Sai Yat Po,* May 30, June 14, 1950.

63. *China Daily News,* June 24, 27, 1950.

64. *Chung Sai Yat Po,* June 4, 1950; *China Daily News,* June 2, 12, 24, 27, 1950.

65. *Chung Sai Yat Po,* June 10, 1950; *China Daily News,* Dec. 26, 1949.

66. *Chinese American Weekly,* June 11, 1953, 6.

67. Renqiu Yu, *To Save China, to Save Ourselves: The Chinese Hand Laundry Alliance of New York* (Philadelphia: Temple University Press, 1992). Many non-party-affiliated newspapers also credited the Communist Revolution in China, although they remained skeptical about certain aspects of the Communist-led reforms.

68. *Chinese Pacific Weekly,* Dec. 25, 1948.

69. *Chinese American Weekly,* Jan. 5, 1950.

70. *Chinese Pacific Weekly,* Jan. 24, 1953.

71. Ibid., Jan. 31, 1953.

72. Ibid., April 4, 1953.

73. Ibid., May 16, 23, 1953.

74. Ibid.
75. Ibid.
76. Wen Ying, "Jiantao ni ziji" [Criticize yourself], *Chinese Pacific Weekly*, May 16, 1953.
77. Ibid., Apr. 11, 1953.
78. Ibid., Apr. 18, 1953.
79. *Chinese Pacific Weekly*, Mar. 20, 1954.
80. Zi Min, "Shixian zhangfu de lixiang" [Realize husband's dreams], *Chinese Pacific Weekly,* Dec. 21, 1950.
81. Zi Min, "*Zhiye funü*" [Career women], *Chinese American Weekly*, Aug. 17, 1950.
82. Wen Qing, "Mali ana, mofan de zhanniang" [Mariana, a model war bride], *Chinese Pacific Weekly*, Aug. 23, 1951.
83. Ibid.
84. Ibid.
85. Ibid.
86. Xiao Min, "*Sanzhong butong dianxing de huaqiao funü*" [Three different types of Chinese American women], *Chinese Pacific Weekly*, June 24, 1950.
87. *Chinese Pacific Weekly*, April 10, 1954.
88. Ibid.
89. Ibid., June 24, 1950.
90. Ibid., May 1, 1954.
91. Aihwa Ong, "Anthropology, China and Modernities: The Geopolitics of Cultural Knowledge" in *The Future of Anthropological Knowledge*, ed. Henrietta L. Moore (New York: Routledge, 1996), 64.
92. *Chinese American Weekly*, Jan 12, 1950.
93. Gilbert Woo, "Huafu Tuanti," [Chinese American community organizations], *Chinese Pacific Weekly*, Jan. 27, 1951.

CHAPTER 7   *In Times of Crisis*

1. Mae M. Ngai, "Legacies of Exclusion: Illegal Chinese Immigration during the Cold War Years," *Journal of Ethnic History* 18:1 (Fall 1998): 4.
2. *Chinese Pacific Weekly*, Nov. 21, 1953.
3. Ibid., March 27, 1954.
4. Everett F. Drumright, "Report on the Problem of Fraud at Hong Kong," Foreign Service Despatch 931, Dec. 9, 1955, 43. National Archives II, College Park, Md., files of the Immigration and Naturalization Service, Central Office, 1949–1958, "Document Fraud," file 56364/51.6, RG 85 (subsequently cited as National Archives II, "Document Fraud").
5. Sidney B. Schatkin, Leon N. Sussman, and Dorris Edward Yarbrough, "Chinese Immigration and Blood Tests," *Criminal Law Review* (Spring 1956): 7, in National Archives II, "Document Fraud", 56364/51.6.
6. *Lue Chow Kon et al. v. Brownell*, 122 Fed. Supp. 370, June 22, 1954.
7. Ibid.; *Chinese Pacific Weekly*, Sept. 29, 1952; Nov. 21, 1953.
8. *Lue Chow Kon v. Brownell*, U.S. Ct. of App., 2d Ct., March 10, 1955.
9. Schatkin, Sussman, and Yarbrough, "Chinese Immigration and Blood Tests," 8.

10. 54 Stat. 876, Act of Oct. 14, 1940, 1171–1172.
11. Ernest L. Hover to Allen C. Devaney, "Declaratory Judgment Cases Filed under Section 503," April 21, 1956, National Archives II, "Document Fraud," file 56364/51.6.
12. Bruce G. Barber, District Director, San Francisco, to W. F. Kelly, Assistant Commissioner, Enforcement Division, Nov. 15, 1951; David H. Carnahan, Regional Commissioner, Southwest Regional Office, to Barber, "Informal Report re: Chinese Section 503 Actions," Apr. 24, 1956, National Archives II, "Document Fraud," file 56364/51.6.
13. Barber to Argyle R. Mackey, Central Office Commissioner, Feb. 15, 1952, National Archives II, "Document Fraud," file 56364/51.6.
14. Ibid.
15. Ibid.
16. Ibid.
17. Ibid.
18. INS Commissioner to Deputy Attorney General Frank Chambers, Chief of the Legal and Legislative Section, "Suits against the Secretary of State under section 503 of the Nationality Act of 1940," Feb. 20, 1952, National Archives II, "Document Fraud," file 56364/51.6.
19. John Patrick Diggings, *The Proud Decades: America in War and in Peace, 1941–1960* (New York: W. W. Norton, 1988), 117–118.
20. *Chinese Pacific Weekly*, Dec. 6, 1952.
21. Hover to Devaney, Apr. 21, 1956.
22. Ibid.
23. Ibid.
24. 110 F. Supp. 50; Hover to Devaney, Apr. 21, 1956.
25. Hover to Devaney, Apr. 21, 1956.
26. Barber to Kelly, Nov. 15, 1951; Carnahan to Barber, Apr. 24, 1956.
27. Hover to Devaney, Apr. 21, 1956.
28. Roger Daniels, *Asian America: Chinese and Japanese in the United States since 1850* (Seattle: University of Washington Press, 1988), 308; Him Mark Lai, "Unfinished Business: The Chinese Confession Program, " in *The Repeal and Its Legacy: Proceedings of the Conference on the 50th Anniversary of the Repeal of the Exclusion Acts. Nov. 12–14, 1993* (San Francisco: Chinese Historical Society of America, 1994); Ngai, "Legacies of Exclusion."
29. Drumright's last post was as ambassador to the Republic of China from 1958 to 1962. See E. J. Kahn, Jr., *The China Hands: American's Foreign Service and What Befell Them* (New York: Viking Press, 1975), 37–38, 309.
30. Drumright, "Report on the Problem of Fraud," Dec. 9, 1955.
31. The consul requested that the report be made available to sixteen government agencies, including the Passport Office, the Visa Office, the INS, the CIA, and the FBI. Drumright, "Report on the Problem of Fraud," Dec. 9, 1955.
32. Robert Griffith, *The Politics of Fear: Joseph R. McCarthy and the Senate* (Lexington: University of Kentucky, 1979), 316.
33. Drumright, "Report on the Problem of Fraud," Dec. 9, 1955.
34. According to his source, a Chinese man, Young John Ming, who was then serving

as a private first class at Fort George Meade, Maryland, in the field of military intelligence, was found to be a paper son. Drumright to State Department, "Memorandum from Chief of Naval Operations," Foreign Service Despatch, 352, Oct. 26, 1956, National Archives II, "Document Fraud," file 56364/51.6.

35. Barber to Mackey, Feb. 15, 1952.

36. This is evident in files of Federal Bureau of Investigation. See FBI file 105–HQ-1332: Chinese American Democratic Youth Club (FBI-CADYC); file 100–HQ-196148: *China Daily News* Cross Reference (FBI-CDN); file 100–HQ-365097: Chinese Hand Laundry Alliance (FBI-CHLA); and FBI file 100–197835, "Chinese Workers Mutual Aid Association" (FBI-CWMAA).

37. J. Austin Murphy, Divisional Investigator, to James F. Greene, Chief, General Investigations Branch, "Hong Kong Seamen's Union," Nov. 16, 1956, National Archives II, "Document Fraud," file 56364/51.6.

38. Raymond F. Farrell, Assistant Commissioner, Investigations Division, to Regional Commissioner, San Pedro, Calif., "Hong Kong Seamen's Union," Nov. 19, 1956, National Archives II, "Document Fraud," file 56364/51.6.

39. Renqiu Yu, *To Save China, to Save Ourselves: The Chinese Hand Laundry Alliance of New York* (Philadelphia: Temple University Press, 1992), 191–192.

40. Farrell to Virginia Richmond, Regional Commissioner, Southeast Region, "Grand Jury Probe at New York Re Chinese Frauds," Mar. 22, 1956, National Archives II, "Document Fraud," file 56364/51.6.

41. Farrell to regional Chief of Investigations, "Report on the Problem of Fraud at Hong Kong," Feb. 14, 1956, National Archives II, "Document Fraud," file 56364/51.6.

42. James F. Greene to Farrell, "Liaison with U.S. Attorney, San Francisco and Seattle," Mar. 21, 1956, National Archives II, "Document Fraud," file 56364/51.6.

43. D. E. Yarbrough, "Grand Jury Investigation of Chinese Passport and Immigration Frauds," Jan. 27, 1956, National Archives II, "Document Fraud," file 56364/51.6.

44. *San Francisco Examiner*, Mar. 3, 1956.

45. Ibid.; Robert F. Cartwright, Acting Administrator, Bureau of Security and Consular Affairs, to J. Walter Yeagley, Chairman, Interdepartmental Committee, "In Reply Refer to F130—Chinese Frauds," Sept. 18, 1956, National Archives II, "Document Fraud," file 56364/51.6; Ngai, "Legacies of Exclusion," 8–9.

46. James F. Greene, "Chinese Fraud Situation at San Francisco," May 8, 1956, National Archives II, "Document Fraud," file 56364/51.6.

47. *Chinese World*, Feb. 15, 1956.

48. *The Call Bulletin*, Mar. 5, 1956, National Archives II, "Document Fraud," file 56364/51.6.

49. O. S. Remington, Deputy Regional Commissioner, St. Paul, Minn., "Use by Chinese Aliens of Fraudulently Obtained Documentation as Citizens of Canada," July 2, 1956, National Archives II, "Document Fraud," file 56364/51.6; Edwin B. Howard, Assistant Commissioner, to all Regional Commissioners, "Intelligence Information, Movement of Chinese to Western Hemisphere Countries outside the United States," Nov. 14, 1956, National Archives II, "Document Fraud," file 56364/51.6.

50. Irvin P. Shrode, Office in Charge, St. Paul, Minn., to Office in Charge at An-

chorage, Alaska, July 5, 1951. National Archives II, "Document Fraud," file 56364/51.6.

51. Edwin B. Howard, Assistant Commissioner, Field Inspection and Security Division, to Frank H. Partridge, Assistant Commissioner, Enforcement Division, "Intelligence Summary, Chinese Fraud and Immigration Problem," Aug. 17, 1956, National Archives II, "Document Fraud," file 56364/51.6.

52. James F. Greene, "George Lee and Eng Wing On," April 19, 1956, National Archives II, "Document Fraud," file 56364/51.6. The press also reported that a lawyer for the Retail Clerks International Union charged that fifty Chinese supermarket employees in Yuba City, California, were "confined to barracks-like quarters" and forced to work ten hours a day, six days a week, and to kick back $265,000 from their wages to their four Chinese employers. See also Stanford M. Lyman, "Marriage and the Family among Chinese Immigrants to America, 1850–1960," in Lyman, *The Asian in North America* (Santa Barbara, Calif.: ABC-Clio, 1970), 71.

53. J. Austin Murphy, Divisional Investigator, to James F. Greene, "Subversive Chinese, Larchmont, New York," May 8, 1956, National Archives II, "Document Fraud," file 56364/51.6.

54. Greene to Farrell, "Meeting at Department of Justice Today," June 15, 1956, National Archives II, "Document Fraud," file 56364/51.6.

55. U.S. Attorney's Office to Joseph M. Swing, INS Commissioner, "Special Grand Jury Investigation in New York of Chinese Passport and Immigration Frauds," May 18, 1956, GLG M10–458, National Archives II, "Document Fraud," file 56364/51.6.

56. Greene to Farrell, June 15, 1956.

57. Yarbrough, "Grand Jury Investigation of Chinese Passport and Immigration Frauds," Apr. 17, 1956, National Archives II, "Document Fraud," file 56364/51.6.

58. See FBI-CWMAA, FBI-CADYC, FBI-CHLA, and FBI-CDN.

59. Han Wee Kee of New York is the only informant identified in the declassified INS files. Han Wee Kee was terminated as a witness because of his confinement to a mental hospital. Regional Chief of Investigations, Burlington, to Assistant Commissioner, Investigations Division, "Evaluation of Confidential Informants," May 25, 1955; INS Report of Investigation, "Han Wee Kee," A-9 555 109, May 9, 1955, National Archives II, "Document Fraud," file 56364/51.6.

60. W. G. Folts, Acting Chief, Investigations Division, Burlington, to New York District Director, "Your A6 798 834; Pan Cho Ying," June 29, 1956, National Archives II, "Document Fraud," file 56364/51.6.

61. FBI San Francisco Report, Apr. 5, 1943, FBI-CWMAAA.

62. Miscellaneous FBI memos and reports, Mar. 1, 1945 to June 19, 1945, FBI-CWMAA.

63. FBI-CADYC, vol. 1.

64. FBI-CDA, vol. 1.

65. Farrell to Regional Commissioners and District Directors, May 19, 1955, National Archives II, "Document Fraud," file 56364/51.6.

66. Ibid.
67. Yu, *To Save China, to Save Ourselves*, 187–188.
68. *China Daily News*, Feb. 8, 10, 1951, in FBI-CDN.
69. Ibid.
70. J. Edgar Hoover, "Chinese Workers Mutual Aid Association," May 23, 1956, in FBI-CWMAA.
71. Ibid.
72. Regional Chief of Investigations, Burlington, to Assistant Commissioner, Investigations Division, "Evaluation of Confidential Informants," May 25, 1955, National Archives II, "Document Fraud," file 56364/51.6. These index cards remain sealed.
73. W. R. Moore, "Fraud in Connection with Chinese Literacy Tests," Dec. 8, 1955, National Archives II, "Document Fraud," file 56364/51.6.
74. San Francisco Report, Oct. 19, 1955, FBI-CWMAA.
75. Interview with Maurice Chuck by the author, Feb. 22, 1998.
76. The author had several discussions with Him Mark Lai on this subject. He was rather surprised to see that the FBI had accumulated seven volumes (about 1,500 pages) of documents regarding Min Qing. See also Franklin Woo interview in Victor G. Nee and Brett de Bary Nee, *Longtime Californ': A Documentary Study of an American Chinatown* (New York: Pantheon Books, 1972), 216. The FBI installed "technical surveillance" on the telephone at the Chinese Hand Laundry Alliance, see Yu, *To Save China, to Save Ourselves,* 191.
77. James M. Sweet, Acting District Director, Helena, Mont., to G. S. Remington, Deputy Regional Commissioner, St. Paul, Minn., "Re Item 6 Monthly Intelligence Report," Nov. 14, 1956, National Archives II, "Document Fraud," file 56364/51.6.
78. M. F. Fargione, Chief, Investigations Division, Burlington, to Raymond F. Farrell, "Smuggling of Chinese into the United States," Apr. 23, 1956; INS Record of Sworn Statement, "Smuggling of Chinese into the United States," Mar. 14, 1956, National Archives II, "Document Fraud," file 56364/51.6.
79. Sidney Fass, "Smuggling of Chinese into the United States," Apr. 11, 1956, National Archives II, "Document Fraud," file 56364/51.6.
80. Bruce G. Barber, "Samuel Gway Choy and Albert Chow," Oct. 24, 1956. Chow was indicted in September 1956, but the case was closed a month later.
81. *Chinese Pacific Weekly*, Mar. 1, 1952.
82. Yarbrough, "Grand Jury Investigation of Chinese Passport and Immigration Frauds," Jan. 27, 1956, National Archives II, "Document Fraud," file 56364/51.6.
83. William F. Thompkins, Assistant Attorney General, to Hoover, Oct. 22, 1956, FBI-CWMAA. On May 1, 1956, FBI agents observed the headquarters of the CWMAA to be vacated.
84. Interview with Laura Jung Lai by the author, May 20, 1997.
85. *San Francisco Examiner*, Mar. 1, 1956.
86. Yarbrough, "Grand Jury Investigation of Chinese Passport and Immigration Frauds," May 8, 1956, National Archives II, "Document Fraud," file 56364/51.6.
87. Ibid.

88. Yarbrough, "Grand Jury Investigation of Chinese Passport and Immigration Frauds," Apr. 24 to May 1, 1956; Greene, "George Lee and Eng Wing On," Apr. 19, 1956, National Archives II, "Document Fraud," file 56364/51.6.

89. Yarbrough, "Grand Jury Investigation of Chinese Passport and Immigration Frauds," Feb. 27, Mar. 1, 16, 1956. See also Affidavit of Chin Seu Loon, Brooklyn, New York, Mar. 13, 1956, 3; National Archives II, "Document Fraud," file 56364/51.6.

90. *Ly Shew v. Acheson*, 110 F. Supp. 50, 1953.

91. J. A. Murphy, "Grand Jury Probe at San Francisco," Mar. 6, 1956, National Archives II, "Document Fraud," file 56364/51.6; Bruce G. Barber to James Greene, "Grand Jury Investigation of Citizenship Frauds in the San Francisco Area," Mar. 5, 1965, National Archives II, "Document Fraud," file 56364/51.6.

92. *San Francisco Examiner*, Mar. 1, 1956.

93. Greene, "George Lee and Eng Wing On," Apr. 19, 1956.

94. INS Report of Investigation, Chinese Frauds Case, May 21–25, 1956, National Archives II, "Document Fraud," file 56364/51.6.

95. *Chinese Pacific Weekly*, Mar. 27, 1954.

96. INS Report of Investigation, "Yee Fong Min and Others," Sept.–Oct. 1955, National Archives II, "Document Fraud," file 56364/51.6; *San Francisco Chronicle*, July 18, 1956.

97. *Daily News*, May 3, 1956.

98. *Oakland Tribune*, Mar. 2, 1956.

99. Shing Tai Liang to Warren G. Magnuson, March 9, 1956, in Warren G. Magnuson Papers, Manuscripts and University Archives Division, University of Washington, Seattle.

100. One report to the State Department indicated that Taiwanese passports were sold in Hong Kong for $25,000 HK apiece, and they were possibly sold through the Chinese Communist-operated China Travel Agency. The source indicated that $2,000 HK from the sale of each passport went back to Taiwan. Aaron R. Coleman, American Consulate at Hong Kong, to Jack B. Minor, State Department, "Chinese Nationalist Passports," Aug. 15, 1956, National Archives II, "Document Fraud," file 56364/51.6.

101. Yarbrough, "Grand Jury Investigation of Chinese Passport and Immigration Fraud," March 9, 1956.

102. Robert K. Lee to Commissioner Joseph M. Swing, Feb. 23, 1956, National Archives II, "Document Fraud," file 56364/51.6.

103. M. F. Fargione, Chief Regional Investigator to Raymond F. Farrell, "Prominent Chinese Fraudulently Bringing Servants to the United States," Aug. 29, 1955, and Farrell to Fargione, Dec. 14, 1955, National Archives II, "Document Fraud," file 56364/51.6.

104. Report of Scott Mcleod, Administrator, Bureau of Security and Consular Affairs, Apr. 12, 1956, National Archives II, "Document Fraud," file 56364/51.6.

105. William H. Bartley, Regional Intelligence Officer, Richmond, Virginia, to Edwin B. Howard, Assistant Commissioner, Field Inspection and Security Division, "Chinese Paper Name Association," Oct. 24, 1956, National Archives II, "Document Fraud," file 56364/51.6.

106. *Chinese Pacific Weekly*, Apr. 3, 1954.

107. *Chinese Journal*, Mar. 2, 6, 8, 1956, English translation, National Archives II, "Document Fraud," file 56364/51.6.

108. Shing-tai Liang to H. Alexander Smith, Mar. 9, 1956, in Smith to J. M. Swing, Mar. 19, 1956, National Archives II, "Document Fraud," file 56364/51.6. Also see Liang to Warren G. Magnuson, Mar. 9, 1956, in Warren G. Magnuson Papers.

109. *Chinese Journal*, Mar. 10, 1956.

110. *Daily News*, May 3, 1956, National Archives II, "Document Fraud," file 56364/51.6.

111. *Chinese American Weekly*, May 17, 1956.

112. Gilbert Woo, "Da peishen tuan chuanxun huafu shetuan" [The grand jury indictment of the Chinese American associations], *Chinese Pacific Weekly*, Mar. 23, 1956.

113. *Hsing Tao Hin Pao*, Mar. 25, 1956, in Drumright to the Department of State, "Reaction in Hong Kong Chinese Language Press to Disclosures of Fraud in Chinese Immigration to United States," Foreign Service Despatch, 1363, Apr. 23, 1956, National Archives II, "Document Fraud," file 56364/51.6.

114. *Vancouver Daily Province*, undated, National Archives II, "Document Fraud," file 56364/51.6.

115. Political Advertisement, "Vote for John F. Shelly, Chinatown's Congressman," *Chinese Pacific Weekly*, May 31, 1952.

116. Everett D. Drumright, "Visit of Congressman Shelly," Foreign Service Despatch 3056, Nov. 30, 1956.

117. William F. Thompkins to FBI Director, "Movement of Communist Chinese Internal Security," Mar. 21, 1956, National Archives II, "Document Fraud," file 56364/51.6; *Chinese Journal*, Mar. 17, 1956.

118. *Chinese Journal*, Mar. 9, 10, 1956.

119. Ibid., Apr. 6, 1956.

120. Ibid., Mar. 16, 20, 1956; Gilbert Woo, "Yimin kongbu" [Immigration terror], *Chinese Pacific Weekly*, Nov. 29, 1947, in Hu Jingnan jinian weiyuan hui, *Hu Jingnan wenji* [Selected works of Gilbert Woo] (Hong Kong: Xiangjiang chuban youxian gongsi, 1991).

121. The ruling was published in community newspapers. See *Chinese Times*, Mar. 21, 1956.

122. *Chinese Journal*, Apr. 4, 1956.

123. Yarbrough, "Grand Jury Investigation of Chinese Passport and Immigration Frauds," Mar. 16, 1956.

124. Drumright to the Department of State, Apr. 23, 1956, National Archives II, "Document Fraud," file 56364/51.6.

125. Schatkin, Sussman, Yarbrough, "Chinese Immigration and Blood Tests," 3.

126. Drumright to the Department of State, "Reaction in Hong Kong Chinese Language Press to Disclosures of Fraud in Chinese Immigration to United States," Apr. 23, 1956.

127. Ralph E. Stanley, Investigator, San Francisco, to Ralph P. Harris, Assistant District Director of Investigation, San Francisco, "Confession Program, Oriental

Fraud Unit," Dec. 19, 1956, National Archives II, "Document Fraud," file 56364/51.6.

128. Ibid.

129. Roy R. Anderson, Acting Supervisor, Oriental Fraud Unit, San Francisco, to Bruce G. Barber, "Through Official Channels," Nov. 15, 1956, National Archives II, "Document Fraud," file 56364/51.6.

130. Stanley to Harris, Dec. 19, 1956.

131. Farrell to Regional Chief of Investigations, "Chinese Frauds—Confession Program," Feb. 6, 1957, National Archives II, "Document Fraud," file 56364/51.6.

132. Stanley to Harris, Dec. 19, 1956. This part was later deleted from the final memo that was distributed to other regions and regional investigative officers. See F. C. Ohswaldt, Regional Chief of Investigations, Southwest Region, to INS Commissioner, "Chinese Frauds—Confession Program," Jan. 14, 1957, National Archives II, "Document Fraud," file 56364/51.6.

133. Stanley to Harris, Dec. 19, 1956.

134. Ibid.

135. Ibid.

136. Ibid.

137. Ibid.

138. American Council for Nationalities Service, "Chinese Confession Program of the Immigration and Naturalization Service," *Interpreter Releases*, 37:2 (Jan. 15, 1960): 6.

139. 71 Stat. 639, Act of Sept. 11, 1957.

140. American Council for Nationalities Service, "Chinese Confession Program of the Immigration and Naturalization Service," *Interpreter Releases*, 7.

141. INS report of investigation on Lee Ying and five others, case file 833 941, Feb. 4, 1957, National Archives II, "Document Fraud," file 56364/51.6.

142. Him Mark Lai, *Cong huaqiao dao huaren: ershi shiji meiguo huaren shehui fazhan shi* [From overseas Chinese to ethnic Chinese: A history of the social development of America's Chinese in the twentieth century] (Hong Kong: Sanlian shudian, 1992), 360.

143. Stanley to Harris, Dec. 19, 1956.

144. Anderson to Barber, "Through Official Channels," Sept. 10, 1956, National Archives II, "Document Fraud," file 56364/51.6.

145. Interview with Shirley Wong by the author, June 15, 1999; INS Record of Sworn Statement, file 12 656 054, San Francisco, June 8, 1962. The author thanks Denise Yee for this source.

146. Interview with Mary Yee by Denise Yee, directed by the author, March 9, 1998.

147. *Chinese American Weekly*, Aug. 4, 1960.

148. Ibid., Oct. 20, 1960.

149. Ibid.

150. Peter Lew, "The Family Immigration History and Genealogy of Lew Chuck Suey (Lew Hawk Yee)," (1997), 3; interview with Peter Lew and Elizabeth Lew Anderson by the author, Nov. 14, 15, 1997.

151. Interview with Maurice Chuck, Feb. 22, 1998. See also Mae M. Ngai, "Legacies of Exclusion: Illegal Chinese Immigration during the Cold War Years," *Journal of American Ethnic History* 18:1 (Fall 1998): 25.

152. Several 503 plaintiffs withdrew their cases and returned to Hong Kong. Yarbrough, "Grand Jury Investigation of Chinese Passport and Immigration Frauds," May 21, 1956.
153. *Dear Wing Jung v. United States*, 312 F. 2d. (1962).
154. Edw. J. Shaughnessy, District Director, New York, to Leland W. Williams, Deputy Regional Commissioner, "Alien Crewmen on Chinese Nationalist Vessels with Regard to Red Effect Program, Illegal Entry, Deportation and Passport Requirements," June 19, 1956, National Archives II, "Document Fraud," file 56364/51.6.
155. Schlem & Burroughs Spar, Counselors at Law, to Godfrey P. Schmidt, June 29, 1956; L. Austin Murphy, "Special Inquiry Officer Hearing under Section 243(h)," July 9, 1956; National Archives II, "Document Fraud," file 56364/51.6; *Annual Report of the Immigration and Naturalization Service*, 1956, 16.
156. Daniels, *Asian America*, 308.
157. *Dear Wing Jung v. United States*.
158. *China Daily News*, Feb. 8, 1951, in FBI-CDN.
159. *Chinese Journal*, Apr. 17, 1956.
160. Ngai, "Legacies of Exclusion," 20; Lai, "Unfinished Business," 13–14.
161. Gilbert Woo, "Quanqiao dahui" [On the Chinese American National Conference], *Chinese Pacific Weekly*, Mar. 1, 1957, in *Hu Jingnan wenji*, 489.
162. Lai, *Cong huaqiao dao huaren*, 361.
163. Edward C. M. Chen, "Historical Highlights: Houston Lodge Chinese American Citizen's Alliance," in *From America to Shangri-li: Chinese American Citizens Alliance 42nd Biennial National Convention, Houston, Texas, August 11–14, 1993* (San Francisco: Chinese American Citizens Alliance, 1993), 13; Sue Fawn Chung, "Fighting for Their American Rights: A History of the Chinese American Citizens Alliance," in *Claiming America: Constructing Chinese American Identities during the Exclusion Era*, ed. K. Scott Wong and Sucheng Chan (Philadelphia: Temple University Press, 1998), 111; Y. C. Hong, *A Brief History of the Chinese American Citizens Alliance* (San Francisco: Chinese American Citizens Alliance, 1955), 2–4.
164. *Annual Report of the Immigration and Naturalization Service*, 1956–1966.
165. News Release, Department of Justice, Dec. 31, 1972.
166. E. P. Hutchinson, *Legislative History of American Immigration Policy, 1798–1965* (Philadelphia: University of Pennsylvania Press, 1981), 511, 517.
167. Ibid.
168. News Release, Department of Justice, Dec. 31, 1972.

Epilogue

1. Interview with Him Mark Lai by the author, July 28, 2000.
2. Him Mark Lai, "To Bring Forth a New China, to Build a Better America: The Chinese Marxist Left in America to the 1960s," *Chinese America: History and Perspectives*, 1992, 56; Renqiu Yu, *To Save China, to Save Ourselves: The Chinese Hand Laundry Alliance of New York* (Philadelphia: Temple University Press, 1992), 191–193.
3. Kate Xiao Zhou, *How the Farmers Changed China: Power of the People* (Boulder: Westview Press, 1996), 26–27.

4. E. J. Kahn, Jr., *The China Hands: American's Foreign Service and What Befell Them* (New York: Viking Press, 1975), 132.

5. See Ross Y. Koen, *The China Lobby in American Politics* (New York: Octagon Books, 1974).

6. FBI file 100–197835, "Chinese Workers Mutual Aid Association" (FBI-CWMAA).

7. Ibid., 224.

8. The *China Daily News* in New York continued to publish, but its circulation dropped sharply after the trial and conviction of editor Eugene Moy and several others. The paper later became a nonpolitical semiweekly: the editorial column disappeared, and Kung Fu stories reprinted from Hong Kong newspapers became an important feature of the paper. See Him Mark Lai, "The Chinese Press in the United States and Canada since World War II: A Diversity of Voices," *Chinese America: History and* Perspectives, 1990, 112.

9. For an abridged edition of the result of the investigation, see *San Francisco Chinese Community Citizens' Survey and Fact Finding Committee Report*, compiled by Lim P. Lee, Albert Lim, and H. K. Wong (San Francisco: H. J. Carle & Sons, 1969).

10. Thomas W. Chinn, H. Mark Lai, and Philip P. Choy, *A History of the Chinese in California: A Syllabus* (San Francisco: Chinese Historical Society of America, 1969).

11. During this time, China politics generated intense political conflict within the community. After organizing a reception for the Chinese Ping-Pong team in San Francisco, Maurice Chuck received death threats in the mail. *Qiao Bao*, July 31, 1997.

12. Nancy Woo, "Father and Daughter," in Hu Jingnan jinian weiyuan hui, *Hu Jingnan wenji* [Selected works of Gilbert Woo] (Hong Kong: Xiangjiang chuban youxian gongsi, 1991), 78.

13. Jade Snow Wong, *No Chinese Stranger* (New York: Harper & Row, 1975), 35, 256–277. Most of these Chinese Americans later returned to the United States.

14. Renqiu Yu, *To Save China, to Save Ourselves*, 98; Lai, "To Bring Forth a New China, to Build a Better America," 56.

15. Sam Yup Benevolent Association History Editorial Committee, *A History of the Sam Yup Benevolent Association in the United States, 1850–2000* (San Francisco: Sam Yup Benevolent Association, 2000), 250–251.

16. Yijun Zheng, *Chuanqi rensheng: ji Cai Fujui zouguo de lu* [A legendary life: The path of Cai Fujiu] (Hong Kong: Haifeng chubanshe, 1997), 251–256; Jiujinshan wanqu gejie huaren qingzhu zhonghua renmin gongheguo guoqing weiyuanhui: *Guanghui licheng, hunxi zhonghau: qingzhu zhonghua renmin gongheguo chengli wushi zhounian* [A glorious journey, with a Chinese spirit: a pictorial collection for the celebration of the fiftieth anniversary of the People's Republic of China] (Jiujinshan wanqui gejie huaren qingzhu zhonghua renmin gongheguo guoqing weiyuanhui, 1999); *Chinese World*, Sept. 18, 26, 1999; *International Daily*, Sept. 21, 1999; *Chinese Times*, Sept. 25, 1999.

GLOSSARY

English	Chinese	Pinyin
PEOPLE		
Cai Nüliang	蔡女良	Cai Nüliang
Chang Xiao	長哮	Chang Xiao
Chen, Jun Hai	陳中海	Chen Zhonghai
Chen Tiemin	陳鐵民	Chen Tiemin
Chiang Kai-shek	蔣介石	Jiang Jie-shi
Chuck, Maurice	黃運基	Huang Yunji
Dai Li	戴笠	Dai Li
Fu Shangwei	傅商偉	Fu Shangwei
Hong, Y. C.	洪耀宗	Hong Yaozong
Huang Cuilian	黃翠蓮	Huang Cuilian
Huang Feng	黃鳳	Huang Feng
Huang Lai	黃來	Huang Lai
Huang Tinghui	黃庭輝	Huang Tinghui
Huang Wang	黃望	Huang Wang
Huang Zunxian	黃遵憲	Huang Zunxian
Ja, Kew Yuen Cai	謝僑遠	Xie Qiao-yuan

Lai, Him Mark	麥禮謙	Mai Li-qian
Lai, Laura Jung	張玉英	Zhang Yu-ying
Lao Heng	老亨	Lao Heng
Lee, Dai Ming	李大明	Li Daming
Lee, Hazel Ah Ying	李月英	Li Yue-ying
Lee, Herbert	李中棠	Bohong (Li Hangling)
Lee, Olden	梁發葉	Li Zhongtang
Leong, Francis	梁錫田	Liang Fa-ye
Leong, Thick Hing	李金堂	Liang Xitian
Li Jingtang	李春輝	Li Jingtang
Li, Chunhui	李柏宏	Li Chunhui
Li Ruiling	黎瑞玲	Li Ruiling
Li, Yizhong	李一中	Li Yizhong
Liang Bixia	梁碧霞	Liang Bixia
Liang, Shing Tai	梁聲泰	Liang, Sheng-tai
Liang Wangxin	梁旺新	Liang Wangxin
Liang Yingyang	梁應陽	Liang Yingyang
Liang Yongyuan	梁永源	Liang Yongyuan
Lim, Happy	林堅夫	Lin Jianfu
Lin, Albert	林登	Lin Deng
Liu Heng	柳亨	Liu Heng
Liu, Pei Chi	劉伯驥	Liu Bo-ji
Ma Bingchang	馬炳昌	Ma Bingchang
Ma Jiliang	馬季良（唐納）	Ma Jiliang (Tang Na)

Ma Siru (Paul Mar)	馬賜汝	Ma Siru
Moy, Eugene	梅參天	Mei Can-tian
Qiu Guanyin	裘冠英	Qiu Guanyin
Shou Yong	守庸	Shou Yong
Sun Yat-sen	孫中山	Sun Zhong-shan
Tan Ying	譚鶯	Tan Ying
Tong, Chu	唐明照	Tang Mingzhao
Tsoi, Henry	蔡福就	Cai Fujiu
Wang Fushi	王福時	Wang Fushi
Wang Shaobi	王少畢	Wang Shaobi
Wen Ying	文鶯	Wen Ying
Wong, Harry	黃傳炎	Huang Chuan-yan
Wong, Jade Snow	黃玉雪	Huang Yu-xue
Wong, Virginia	黃桂燕	Huang Guiyan
Woo, Chin-Fu	吳敬敷	Wu Jing-fu
Woo, Gilbert	胡景南	Hu Jing-nan
Woo, Norbert	胡景濤	Hu Jingtao
Wu Boxiang	伍伯祥	Wu Boxiang
Xiang Yun	湘雲	Xiang Yun
Xiao Min	小敏	Xiao Min
Yan Xin	燕心	Yan Xin
Xishi	西施	Xishi
Ye Miaolan	葉妙蘭	Ye Miaolan
Yu, Renqiu	于仁秋	Yu Renqiu

Yu, Yun Shan	余仁山	Yu Ren-shan
Yuey, Joe	周銳	Zhou Rui
Zheng Hele	鄭和樂	Zheng Hele
Zheng Yijun	鄭奕鈞	Zheng Yijun
Zhu Yushi	朱余氏	Zhu Yushi
Zhu, Rucong	朱汝聰	Zhu Rucong
Zi Ming	紫明	Zi Ming
Zun Ni	尊尼	Zun Ni

PLACES

Kaiping	開平	Kai Ping
Marco Polo Bridge	蘆溝橋	Lugou qiao
Toishan	台山	Taishan
Xinhui	新會	Xinhui

INSTITUTIONS

Chick Char Society	叱吒社	Chizha she
China War Relief Association	旅美華僑統一義揵救國總會	Lümei huaqiao tongyi yijuan jiuguo zonghui
Chinese American Citizens Alliance	同源會	Tongyuan hui
Chinese Central High School	中華中學校	Zhonghua zhongxuexiao
Chinese Chamber of Commerce	中華總商會	Zhonghua zongshanghui
Chinese Consolidated Benevolent Association	中華公所	zhonghua gongsuo
Chinese Hand Laundry Alliance	紐約衣館聯合會	Niuyue yiguan lianhehui

Chinese Hospital	東華醫院	Donghua yiyuan
Chinese Youth Club	紐約華僑青年救國團	Niuyue huaqiao qingnian jiuguo tuan
Chinese Workers Mutual Aid Association	加省華工合作會	Jiasheng huagong hezuohui
Committee to challenge the 1924 Immigration Act	駁例局	Boli ju
district association	會館	huiguan
FBI	聯邦調查局	Lianbang diaocha ju
grand jury	大陪審團	da peishengtuan
INS	移民局	Yimin ju
Kuomintang	國民黨	Guomindang
Ning Yung Association	寧陽會館	Ningyang huiguan
Oasis Bookstore	綠園書店	Lüyuan shudian
Suey Sing Tong	萃勝工商總會	Cuisheng gongshang zonghui

PUBLICATIONS

China Tribune	紐約新報	*Niuyue xinbao*
China Weekly	金門僑報	*Jinmen qiaobao*
Chinese American Weekly	中美周報	*Zhongmei zhoubao*
Chinese Journal	商報	*Shangbao*
Chinese Journal	美洲日報	*Meizhou ribao*
Chinese National	國民日報	*Guomin ribao*
Chinese Nationalist Daily (Mun Hey Yat Po)	民氣日報	*Minqi ribao*
Chinese Nationalist Daily (Kuo Min Yat Po)	美洲國民	*Meizhou guomin ribao*

Chinese Pacific Weekly	太平洋周報	*Taipingyang zhoubao*
Chinese Times	金山時報	*Jinshan shibao*
Chinese Vanguard	先鋒報	*Xianfeng bao*
Chinese World (Sai Gai Yat Po)	世界日報	*Shijie ribao*
Chinese Youth	中國青年	*Zhongguo qingnian*
Chung Sai Yat Po	中西日報	*Zhongxi ribao*
East/West	東西報	*Dongxi bao*
Honolulu Chinese Press	夏威夷檀山日報	*Xiaweiyi tanshan ribao*
International Daily News	國際日報	*Guoji ribao*
Light Cavalry	輕騎	*Qingqi*
New Life	新生	*Xinsheng*
Oasis	綠州	*Lüzhou*
San Min Morning Post	三民日報	*Sanmin Ribao*
United Journal	聯合日報	*Lianhe ribao*
Young China Morning Paper (Young China Daily)	少年中國晨報	*Shaonian zhongguo chenbao*

TERMS

America	美國	Meiguo
American-born Chinese girl	土生女	tusheng nü
Chinese-born girl	唐山女	tangshan nü
choaching paper	口供	kougong
confession	坦白	tanbai
Everyone's Literature Forum	大眾文學論壇	Dazhong wenxue luntan

false paper	假祇	jiazhi
good value	價廉物美	jialian wumei
husband	老公	laogong
I Wish to Inform You	啓者	Qizhe
Informal Essays from the Military	軍中隨筆	Junzhong suibi
literature of pouring out grievances	訴冤文學	suyuan wenxue
model war bride	模範的戰娘	mofan de zhanniang
old Chinese woman	唐山婆	tangshan po
a plate of loose sand	一盤散沙	yipan sansha
principles of three obediences and four virtues	三從四德	sancong side
solemn pledge of love	山盟海誓	shanmeng haishi
To the Husbands	獻給丈夫們	Xiangei zhangfumen
transferring paper	調祇	diaozhi
war bride	戰娘	zhanniang
wife	老婆	laopo
wife from China	唐山太太	tangshan taitai
Women's Column	婦女欄	Funü lan
Yellow River Cantata	黃河大合唱	*Huanghe da hechang*

SELECTED BIBLIOGRAPHY

Manuscripts and Archival Collections

California State Emergency Relief Administration (CSERA). "Survey of Social Work Needs of the Chinese Population of San Francisco, California." 1935. Bancroft Library, University of California, Berkeley.

Chinese American Citizens Alliance. Minutes, reports, and papers. Files of CACA Archivist, Suellen Cheng.

Federal Bureau of Investigation. Freedom of Information/Privacy Acts Section. Chinese American Democratic Youth Club (CADYC). File: 105–HQ-1332, 7 vols.

———. *China Daily News* (CDN) File: 100–HQ-196148, 2 vols.

———. Chinese Hand Laundry Alliance (CHLA). File: 100–HQ-365097, 4 vols.

———. Chinese Workers Mutual Aid Association(CWMAA). File: 100–HQ-197835.

Immigration and Naturalization Service. Files of the History Office, Washington, D.C. Miscellaneous files on Chinese immigration.

Johnson, Charles S. *The Negro War Workers in San Francisco: A Local Survey.* San Francisco, 1944. Bancroft Library, University of California, Berkeley.

Lew, Peter. "The Family Immigration History and Genealogy of Lew Chuck Suey (Lew Hawk Yee)." 1997. In author's possession.

Warren G. Magnuson Papers. Manuscripts and University Archives Division, University of Washington, Seattle.

National Archives II, College Park, Md. Files of the Immigration and Naturalization Service, Central Office, 1949–1958, "Document Fraud." RG 85.

National Archives, San Bruno, Calif. Records of the Immigration and Naturalization Service, 1945–1952. RG 85.

Newspapers, Periodicals, and Newsletters

California Chinese Press, 1940–1945.
China Daily News, 1945–1952.
China Weekly, 1949–1950.
Chinese American Weekly, 1942–1965.
Chinese Pacific Weekly, 1947–1965.
Chinese Times, 1928–1950.

Chung Sai Yat Po, 1945–1950.
Fore 'n' Aft, Richmond Shipyard, Richmond, Calif., 1942–1946.
Hawaii Chinese Journal, 1942.
Longgang Magazine, 1956–1965.
Marin-er, Marinship Corporation, Sausalito, Calif., 1943–1945.
Minqing, 1949–1959.

United States Statutes

2 Stat. 153, Act of Apr. 14, 1802.
10 Stat. 604, Act of Feb. 10, 1855.
18 Stat. 477, Act of Mar. 3, 1875.
22 Stat. 58, Act of May 6, 1882.
23 Stat. 115, Act of July 5, 1884.
25 Stat. 504, Act of Oct. 1, 1888.
27 Stat. 25, Act of May 5, 1892.
32 Stat. 176, Act of Apr. 29, 1902.
33 Stat. 428, Act of Apr. 27, 1904.
34 Stat. 898, Act of Feb. 20, 1907.
34 Stat. 1228, Act of Mar. 2, 1907.
42 Stat. 1021, Act of Sept. 22, 1922.
43 Stat. 153, Act of May 26, 1924.
46 Stat. 581, Act of June 13, 1930.
46 Stat. 849, Act of July 3, 1930.
46 Stat. 1551, Act of Mar. 3, 1931.
47 Stat. 656, Act of May 19, 1948.
48 Stat. 797, Act of May 24, 1934.
54 Stat. 876, Act of Oct. 14, 1940.
57 Stat. 600, Act of Dec. 17, 1943.
59 Stat. 659, Act of Dec. 28, 1945.
60 Stat. 339, Act of June 29, 1946.
60 Stat. 975, Act of Aug. 9, 1946.
66 Stat. 163, Act of June 27, 1952.
71 Stat. 639, Act of Sept. 11, 1957.
Rev. Stat. Sect. 1993, 1878.

Legal Cases

Ah Moy, In re, 21 F. 785 (1884).
Ah Quan, 21 F. 182 (1884).
Case of the Chinese Wife, 21 F. 785 (1884).
Chan Shee et al., Ex parte, 2 F. 2d 995 (1924).
Chang Chan et al. v. John Nagle, 268 U.S. 346 (1925).
Cheung Sum Shee v. Nagle, 268 U.S. 336 (1925).
Chiu Shee, Ex parte, 1 F. 798 (1924).
Chung Toy Ho and Wong Choy Sin, In re, 42 F. 398 (1890).

Dear Wing Jung v. United States, 312 F. 2d. (1962).
Fong Yue Ting v. United States, 149 U.S. 698 (1893).
Lue Chow Kon et al. v. Brownell, 122 F. Supp. 370 (1954).
Lue Chow Kon v. Brownell, U.S. Ct. of App., 2d Ct. (1955).
Ly Shew v. Acheson, 110 F. Supp. 50 (1953).
Mackenzie v. Hare, 239 U.S. 299 (1915).
(NG) Fung Sing, Ex parte, 6 F. 2 (1925).
Tsoi Sim v. United States, 116 F. 738 (1902).
United States v. Gue Lim. 88 F.136 (1897).
United States v. Mrs. Gue Lim, 176 U.S. 459 (1900).
United States v. Thind, 261 U.S. 294 (1923).

U.S. Government Publications

U.S. Department of Commerce. Bureau of the Census. *Fourteenth Census of the United States*, 1924. Washington, D.C.: Government Printing Office.
————. *Seventeenth Census of the United States*. Census of the Population, 1950. Washington, D.C.: Government Printing Office.
————. *Sixteenth Census of the United States*, Population, 1940. Washington, D.C.: Government Printing Office.
U.S. Department of Justice. *Annual Report of the Immigration and Naturalization Service*. 1944–1954. Philadelphia: Immigration and Naturalization Service.
————. Immigration and Naturalization Service. *Annual Report*. 1955–1966. Washington D.C.: Government Printing Office.
————. Immigration and Naturalization Service. "Repeal of the Chinese Exclusion Act." *Monthly Review*. Aug. 1943, 16.
————. News Release. Dec. 27, 1959.
————. News Release. Dec. 31, 1972
U.S. Department of Labor. Bureau of Apprenticeship. *Apprenticeship Statistics: A Summary of National Data on Registered Apprentices and Apprenticeship Systems in the United States, 1949–1952*. Technical Bulletin, no. T-137. Washington, D.C., 1953.
————. Bureau of Immigration. *Annual Report, 1913–1931*. Washington D.C.: Government Printing Office.
U.S. House. *Admission of Wives of American Citizens of Oriental Ancestry: Hearings before the Committee on Immigration and Naturalization on H.R. 6544*. 69th Cong., 1st sess., 1926.
————. *Hearings before the Committee on Immigration and Naturalization*. 78th Cong., 1st sess., 1943.
————. *Hearings before the Committee on Immigration and Naturalization on H.R. 2404, H.R. 5654, H.R. 10524*. 71st Cong., 2nd sess., 1930.
————. *Hearings before Subcommittee on Immigration and Naturalization of the Committee on the Judiciary, House of Representatives, on H.R. 5004, a Bill to Provide the Privilege of Becoming a Naturalized Citizen of the United States to All Immigrants Having a Legal Right to Permanent Residence, to Make Immigration Quotas Available to Asiatic and Pacific People*. 80th Cong., 2nd sess., April 19 and 21, 1948.

U.S. Senate. *Admission as Nonquota Immigrants of Certain Alien Wives and Children of United States Citizens: Hearing before a Subcommittee of the Committee on Immigration on S. 2271.* 70th Cong., 1st sess., 1928.

Oral History Interviews

Anderson, Elizabeth Lew. Interview with the author, Nov. 14, 15, 1997.
Chen, Aimei.* Interview with the author, July 11, 1994.
Chin, Tenley. Interview with Kristen Martin directed by the author, May 29, 1997.
Chu, Tuen Ock. Interview with Jeff Wong directed by the author, Nov. 20, 1995, and Feb. 27, 1996.
Chuck, Maurice. Interview with the author, Feb. 22, 1998.
Doyle, Janet. Interview with the author, July 26, 1990.
Fu, Yuqin.* Interview with the author, Aug. 19, 1994.
Gee, Maggie. Interview with the author, Feb. 20, Mar. 27, 1994; June 20, 1998.
Gin, Danny. Interview with Britton Yee directed by the author, May 8, 1998.
Jeu, Lauren. Interview with the author, May 15, 1994.
Lai, Him Mark. Interview with the author, July 27, 2000.
Lai, Laura Jung. Interview with the author, May 20, 1997.
Leong, Chiu Yuk. Interview with the author, Aug. 22, 1994.
Lew, Betty. Interview with the author, Dec. 2, 1997.
Lew, Chen. Interview with the author, Apr. 5, 2000.
Lew, Helen. Interview with the author, June 1, 1998.
Lew, Lai. Interview with the author, Apr. 5, 2000.
Lew, Peter. Interview with the author, Aug. 23, 1994; Nov. 14, 15, 1997.
Liu, Yulan.* Interview with the author, Jan. 8, 1993.
Louie, Luella (Chinn). Interview with Andrea L. Chow and the author, Oct. 21, 1998.
Louie, Susan. Interview with the author, Dec. 2, 1997.
Ma, Mary (Gin). Interview with the author, Aug. 8, 1994.
Low, Sam Sik. Inteview with the author, Aug. 5, 2000.
Tom, Florence Gee. Interview with the author, July 15, Aug. 23, 1994.
Wong, Chiu Chun Ma. Interview with Denise Yee directed by the author, Jan. 30, 1998.
Wong, Jade Snow. Interview with the author, Nov. 25, 1991.
Wong, Lanfang.* Interview with the author, Aug. 20, 1994.
Wong, Lili.* Interview with the author, Aug. 10, 1994.
Wong, Limin.* Interview with the author, July 19, 1994.
Wong, Shirley. Interview with the author, June 15, 1999.
Yee, Eddie. Interview with Denise Yee directed by the author, Mar. 9, 1998.
Yee, Joy. Interview with the author, Aug. 18, 23, 1994.
Yee, Mary. Interview with Denise Yee directed by the author, Mar. 9, 1998.
Zhou, Lihua.* Interview with the author, Aug. 10, 1994.

Secondary Sources

Anderson, Benedict. *Imagined Communities: Reflections on the Origin and Spread of Nationalism.* Rev. ed. New York: Verso, 1991.

Aptheker, Bettina. *Tapestries of Life: Women's Work, Women's Consciousness, and the Meaning of Daily Experience.* Amherst: University of Massachusetts Press, 1989.

Archibald, Katherine. *Wartime Shipyard: A Study in Social Disunity.* Berkeley: University of California Press, 1947.

Bao, Xiaolan. "Holding Up More than Half the Sky: A History of Women Garment Workers in New York's Chinatown, 1948–1991." Ph.D. diss., New York University, 1991.

———. "When Women Arrived: The Transformation of New York's Chinatown." In *Not June Cleaver: Women and Gender in Postwar America, 1945–1960,* edited by Joanne Meyerowitz, 19–39. Philadelphia: Temple University Press, 1994.

Barth, Gunther. *Bitter Strength: A History of the Chinese in the United States, 1850–1870.* Cambridge, Mass.: Harvard University Press, 1964.

Baum, Dale. "Woman Suffrage and the 'Chinese Question': The Limits of Radical Republicanism in Massachusetts, 1865–1876." *New England Quarterly,* 56:1 (Mar. 1983): 60–77.

Berkeley Historical Society. *Looking Back at Berkeley: A Pictorial History of a Diverse City.* Berkeley: Book Committee of the Berkeley Historical Society, 1984.

Bredbenner, Candice Lewis. *A Nationality of Her Own: Women, Marriage, and the Law of Citizenship.* Berkeley: University of California Press, 1998.

Bullock, Mary Brown. *An American Transplant: The Rockefeller Foundation and Peking Union Medical College.* Berkeley: University of California Press, 1980.

Butler, Anne. *Daughters of Joy, Sisters of Misery: Prostitution in the American West, 1865–90.* Urbana: University of Illinois Press, 1985.

Chafe, William H. *The American Woman: Her Changing Social, Economic, and Political Roles, 1920–1970.* New York: Oxford University Press, 1972.

Chan, Sucheng. "Chinese Livelihood in Rural California: The Impact of Economic Change, 1860–1880." In *Working People of California,* edited by Daniel Cornford, 57–81. Berkeley: University of California Press, 1995.

———. "The Exclusion of Chinese Women, 1870–1943." In *Entry Denied: Exclusion and the Chinese Community in America, 1882–1943,* edited by Sucheng Chan, 94–146. Philadelphia: Temple University Press, 1991.

———. *This Bittersweet Soil: The Chinese in California Agriculture, 1860–1910.* Berkeley: University of California Press, 1926.

Chen, Edward C. M. "Historical Highlights: Houston Lodge Chinese American Citizen's Alliance." In *From America to Shangri-li: Chinese American Citizens Alliance 42nd Biennial National Convention, Houston, Texas, August 11–14, 1993.* San Francisco: Chinese American Citizens Alliance, 1993.

Chen, Helen. "Chinese Immigration into the United States: An Analysis of Changes in Immigration Policies." Ph.D. diss., Brandeis University, 1980.

Chen, Serena. "Special Report: A Look Back at the Chinese Confession Program." *East/West* 21:16 (Apr. 23, 1987): 6–9.

Ch'en Ta. *Emigrant Communities in South China: A Study of Overseas Migration and Its Influence on Standards of Living and Social Change.* Shanghai: Kelly and Walsh, 1939.

Chen, Wen-Hsien. "Chinese under Both Exclusion and Immigration Laws." Ph.D. diss., University of Chicago, 1940.

Chen, Yong. *Chinese San Francisco, 1850–1943: A Trans-Pacific Community*. Stanford: Stanford University Press, 2000.

Chesneaux, Jean, Françoise Le Barbier, and Marie-Claire Bergère. *China from the 1911 Revolution to Liberation*. Translated by Paul Auster and Lydia Davis. New York: Pantheon Books, 1977.

Chih, Ginger. "Immigration of Chinese Women to the U.S.A." M.A. thesis, Sarah Lawrence College, 1977.

Chinese American Citizens Alliance. *Biennial National Convention Reports*. 1985–1999.

Chinn, Thomas W. *Bridging the Pacific: San Francisco's Chinatown and Its People*. San Francisco: Chinese Historical Society of America, 1989.

Chinn, Thomas W., Him Mark Lai, and Philip P. Choy. *A History of the Chinese in California: A Syllabus*. San Francisco: Chinese Historical Society of America, 1969.

Chiu, Ping. *Chinese Labor in California, 1850–1880: An Economic Study*. Madison: State Historical Society of Wisconsin for the Department of History, University of Wisconsin, 1967.

Chu, Louis. *Eat a Bowl of Tea*. New Jersey: Lyle Stuart, 1961.

Chung, Sue Fawn. "Fighting for Their American Rights: A History of the Chinese American Citizens Alliance." In *Claiming America: Constructing Chinese American Identities during the Exclusion Era*, edited by K. Scott Wong and Sucheng Chan, 95–126. Philadelphia: Temple University Press, 1998.

Coolidge, Mary Roberts. *Chinese Immigration*. New York: Henry Holt, 1909.

Cott, Nancy F. *Public Vows: A History of Marriage and the Nation*. Cambridge, Mass.: Harvard University Press, 2000.

Danaher, Eugene. *Apprenticeship Practice in the United States*. Stanford: Graduate School of Business, 1945.

Daniels, Roger. *Asian America: Chinese and Japanese in the United States since 1850*. Seattle: University of Washington Press, 1988.

Dare, Richard Kock. "The Economic and Social Adjustment of the San Francisco Chinese for the Past Fifty Years." M.A. thesis, University of California, Berkeley, 1959.

Diggings, John Patrick. *The Proud Decades: America in War and in Peace, 1941–1960*. New York: W. W. Norton, 1988.

Dong, Lorraine. "Him Mark Lai: Historian." San Francisco: Chinese Historical Society of America, 1995.

Fang Di. "Cong renkou pucha ziliao zhong fanying chulai de qiaoxiang laonian nuqiaoshu tedian" [Characteristics of elderly women among the overseas families as reflected in the census]. In *Huaqiao huaren shi yanjiu ji* [A history of overseas Chinese], edited by Zheng Min and Lian Cumin, 304–314. Beijing: Haiyang chuban she, 1989.

Fass, Paula. *The Damned and the Beautiful: American Youth in the 1920s*. New York: Oxford University Press, 1977.

Fong, Timothy P. *The First Suburban Chinatown: The Remaking of Monterey Park, California*. Philadelphia: Temple University Press, 1994.

Frank, Miriam, Marilyn Ziebarth, and Connie Field. *The Life and Times of Rosie the Riveter: The Story of Three Million Working Women during World War Two*. Clarity Educational Productions, 1982.

Geiger, J. C., et al. *The Health of the Chinese in an American City: San Francisco*. San Francisco: Department of Public Health, 1939.

Glenn, Evelyn Nakano. *Issei, Nisei, Warbride: Three Generations of Japanese American Women in Domestic Service*. Philadelphia: Temple University Press, 1986.

———. "Split Household, Small Producer, and Dual Wage Earner: An Analysis of Chinese-American Family Strategies." *Journal of Marriage and Family* 45:1 (Feb. 1983): 35–48.

Glick, Clarence E. *Sojourners and Settlers: Chinese Migrants in Hawaii*. Honolulu: University of Hawaii Press, 1980.

Gluck, Sherna Berger. *Rosie the Riveter Revisited: Women, the War, and Social Change*. Boston: Twayne Publishers, 1987.

Goodman, Bryna. *Native Place, City, and Nation: Regional Networks and Identities in Shanghai, 1853–1937*. Berkeley: University of California Press, 1995.

Griffith, Robert. *The Politics of Fear: Joseph R. McCarthy and the Senate*. Lexington: University of Kentucky, 1979.

Hill, Cyril D. "Citizenship of Married Women." *American Journal of International Law* 18 (1924): 720–736.

Hing, Bill Ong. *Making and Remaking Asian America through Immigration Policy, 1850–1990*. Stanford: Stanford University Press, 1993.

Hirata, Lucie Cheng. "Chinese Immigrant Women in Nineteenth-Century California." In *Women of America: A History*, edited by C. R. Berkin and M. B. Norton, 223–244. Boston: Houghton-Mifflin, 1979.

———. "Free, Indentured, Enslaved: Chinese Prostitutes in Nineteenth-Century America." *Signs: Journal of Women in Culture and Society* 5:1(Autumn 1979): 3–29.

Hirshfield, Debrah Ann. "Rosie Also Welded: Women and Technology in Shipbuilding during World War II." Ph.D. diss., University of California, Irvine, 1987.

Hong, Y. C. *A Brief History of the Chinese American Citizens Alliance*. San Francisco: Chinese American Citizens Alliance, Nov. 1955.

———. "Milestones of the Chinese-American Citizens Alliance," 1963. Reprinted in *Chinese American Citizens Alliance 38th Biennial National Convention, August 7–10, 1985*, pp. 32–39. Los Angeles: Chinese American Citizens Alliance, 1985.

Honig, Emily, and Gail Hershatter. *Personal Voices: Chinese Women in the 1980s*. Stanford: Stanford University, 1988.

Horton, John. *The Politics of Diversity: Immigration, Resistance, and Change in Monterey Park, California*. Philadelphia: Temple University Press, 1995.

Hsu, Madeline Yuan-yin. " 'Living Abroad and Faring Well': Migration and Transnationalism in Taishan County, Guangdong, 1904–1939." Ph.D. diss., Yale University, 1996.

———. "Gold Mountain Dreams and Paper Son Schemes: Chinese Immigration under Exclusion." *Chinese America: History and Perspectives*, 1997, 46–60.

Hu Jingnan jinian weiyuan hui. *Hu Jingnan wenji* [Selected works of Gilbert Woo]. Hong Kong: Xiangjiang chuban youxian gongsi, 1991.

Huang, Lucy Jen. "The Chinese American Family." *In Ethnic Families in America.*, edited by Charles M. Mindel and Robert W. Habenstein. New York: Elsevier, 1982.

Huang Wang. "Xiangei Lao Heng xiansheng fuzheng" [A debate with Mr. Lao Heng]. *Chinese Pacific Weekly*, May 22, 1948.

Huang Yunji (Maurice Chuck). *Benliu—yixiangqu diyi bu.* Shengyang: Shengyang chuban she, 1996.

———. *Huang yunquan xuanji.* 2 vols. San Francisco: Meiguo shidai youxian gongsi, 1996.

Hutchinson, E. P. *Legislative History of American Immigration Policy, 1798–1965.* Philadelphia: University of Pennsylvania Press, 1981.

I Was a Male War Bride (film). Directed by Howard Hawks. 1949.

Jiujinshan wanqu gejie huaren qingzhu zhonghua renmin gongheguo guoqing weiyuanhui. *Guanghui licheng, hunxi zhonghau: qingzhu zhonghua renmin gongheguo chengli wushi zhounian* [A glorious journey, with a Chinese spirit: a pictorial collection for the celebration of the fiftieth anniversary of the People's Republic of China]. Jiujinshan wanqui gejie huaren qingzhu zhonghua renmin gongheguo guoqing weiyuanhui, 1999.

Johnson, J. Percy H., ed. *Ayer Directory of Newspapers and Periodicals.* Philadelphia: N. W. Ayer & Son, 1925–1965.

Johnson, Marilynn S. *The Second Gold Rush: Oakland and the East Bay in World War II.* Berkeley: University of California Press, 1993.

Kahn, E. J., Jr. *The China Hands: America's Foreign Service and What Befell Them.* New York: Viking Press, 1975.

Kessler-Harris, Alice. *Out to Work: A History of Wage-Earning Women in the United States.* Oxford: Oxford University Press, 1982.

Kim, Elaine H. *Asian American Literature: An Introduction to the Writings and Their Social Context.* Philadelphia: Temple University Press, 1982.

Koen, Ross Y. *The China Lobby in American Politics.* New York: Octagon Books, 1974.

Kung, S. W. *Chinese in America.* Seattle: University of Washington Press, 1962.

Kwok, Munson. "Walter Urian Lum, Founder of the *Chinese Times* (Interview with Mabel Lum Lew)," *Gum Saan Journal* 1:1 (Aug. 1977).

Kwong, Peter. *Chinatown, New York: Labor and Politics, 1930–1950.* New York: Monthly Review Press, 1979.

———. *The New Chinatown.* New York: Hill & Wang, 1987.

Lai, Him Mark. "China Politics and the U.S. Chinese Communities." In *Counterpoint: Perspectives on Asian America*, edited by Emma Gee et al. Los Angeles: Asian American Studies Center, 1976.

———. "The Chinese American Press." In *The Ethnic Press in the United States: A Historical Analysis and Handbook*, edited by Sally M. Miller, 27–43. New York: Greenwood Press, 1987.

———. "The Chinese Press in the United States and Canada since World War II: A Diversity of Voices." *Chinese America: History and Perspectives*, 1990, 107–156.

———. "The Chinese Vernacular Press in North America, 1900–1950: Their Role in Social Cohesion." *Annals of the Chinese Historical Society of the Pacific Northwest* (1984): 170–178.

———. *Cong huaqiao dao huaren: ershi shiji meiguo huaren shehui fazhan shi* [From overseas Chinese to ethnic Chinese: A history of the social development of America's Chinese in the twentieth century]. Hong Kong: Sanlian shudian, 1992.

———. "Historical Development of the Chinese Consolidated Benevolent Association/ Huiguan System." In *Chinese America: History and Perspectives*, 1987, 13–52.

———. "A Historical Survey of the Chinese Left in America." In *Counterpoint: Perspectives on Asia America,* edited by Emma Gee et al., 63–80. Los Angeles: Asian American Studies Center, University of California, Los Angeles, 1976.

———. *A History Reclaimed: An Annotated Bibliography of Chinese Language Materials on the Chinese of America.* Los Angeles: Asian American Studies Center, University of California, Los Angeles, 1986.

———. "Kuomingtang in Chinese American Communities. In *Entry Denied: Exclusion and the Chinese Community in America, 1882–1943*, edited by Sucheng Chan, 170–212. Philadelphia: Temple University Press, 1991.

———. "Roles Played by Chinese in America during China's Resistance to Japanese Aggression during World War II." *Chinese America: History and Perspectives*, 1997.

———. "To Bring Forth a New China, to Build a Better America: The Chinese Marxist Left in America to the 1960s." *Chinese America: History and Perspectives*, 1992, 3–82.

———. "Unfinished Business: The Chinese Confession Program." *The Repeal and Its Legacy: Proceedings of the Conference on the 50th Anniversary of the Repeal of the Exclusion Acts. Nov. 12–14, 1993*, 47–57. San Francisco: Chinese Historical Society of America, 1994.

Lai, Him Mark and Betty Lim. "Gilbert Woo, Chinese American Journalist." In Hu Jingnan jinian weiyuan hui, *Hu Jingnan wenji*, 39–40. Hong Kong: Xiangjiang chuban youxian gongsi, 1991.

Lai, Him Mark, Genny Lim, and Judy Yung. *Island: Poetry and History of Chinese Immigrants on Angel Island, 1910–1940.* San Francisco: HOCDOI, 1986.

Lam, Julie Shuk-yee. "The *Chinese Digest*, 1935–1940." *Chinese America: History and Perspectives*, 1987, 120–121.

Lao Heng. "Daling" [Darling]. *Chinese Pacific Weekly*, Feb. 28, 1948.

———. "Guxi zhijian" [Between mother- and daughter-in-law]. Mar. 6, 1948.

———. "Hanxu" [Reserving]. *Chinese Pacific Weekly*, Mar. 27, 1948.

———. "Lengnuan fuqi" [Cold or warm couples]. *Chinese Pacific Weekly*, Nov. 15, 1945.

———. "Maipiao" [Buying lottery tickets]. *Chinese Pacific Weekly*, Mar. 13, 1948.

———. "Songli" [Gifts]. *Chinese Pacific Weekly*, Sept. 13, 1947.

———. "Youmo gan" [A sense of humor]. *Chinese Pacific Weekly*, Nov. 22, 1947.

———. "Zhangfu fa piqi" [Husband's temperament]. *Chinese Pacific Weekly*, Oct. 18, 1947.

———. "Ziman" [Complacency]. Mar. 20, 1948.

Lark, Regina Frances. "They Challenged Two Notions: Marriage between Japanese Women and American GIs, 1945 to present." Ph.D. diss., University of Southern California, 1999.

Lee, Erika. "At America's Gates: Chinese Immigration during the Exclusion Era, 1882–1943." Ph.D. diss., University of California, Berkeley, 1998.

———. "Enforcing and Challenging Exclusion in San Francisco: U.S. Immigration Officials and Chinese Immigrants, 1882–1905." *Chinese America: History and Perspectives*, 1997, 1–15.

Lee, Rose Hum. *The Chinese in the United States of America*. Hong Kong: Hong Kong University Press, 1960.

———. "The Recent Immigrant Chinese Families of the San Francisco–Oakland Area." *Marriage and Family Living* 18 (1956): 14–24.

Leong Think Hing. "Nanwang de ta—dao Jing Nan" [The Unforgettable Jing Nan]. In Hu Jingnan jinian weiyuan hui, *Hu Jingnan wenji*, 67–68. Hong Kong: Xiangjiang chuban youxian gongsi, 1991.

Lew Ling. *Huaqiao renwu zhi* [The Chinese in North America: A guide to their life and progress]. Los Angeles: Dongsi wenhua chuban she, 1948.

Li, Peter S. "Fictive Kinship, Conjugal Tie, and Kinship Chain among Chinese Immigrants in the United States." *Journal of Comparative Family Studies* 8:1 (Spring 1997): 47–63.

Liang, Hua. "Fighting for a New Life: Social and Patriotic Activism of Chinese American Women in New York City, 1900 to 1945." *Journal of American Ethnic History* 17:2 (Winter 1998): 22–38.

Lichtman, Sheila Tropp. "Women at Work, 1941–1945: Wartime Employment in the San Francisco Bay Area." Ph.D. diss., University of California, Davis, 1981.

Light, Ivan. "From Vice District to Tourist Attraction: The Moral Career of American Chinatowns." *Pacific Historical Review* 43:3 (Aug. 1974): 367–394.

Lim, Albert. "Baoren Hu Jingnan yu wo" [My friendship with Gilbert Woo the journalist]. In Hu Jingnan jinian weiyuan hui, *Hu Jingnan wenji*, 64. Hong Kong: Xiangjiang chuban youxian gongsi, 1991.

Liu, Haiming. "The Trans-Pacific Family: A Case Study of Sam Chang's Family History." *Amerasia* 18:2 (1992): 1–34.

———. "Between China and America: The Trans-Pacific History of the Chang Family." Ph.D. diss., University of California, Irvine, 1996.

Liu Heng. "Wo yao qu ge cungu" [I shall marry a Chinese country girl]. *Chinese Pacific Weekly*, Nov. 13, 1948.

Liu, Pei Chi. *Meiguo huaqiaoshi* [A history of the Chinese in the United States of America, 1848–1911]. Taipei: Commission of Overseas Chinese Affairs, 1976.

———. *Meiguo huaqiaoshi xubian* [A history of the Chinese in the United States of America, II]. Taipei: Limin wenhua qiye gongsi, 1981.

Lo, Karl, and H. M. Lai. *Chinese Newspapers Published in North America, 1854–1975*. Washington, D.C.: Center for Chinese Research Materials, Association of Research Libraries, 1977.

Low, Victor. *The Unimpressible Race: A Century of Educational Struggle by the Chinese in San Francisco*. San Francisco: East/West, 1982.

Lowell, Waverly B. *Chinese Immigration and Chinese in the United States: Records in the Regional Archives of the National Archives and Records Administration*. Washington, D.C.: National Archives and Records Administration, 1996.

Lydon, Sandy. *Chinese Gold: The Chinese in the Monterey Bay Region*. Capitola, Calif.: Capitola Book Company, 1985.

Lyman, Stanford M. *Chinese Americans*. New York: Random House, 1974.

————. "Conflict and the Web of Group Affiliation in San Francisco's Chinatown, 1850–1910," *Pacific Historical Review* 43:4 (Nov. 1974): 473–499

————. "Marriage and the Family among Chinese Immigrants to America, 1850–1960." In Lyman, *The Asian in North America*, 67–76. Santa Barbara, Calif.: ABC-Clio, 1977.

————. "The Structure of Chinese Society in Nineteenth Century America." Ph.D. diss., University of California, Berkeley, 1961.

Mark, Diane Mei Lin, and Ginger Chih. *A Place Called Chinese America*. Dubuque: Kendall/Hunt, 1982.

Maslin, Marshall, ed. *Western Shipbuilders in World War II*. Oakland, Calif., 1954.

Matsumoto, Valerie. "Desperately Seeking 'Deirdre': Gender Roles, Multicultural Relations, and Nisei Women Writers of the 1930s." *Frontiers: A Journal of Women Studies* 12:1 (1991): 19–32.

————. "Japanese American Women during World War II." *Frontiers: A Journal of Women Studies* 8:1 (1984): 6–14.

McCarthy, Ethel. "Shipbuilder and Seaman Training: A Clearing House for Ideas on the War-Winning Job of Wholesale Production of Skill in the Maritime Crafts." *Pacific Marine Review* 51 (Feb. 1943).

McClain, Charles J. *In Search of Equality: The Chinese Struggle against Discrimination in Nineteenth-Century America*. Berkeley: University of California Press, 1994.

McClain, Charles J., and Laurene Wu McClain. "The Chinese Contribution to the Development of American Law." In *Entry Denied: Exclusion and the Chinese Community in America, 1882–1943*, edited by Sucheng Chan, 3–24. Philadelphia: Temple University Press, 1991.

McCunn, Ruthanne Lum. *Chinese American Portraits: Personal Histories, 1828–1988*. San Francisco: Chronicle Books, 1988.

McKeown, Adam. "Transnational Chinese Families and Chinese Exclusion, 1875–1943." *Journal of American Ethnic History* 18 (Winter 1999): 73–110.

Milkman, Ruth. *Gender at Work: The Dynamics of Job Segregation by Sex during World War II*. Urbana: University of Illinois Press, 1987.

————. "Women's Work and the Economic Crisis: Some Lessons from the Great Depression." In *A Heritage of Her Own: Toward a New Social History of American Women*, edited by Nancy F. Cott and Elizabeth Pleck, 507–541. New York: Simon & Schuster, 1979.

Morokvasic, Mirjana. "Women in Migration: Beyond the Reductionist Outlook." In *One Way Ticket: Migration and Female Labor*, edited by Annie Phizacklea, 13–32. Boston: Routledge & Kegan Paul, 1983.

Nee, Victor G., and Brett de Bary Nee. *Longtime Californ': A Documentary Study of an American Chinatown*. New York: Pantheon Books, 1972.

Ngai, Mae M. "The Architecture of Race in American Immigration Law: A Reexamination of the Immigration Act of 1924." *Journal of American History*, 86:1 (June 1999): 80–88.

————. "Legacies of Exclusion: Illegal Chinese Immigration during the Cold War Years." *Journal of American Ethnic History* 18:1 (Fall 1998): 1–35.

Ong, Aihwa. "Anthropology, China, and Modernities: The Geopolitics of Cultural

Knowledge." In *The Future of Anthropological Knowledge*, edited by Henrietta L. Moore, 60–91. New York: Routledge, 1996.

Pascoe, Peggy. *Relations of Rescue: The Search for Female Moral Authority in the American West, 1874–1939*. New York: Oxford University Press, 1990.

Peffer, George Anthony. "Forbidden Families: Emigration Experiences of Chinese Women under the Page Law, 1875–1882." *Journal of American Ethnic History* 6 (Fall 1986): 28–46.

———. "The Forces Without: The Regulation of Chinese Female Immigration to America, 1852–1882." Ph.D. diss., Carnegie-Mellon University, 1988.

———. *If They Don't Bring Their Women Here: Chinese Female Immigration before Exclusion*. Urbana: University of Illinois Press, 1999.

Portes, Alejandro, and Ruben G. Rumbaut, *Immigrant America: A Portrait*. 2nd ed. Berkeley: University of California Press, 1996.

Purcell, Victor. *The Chinese in Southeast Asia*. New York: Oxford University Press, 1951.

Quan, Wen. "Chinatown Literature during the Last Ten Years (1939–1949)." Translated by Marlon K. Hom. *Amerasia* 9:1 (1982): 75–100.

Rasmussen, Cicillia. "China's Amelia Earhart Got Her Wings Here." *Los Angeles Times*, Apr. 12, 1998.

Reinhardt, Richard. *Chinatown, San Francisco*. Berkeley: Lancaster-Miller Publishers, 1981.

Riggs, Fred W. *Pressure on Congress: A Study of the Repeal of Chinese Exclusion*. New York: Columbia University Press, 1950.

Roedinger, David. *The Wages of Whiteness*. New York: Verso, 1991.

Rowe, William T. *Hankow: Conflict and Community in a Chinese City, 1796–1895*. Stanford: Stanford University Press, 1989.

———. *Hankow: Commerce and Society in a Chinese City, 1796–1889*. Stanford: Stanford University Press, 1984.

Ryan, Mary P. *Womanhood in America: From Colonial Times to the Present*. 3rd ed. New York: Franklin Watts, 1983.

Salyer, Lucy E. "'Laws Harsh as Tigers': Enforcement of the Chinese Exclusion Laws, 1891–1941." In *Entry Denied: Exclusion and the Chinese Community in America, 1882–1943*, edited by Sucheng Chan, 57–93. Philadelphia: Temple University Press, 1991.

———. *Laws Harsh as Tigers: Chinese Immigrants and the Shaping of Modern Immigration Law*. Chapel Hill: University of North Carolina Press, 1995.

Sam Yup Benevolent Association History Editorial Committee. *A History of the Sam Yup Benevolent Association in the United States, 1850–2000*. San Francisco: Sam Yup Benevolent Association, 2000.

San Francisco Chinese Community Citizens' Survey and Fact Finding Committee. *Report of the San Francisco Chinese Community Citizens' Survey and Fact Finding Committee*, compiled by Lim P. Lee, Albert Lim, and H. K. Wong. San Francisco: H. J. Carle & Sons, 1969.

Sandmeyer, Elmer Clarence. *The Anti-Chinese Movement in California*. Reprint. Urbana: University of Illinois Press, 1973.

Saxton, Alexander. *The Indispensable Enemy: Labor and the Anti-Chinese Movement in California*. Berkeley: University of California Press, 1971.

Schatkin, Sidney B., Leon N. Sussman, and Dorris Edward Yarbrough. "Chinese Immigration and Blood Tests." *Criminal Law Review* (Spring 1956).

Schurmann, Franz. *The Logic of World Power: An Inquiry into the Origins, Currents, and Contradictions of World Politics*. New York: Pantheon Books, 1974.

Schwartz, Shephard. "Mate-Selection among New York City's Chinese Males, 1931–38." *American Journal of Sociology* 66 (July 1950–May 1951): 562–568.

See, Lisa. *On Gold Mountain: The One-Hundred-Year Odyssey of My Chinese-American Family*. New York: Vintage Books, 1995.

Sewing Women (film). Directed by Arthur Dong. Deepfocus Production, 1982.

Shou Yong. "Xiezai guxi zhijian hou" [Some afterthoughts about Lao Heng's "mother- and daughter-in-law"]. *Chinese Pacific Weekly*, Mar. 20, 1948.

Siu, Paul C. P. *The Chinese Laundryman: A Study of Social Isolation*. New York: New York University Press, 1987.

Sung, Betty Lee. *The Adjustment Experience of Chinese Immigrant Children in New York City*. New York: Center for Migration Studies, 1987.

Tong, Benson. *Unsubmissive Women: Chinese Prostitutes in Nineteenth-Century San Francisco*. Norman: University of Oklahoma Press, 1994.

Tsai, Henry Shih-shan. *China and the Overseas Chinese in the U.S., 1868–1911*. Fayetteville: University of Arkansas Press, 1983.

———. *The Chinese Experience in America*. Bloomington: Indiana University Press, 1986.

Verges, Marianne. *On Silver Wings: The Women Airforce Service Pilots of World War II, 1942–1944*. New York: Ballantine Books, 1991.

Virden, Jenel. *Good-bye, Piccadilly: British War Brides in America*. Urbana: University of Illinois Press, 1996.

Wen Qing, "Mali ana, mofan de zhanniang" [Mariana, a model war bride]. *Chinese Pacific Weekly*, Aug. 23, 1951.

Wen Ying. "Jiantao ni ziji" [Self-criticism]. *Chinese Pacific Weekly*, May 16, 1953.

Williams, Vera S. *WASPs: Women Airforce Service Pilots of World War II*. Osceola, Wisc.: Motorbooks International Publishers & Wholesalers, 1994.

Wollenberg, Charles M. *All Deliberate Speed: Segregation and Exclusion in California Schools, 1855–1975*. Berkeley: University of California Press, 1976.

———. "James v. Marinship: Trouble on the New Black Frontier." *California History* 60 (Fall 1981).

———. *Marinship at War: Shipbuilding and Social Change in Wartime Sausalito*. Berkeley: Western Heritage Press, 1990.

Wong, Constance. "Marinship Chinese Workers Are Building Ships to Free Their Home Land." *Marin-er*, June 26, 1943, 3.

Wong, Harry. "Zhuiyi Hu Jingnan xiansheng" [Reminiscing of Mr. Gilbert Woo]. In Hu Jingnan jinian weiyuan hui, *Hu Jingna wenji*, 76–77. Hong Kong: Xiangjiang chuban youxian gongsi, 1991.

Wong, Jade Snow. *Fifth Chinese Daughter*. 2nd ed. 1950; Seattle: University of Washington Press, 1990.

———. *No Chinese Stranger*. New York: Harper & Row, 1975.

Wong, Sandra M. J. "For the Sake of Kinship: The Overseas Chinese Family." Ph.D. diss., Department of Anthropology, Stanford University, 1987.

Wong, Sau-Ling C. "Tales of Postwar Chinatown: Short Stories of *The But*, 1947–1948." *Amerasia* 14:2 (1988): 61–79.

Wong Tik Wah. "Dao Hu Jingnan jun" [Mourning Gilbert Woo]. In Hu Jingnan jinian weiyuan hui, *Hu Jingna wenji*, 59–60. Hong Kong: Xiangjiang chuban youxian gongsi, 1991.

Woo, Gilbert. "Baoren Li Daming" [Newspaperman Dai Ming Lee]. *Chinese Pacific Weekly*, March 23, 1961. In Hu Jingnan jinian weiyuan hui, *Hu Jingnan wenji*, 163–165. Hong Kong: Xiangjiang chuban youxian gongsi, 1991.

———. "Da peishen tuan chuanxun huafu shetuan" [The grand jury indictment of the Chinese American associations]. *Chinese Pacific Weekly*, Mar. 23, 1956.

———. "Feichu paihua lü" [On repeal of the Chinese exclusion acts]. *Chinese Times*, Dec. 1, 1943. In Hu Jingnan jinian weiyuan hui, *Hu Jingnan wenji*, 41–42. Hong Kong: Xiangjiang chuban youxian gongsi, 1991.

———. "Huafu Tuanti" [Chinese American community organizations]." *Chinese Pacific Weekly*, Jan. 27, 1951. In Hu Jingnan jinian weiyuan hui, *Hu Jingnan Wenji*, 279. Hong Kong: Xiangjiang chuban youxian gongsi, 1991.

———. "Quanqiao dahui" [On the Chinese American National Conference]. *Chinese Pacific Weekly*, Nov. 29, 1929. In Hu Jingnan jinian weiyuan hui, *Hu Jingnan wenji*, 488–489. Hong Kong: Xiangjiang chuban youxian gongsi, 1991.

———. "Tongyuanhui shijian" [The CACA incident]. *Chinese Pacific Weekly*, July 1 to Aug. 5, 1971.

———. "Yimin kongbu" [Immigration terror]. *Chinese Pacific Weekly*, Nov. 29, 1947. In Hu Jingnan jinian weiyuan hui, *Hu Jingnan wenji*, 455–456. Hong Kong: Xiangjiang chuban youxian gongsi, 1991.

———. "Zagan" [Some afterthoughts]. *Chinese Pacific Weekly*, July 1, 1948.

Woo, Nancy. "Father and Daughter." In Hu Jingnan jinian weiyuan hui, *Hu Jingnan wenji* [Selected works of Gilbert Woo]. Hong Kong: Xiangjiang Chuban youxian gongsi, 1991.

Wynar, Lubomyr R., and Anna T. Wynar, eds. *Encyclopedic Directory of Ethnic Newspapers and Periodicals in the United States*. 2nd ed. Littleton, Colo.: Libraries Unlimited, 1976.

Xiao Min. "Sanzhong butong dianxing de huaqiao funü" [Three different types of Chinese American women]. *Chinese Pacific Weekly*, June 24, 1950.

Xue, Suzhen, and Chen, Jingying. *Chinese American Families in New York*. Shanghai: Sanlian shudian. 1993.

Yanagisako, Sylvia. "Transforming Orientalism: Gender, Nationality, and Class in Asian American Studies." In *Naturalizing Power: Essays in Feminist Cultural Analysis*, edited by Sylvia Yanagisako and Carol Delaney, 275–300. New York: Routledge, 1995.

Yu, Renqiu. "Little Heard Voices: The Chinese Hand Laundry Alliance and the *China Daily News'* Appeal for Repeal of the Chinese Exclusion Act in 1943." *Chinese America: History and Perspectives*, 1990, 21–35.

————. *To Save China, to Save Ourselves: The Chinese Hand Laundry Alliance of New York*. Philadelphia: Temple University Press, 1992.

Yung, Judy. *Chinese Women of America: A Pictorial History*. Seattle: University of Washington Press, 1986.

————. "The Fake and the True: Researching Chinese Women's Immigration History." *Chinese America: History and Perspectives*, 1998, 25–56.

————. "The Social Awakening of Chinese American Women as Reported in *Chung Sai Yat Po*, 1900–1911." In *Unequal Sisters: A Multicultural Reader in U.S. Women's History*, edited by Ellen Carol Dubois and Vicki L. Ruiz, 195–207. New York: Routledge, 1990.

————. *Unbound Feet: A Social History of Chinese Women in San Francisco*. Berkeley: University of California Press, 1995.

————. *Unbound Voices: A Documentary History of Chinese Women in San Francisco*. Berkeley: University of California Press, 1999.

Zhao, Xiaojian. "Chinese American Women Defense Workers in World War II." *California History* 75:2 (Summer 1996): 138–153, 182–184.

————. "Women and Defense Industries in World War II." Ph.D. diss., University of California, Berkeley, 1993.

Zheng Yijun. *Chuanqi rensheng: ji Cai Fujiu zouguo de lu* [A legendary life: The path of Cai Fujiu]. Hong Kong: Haifeng chubanshe, 1997.

Zhong Guoren. "Jialian wumei de Taipingyang zhoubao" [A well-priced high-quality *Chinese Pacific Weekly*]. *Chinese Pacific Weekly*, Oct. 8, 1949.

Zhou, Kate Xiao. *How the Farmers Changed China: Power of the People*. Boulder: Westview Press, 1996.

Zhou, Min. *Chinatown: The Socioeconomic Potential of an Urban Enclave*. Philadelphia: Temple University Press, 1992.

Zi Min. "Shixian zhangfu de lixiang" [Realizing husband's dreams]. *Chinese Pacific Weekly*, Dec. 21, 1950.

————. "Zhiye funü" [Career women]. *Chinese American Weekly*, Aug. 17, 1950.

INDEX

advice columns, 140–144; and culture gap, 140; and marital problems, 140

African Americans, and World War II, 111, 205n70

Ah Moy, 11–12

Ah Quan, 11

Ah Yoke Gee, 50–51, 63, 71, 72, 74; citizenship, 204n32; defense work, 56, 56–57, 59; in press stories, 69

Aihwa Ong, 150–151

Alien Fiancées and Fiancés Act (1946), 25, 78, 80

American Communist Party, investigation of, 162

American Federation of Labor, 23

American Legion, 23

American Veterans Association, California branch, 91

American Women's Voluntary Service, 71

Anderson, Wallace, 70

anti-Chinese movement, and Cold War, 152, 173

apprenticeship training, 73

Archibald, Katherine, 68

Army Nurse Corps, and Chinese American women, 65–66

Arnold, Hap, 73

Artkino, 179

"Art of Life, The" (column in *Chinese American Weekly*), 147–148

Asian Indians, end of exclusion of, 197n85

Asian Shirt Press Company, 169

Atwood, Raymond, 164–165

bachelor society, 9; transition to a family society, 78, 126, 141

Barber, Bruce G., 157–158, 161

Benliu (Chuck), 35

Bernstein, Samuel, 170

Bingham (Conn.), 21

Bing Kung Cong, 116

blood tests, and immigration cases, 154–157. *See also* derivative citizenship; document fraud

Boli ju (Committee to Challenge the 1924 Immigration Act), 16, 20–21

Butler, Nicholas Murray, 18

Cable Act (1922), 15, 17, 37–38, 39

CACA. *See* Chinese American Citizens Alliance

Cai Fujiu (Henry Tsoi), 45, 85, 119, 120, 185; and *China Weekly*, 189; and independent press, 108, 116

Cai Nüliang, 85

Cai Tingkai, and Chinese Americans, 101

California Labor School, 117, 119; investigation of, 162

California League of Women Voters, 196n68

California Supreme Court, 51

Carter, Jimmy, 76

Carter, Oliver H., 175

ABOUT THE AUTHOR

Xiaojian Zhao is an associate professor of Asian American studies and history at the University of California, Santa Barbara. A graduate of Fudan University in Shanghai, China, she received her M.A. degree from the University of Rochester and a Ph.D. from the University of California, Berkeley.

CPSIA information can be obtained at www.ICGtesting.com
Printed in the USA
267371BV00001B/95/A